Professional Recommendations
for 'The Murray Method'

Marcus Earle, PhD, LMFT, CSAT, S-PSB
Psychological Counseling Services, Clinical Director

Many people may not be aware Marilyn Murray is one of the pioneers in the treatment of trauma. Psychological Counseling Services has been utilizing her model and tools for over 25 years. Our clients are relieved to finally discover answers to what has created barriers to fully experiencing intimacy with themselves and those they love. The Murray Method presents a straight forward and easy to understand theory which bridges the gap between a clinician and a client. This book is a critical resource providing a path toward healing the traumas which limit us from becoming the "Healthy Balanced Person" we are intended to be.

Alexandra Katehakis, MFT, CSAT-S, CST-S
The Center for Health Sex, Clinical Director

The Murray Method is unsurpassed in its rapid ability to reveal the past in the present. By accessing the right side of the brain, implicit memories sequestered long ago are revealed and regulated. This powerful process facilitates neural integration necessary for long-term change. Everyone should experience this modality!

Boris Bratus, PhD
General Psychology, Department Head and Professor; Moscow State University, Moscow, Russia

World famous psychologists have come to Russia, and I have had the pleasure of meeting them: Viktor Frankl, Carl Rogers, Rollo May and Virginia Satir. They all had a unique way of treating people—an inner transparency—like an archetype. Marilyn Murray also has this special quality. But, she did not come to Russia for just a few weeks—she has brought her love and knowledge to us for 15 years. She is regarded as a high authority psychologically in Russia and has touched and transformed many lives here.

Soozi Bolte MC, LPC, LISAC

The Murray Method has given me a structure to invite clients into their own healing journey—one that I have experienced and have practiced for the past 14 years. It's a method that works.

Christopher J. Charleton, MA, LCSW, Fulbright Scholar

Marilyn's method was instrumental in transforming my life from the ravages of childhood trauma. The Murray Method had has enabled me to embrace, celebrate and unleash the person God ordained me to be. Professionally I have employed the Murray Method for 18 years. My personal transformation experience utilizing the Murray Method has been replicated hundreds of times in the clients I have been able to serve.

Gayle Cordes, DBH, LPC, LISAC

Most people think *"Trauma? Not me. I've never been in combat or at the site of some disaster."* Marilyn's book helps people understand that trauma happens to all of us, and that trauma, left unhealed, follows us through the years, damaging our relationships, our health, and our ability to be our optimal selves. She offers a pathway, a course, that if followed, guides us to a life of balance and a chance to experience real joy.

Greg Crow, PhD

Marilyn Murray's methods are understandable, memorable and transferable—that is why it is popular—it is effective—and it is effective over a long period of time. I have known and worked with Marilyn for 30 years and was in her first training session. I have witnessed her phenomenal track record working in the field of trauma and addictions. She has made an enormous impact on professionals and clients here in the United States and in Russia.

Victoria Bartsalkina, PhD
Psychologist, Professor; Moscow University of Psychology and Education; Moscow, Russia

As a victim of a terrorist attack as a child, I felt as though I had waited all my life for someone like Marilyn to come and help me work through this horrific trauma. When I finally had the opportunity to attend Marilyn's classes, I gained a long-desired healing at a very deep level. As I worked on my own issues, I also acquired many new instruments which I now regularly use with great effectiveness with my clients and students.

Uriy Zabordin, PhD
Vice Rector, Scientific Research Division
Moscow University of Psychology and Education; Moscow, Russia

Moscow State University of Psychology and Education expresses its deep gratitude to Professor Marilyn Murray for the series of trainings she has conducted for our university in Russia and for her altruistic and highly professional help. The knowledge and skills that our psychologists acquired during these trainings is being successfully used in their personal lives as well as in their professional work with adults, children and families.

Mike Tyson,
World Champion Boxer, Entertainer
Excerpts regarding his therapeutic work with Marilyn Murray from his autobiography: The Undisputed Truth (2013)

It was obvious to me after a while that Marilyn's job in life was to help people. Marilyn's job was to take big strong scary men that society had rejected and make society accept them again and make them excel while they're being accepted. She was talking the right talk a hundred percent to me. I owe Marilyn a debt that can never be repaid for getting me into the recovery world. Marilyn took me to a place that I could never have been able to go. She believed in me.

Amazon Reader Reviews for The Murray Method

★ ★ ★ ★ ★ I love this book

I love this book. It helps me put together and apply everything I have been learning in therapy over the last 6 months. I bought one for each of my children. I highly recommend it for anyone that would like to heal from any kind of trauma experienced in childhood or in their adult life.

★ ★ ★ ★ ★   **The best book I've read on the topic of inner healing**

The author's description of how trauma affects the whole person is helpful, but the fact that she offers a very practical way of dealing with those effects is even more so. I am currently working through the exercises she includes, and finding them extremely insightful and inspiring.

★ ★ ★ ★ ★   **Balanced!**

The Murray Method is an excellent read filled with teachings through example and skilled advice on how to obtain a balanced life through healing methods Marilyn Murray guides you through beautifully!

★ ★ ★ ★ ★   **Dynamic book!**

This is one of the 3 most important books I've ever read! It simplifies the healing journey for the person who desires to understand what could be going wrong inside of them, why it is like that, and simple refreshing solutions for healing. This book is a light touch and a blessing to a subject that can be so scary and discouraging...inner-healing. I highly recommend this book.

★ ★ ★ ★ ★   **Inspiring ... Hopeful ... Uplifting,**

An amazing book written by a woman with keen insight into dealing with trauma and its lasting effects. The author created a 'method' for dealing with abuse and trauma that treats the whole person without giving in to any wallowing in victimhood. She approaches the whole picture with the attitude of 'it sucks, now let's deal with it'. I love that.

The book is set up with over 30 exercises - the suggestion is to read the book first then go back and do the exercises as you re-read it. It requires a lot of soul searching and real desire, but there's so much to be gained. She suggests the reader have a friend or therapist be a part of the process - a great way to stay grounded - and encourages seeking out therapy if you become 'stuck'. Lots of good common sense in that advice. Overall an amazing book.

The
Murray
Method

Also by Marilyn Murray

Prisoner of Another War—A Remarkable Journey of Healing from Childhood Trauma (PageMill Press, 1991, 2021)

The
Murray
Method

Creating Wholeness Beyond Trauma, Abuse, Neglect, and Addiction

THE INTERNATIONALLY ACCLAIMED APPROACH
TO BECOMING A HEALTHY BALANCED PERSON

VIVO PUBLICATIONS
VP

Marilyn Murray

Printed in the United States of America

For special orders or information, contact:
Vivo Publications
7349 N. Via Paseo Del Sur, Suite 515-275
Scottsdale, AZ 85258

Editor's note: The illustration concerning the author's clients and students have been either slightly changed or combined for reasons of confidentiality.

The use of the terms "God" and "Higher Power" have been used interchangeably to denote the Supreme Being. However, readers may feel free to use terms with which they are most comfortable.

Library of Congress Cataloging-in-Publication Data
Hard Cover ISBN: 978-0-9855093-1-6
E-book ISBN: 978-0-9855093-3-0
1 2 3 4 5 6 7 8 9 10   27 26 25 24 23 22 21

Psychology|Psychotherapy|Self-Help

To my clients and students who have had the courage to share their pain, to risk, and to grow...

Table of Contents

How to Use This Book...

You may desire to read this book for general information without using it as a guide for personal growth. A number of exercises, however, are included which you may wish to consider. These simple, helpful tools have been used effectively with individuals ages 13 to 80 who come from a wide range of ethnicities and educational backgrounds across the social stratum.

This text is designed for use by individuals or within support groups or classes. It is recommended that you first read the book in its entirety without addressing the exercises. Then, reread the text and consider each exercise to decide whether or not you wish to complete it as part of your healing journey. If you choose to participate in the exercises, allow yourself adequate time to contemplate the questions and complete your answers in each assignment.

These exercises are most beneficial when done with another person—either a caring friend, a family member, a support group, or a psychologist or counselor. If at any time during the reading of the text or in answering the exercise questions you feel distressed, please stop and give yourself time to rest. *If your discomfort continues, contact a professional therapist.*

This book is not to be considered a substitute for therapy, and if the reader is undergoing psychological or psychiatric care, he/she should consult with his or her clinician before completing the exercises.

EXERCISE INDEX

Recommended Materials for Exercises:

1. Plain paper (such as unlined typing paper)
2. Large easel pad or two rolls smooth wallpaper
3. One box colored felt-tip pens; purchase extras of black and red
4. Small Post-it notes
5. Journal

ILLUSTRATION INDEX

GLOSSARY

Murray Method Terminology

Original Child:
- is who you were created to be
- contains your soul and your true spirituality, with its inherent desire to connect with God
- includes your innate intelligence, talent, personality, creativity, and physical appearance
- is an emotionally unfragmented child at conception with the capacity to feel all emotions, appropriately and inappropriately
- has free will and the capacity to choose good or evil

Sobbing Child:
- contains all your painful feelings (fear, hurt, sadness, anger, resentment, loneliness, helplessness, shame, and so on)
- is created by negative outside influences such as trauma, abuse, neglect, or illness
- is created from your Original Child
- contains a positive element in that it enables you to feel compassion and empathy, and to be tender and caring

Controlling Child:
- is necessary as your innate defense mechanism, including physical and emotional shock
- is created out of your Original Child to protect your Sobbing Child
- is meant to be a temporary help in time of pain and distress, but can become unhealthy if it develops into a permanent status

- will use whatever is available in your environment or your innate abilities to manage pain
- uses several basic defenses:
    - repression
    - anesthetizers (such as nicotine, alcohol, drugs, sex, or food in excess); can become destructive when applying these defenses
    - diversionary tactics (such as relationships, work, reading, television, music, sports, school, church, or computers when they are used to avoid dealing with pain and difficult issues)
- when healthy, contains additional positive elements: it keeps you responsible and also helps you set appropriate boundaries (keeps others from victimizing you and you from victimizing others)

The Angry Rebellious Child:
- occurs when the Sobbing Child's needs are being ignored and the impatient Controlling Child is no longer able to repress this crying child and he reacts by joining him; when they connect, they resemble two electrical live wires, arcing as they touch
- is aggressive
- is overtly hostile
- is demanding
- operates with a very short fuse
- is into power and control

The Stubborn Selfish Child:
- occurs when the Sobbing Childs feelings are disregarded and the Controlling Child is weary of his responsibilities, and they join with the Original Child into a very unhealthy trio
- is covert
- is passive-aggressive
- is manipulative

- is a game player
- is sneaky
- is revengeful
- is sometimes seductive and promiscuous; sexual addiction can start here
- has a sense of entitlement and grandiosity (fueled by the Original Child)

Both The Angry Rebellious Child and The Stubborn Selfish Child:

- are unreasonable
- will rationalize to justify their behavior
- are unwilling to look at the consequences of their actions
- refuse to take responsibility for their behavior
- consistently blame other people or events for their deeds
- will do whatever they want even though they know their actions will be destructive to themselves and/or others (we often refer to this as "crawling out on a limb and sawing it off behind you.")
- see themselves as the victim, but become the victimizer, to themselves and to others
- The Angry Rebellious Child and the Stubborn Selfish Child behave in harmful manners due to the unhealthy combination of the Sobbing Child, the Controlling Child and the Original Child, and they must be eliminated. Addictions are born here.

Healthy Balanced Person:

- is your goal in your healing journey of recovery
- is integrated as a deeply feeling person who also is reasonable, thinking, and responsible
- is an effective synthesis of head (intellect) and gut (emotions)
- combines your Original Child with the positive strengths of your Sobbing Child and Controlling Child in a balanced, healthy way

- is capable of feeling all emotions appropriately
- generates maturity and therefore is part of a lifelong process

External Positive Influences (EPI):

Any favorable, affirmative influences upon the individual that nurture it and accept it as an individuated self (e.g. relative, teacher, friend, church, award)

Internal Positive Influences (IPI):

All the positive attributes of the Original Child—the innate talents and traits which are incorporated into each human at conception (e.g., intelligence, physical attributes, emotions, spirituality, unique personality, skills, and abilities in music, art, sports, etc.)

Pool of Pain:

Contains painful events experienced through a person's life in which the resulting feelings have not been appropriately dealt with; they have either been denied or released in a destructive manner.

Scindo:

Latin term denoting the "split" for survival which is common and normal; the human organism's natural, innate defense mechanism in times of trauma and/or deprivation; this "emotional shock" defense mechanism is likened to physical shock that represses pain and occurs in times of physical trauma.

Additional definitions:

Addiction:

Being abnormally tolerant of and dependent on something that is psychologically or physically habit-forming; an excessive behavior that controls your life instead you controlling it (the behavior or your life); a bad habit, compulsion, dependency, need, obsession, craving, or infatuation.

Codependency:

Sacrificing one's self-worth by submitting to and taking responsibility for another person, which enables the other person to engage in destructive behavior; doing something for someone else
that he should be doing for himself. It also means being excessively
focused on others, not only in caretaking but in blaming. It is attempting to manage the behavior of others rather than your own.

INTRODUCTION

Understanding the Journey

There can be no knowledge without emotion.
We may be aware of a truth,
Yet until we have felt its force,
It is not ours.
To the cognition of the brain must be added
The experience of the soul.

—Arnold Bennett (1867–1931)

A Personal Passage

Knowledge plus Experience plus Understanding equals Wisdom.
—Marilyn Murray

Wisdom is a cumulative gift we receive throughout our lives and is one of the most indispensable benefits of our lifelong journey. By the time I reached age 44 in 1980, I had a great deal of knowledge and experience regarding many things. I did not, however, have much understanding about my life, and I certainly was not wise.

I was a successful art dealer and had co-founded a national organization of support groups for women called "More Than Friends." I was also a highly visible leader in my community and was married with two beautiful daughters, a wonderful son-in-law, and an adorable grandson. People who knew me thought I had everything. But most people were not aware that I suffered from intense physical pain from which I could not escape. They did not know that I was becoming suicidal. Fortunately, a close friend insisted I go into therapy and, as a result, my life changed radically.

As I began my healing journey, I often became frustrated because I wanted explanations regarding my therapeutic process. I wanted to understand what was happening to me and why. I wanted practical guides. Despite my copious questions, few were able to explain my experience in language that made sense to me.

In my search for understanding, I returned to school and received undergraduate and graduate degrees in psychology. By applying the knowledge and experience I had gained not only from my own therapeutic process but also from my long years in the business world, I endeavored to gain some insight into why I did what I did in life. As a result, I developed a psychological theory that explained human behavior, which I thought only applied to me. Much to my great surprise, I found that my theory applied to other people as well.

Since the 1980s, in addition to my private practice in intensive psychotherapy, I have taught my theory—the Murray Method, featuring the Scindo Syndrome—to mental health professionals, clergy, and the general public. It has now been used with clients worldwide.

Intimacy and Reclamation

This is an intimate book. In it, I will share bits of my personal journey with you, as everything I teach comes out of a search to understand myself and my relationships. As you read this book, I will ask you to participate in the exercises and share your journey with me. My own healing journey—which has at times been long, difficult, and painful—has also contained great joy, valuable insights, and rewarding experiences as I have sought to reclaim the person God created me to be.

I invite you to join me on this journey so you may become everything you were designed to be. When you do, you will deeply connect with your soul—that amazingly talented, beautiful part of you that is unique only to you and desires a meaningful spiritual connection with God in your life.

For many of us, our souls have been covered over by years of pain and trauma, so they have remained ever-illusive. I hope that within these pages you will find simple guidelines and tools that will help you reclaim your own soul as you proceed on your personal healing journey. Traversing this journey can be the most rewarding experience of your existence, but it can also be overwhelming and intimidating if attempted alone and without guideposts to conduct you safely to your destination.

Guideposts and Stepping Stones

I am including words of wisdom from many who have had a profound influence on me over the years. Throughout the book, you will find quotations that have inspired me—from the words of Jesus in the Bible to the poetry of Goethe and Maya Angelou, and from the thoughts of Blaise Pascal and Carl Jung to the observations of Helen Keller. It is my desire that this wisdom will serve as stepping stones to support you as you travel along your own healing path.

The book begins with a Prologue, which lays the foundation for the theoretical concepts within the book. I will also share some of my personal story and introduce the Murray Method and its components.

Starting with Chapter One, I have divided this book into five parts based upon five guideposts:

- **Purpose and Process**—discusses the necessity of accepting the need for a personal healing journey in one's life, trusting in the process of that healing, and being willing to actively participate by taking action.

- **Balance and Health**—initiates methods to create a healthy, balanced person: physically, emotionally, intellectually, and spiritually. At this guidepost, you are challenged to discover what experiences have wounded your spirit and to contemplate developing a relationship with God or deepening an existing bond.
- **Faith and Values**—brings healing to your soul and presents the foundational basics for a healthy journey based upon love and respect of God, self, and others; challenges personal values based upon behaviors.
- **Actions and Accountability**—evaluates actions which are outward indications of inward attitudes; addresses addictions; encourages behavioral accountability to reflect a commitment toward transforming actions and attitudes.
- **Wisdom and Maturity**—defines and analyzes the concept of wisdom as a combination of knowledge plus experience plus understanding and maturity as the application of that wisdom. This guidepost offers an appraisal of this healing journey and points to the resulting over-arching legacy of life's destination: the development of character as you reclaim who you were created to be.

A Journey or a Contest?

While these guideposts will help you on the path, your healing journey cannot begin unless you are willing to challenge your old views and attitudes. If you accept that challenge, one of the first questions you must honestly answer is this: Do you view life as a journey or a contest?

Many people see life as a contest or a game in which we attempt to defeat our opponent; there is a winner and a loser. Perhaps you have been raised to view life only as a competition or a fight for supremacy. But life is not a contest or a game; life is a journey—one in which everyone can be a winner.

Other people say they view life as a journey, but they live their lives like a contest and, consequently, they feel like either winners or losers. In such a contest, each person has his or her own standard that determines who wins or loses and a personal definition for the meaning of success or failure. Those standards are determined by each person's experiences, their families, their culture, their era, and so on.

Is it possible to shift your own perceptions from perceiving life as a contest or a game to viewing life as a journey—a journey in which you can be a winner, a success, but not at the expense of another's failure? Are you willing to initiate a "win-win" approach to life and to take the first steps toward healing and wholeness?

A Vertical, Not a Horizontal Journey

Have you ever done a timeline of your life by listing important events on a long horizontal line? If you have, you know it is sometimes hard to understand why something that happened "way back when" could affect what you do in your life today or will affect what you do in your future. I have my clients list personal events in a large oval that represents their lives, starting at the bottom first and moving upward. This exercise helps them envision the process of living their lives in a vertical rather than a horizontal manner.

Each event in your life is stacked upon prior events—not only events in your life, but also those from your parents' lives—and as such is heavily impacted by preceding incidents. It reminds me of the old fairy tale "The Princess and the Pea," in which the heroine could feel a tiny pea in her bed even though it was covered by a multitude of mattresses piled one on top of the other.

Just as the events of your life are stacked, the concepts introduced in this material are intentionally layered one upon the other as you begin your vertical journey. The information in this book works like a map, helping you choose your destination and giving you skills and tools to aid you on your journey and help you identify possible detours, dead-ends, and potentially dangerous areas.

A traditional map only has general lines showing ways to travel from point A to point B. There may be several options, some long, some short. The material in this book is similar to that type of map. It is not designed to explain every nuance of each person's journey. Should you decide to use this guide, it will challenge you to think and to feel. This is a map toward integration and health, but you will design your own itinerary and choose the path on which you travel.

Do you already have a clearly defined goal and destination for your life, or is that still a vast uncharted area for you? In either case, this book will assist you in your journey.

The Destination: To Live a Worthwhile Life

Don't be afraid of death so much as an inadequate life.
—Bertolt Brecht (1898–1956)

What defines a "worthwhile life" for you? Your definition may fluctuate over time as your age and circumstances change. At this very moment, which of the items on this list make you feel successful in life?

- just staying alive
- healthy relationships
- happy children and grandchildren
- physical health and strength
- being creative
- accomplishment in your profession
- recognition
- power and control
- home
- possessions

- money
- ministering to others

For scores of individuals, success means merely surviving—simply staying alive one more day. For some, it means being able to provide food and shelter for themselves and their families. For many people, success is defined as enjoying good relationships with friends and family. Or, success may mean doing something very creative or accomplishing a major goal, perhaps as an athlete, a businessperson, or a military officer. Many of these goal-oriented individuals often think they will take time to work on their own well-being and/or on their relationships sometime later in life. But that chance may never come. They do not realize that it is possible to live a balanced, healthy life and be successful in their relationships while also achieving other goals.

How about you? I look forward to helping you feel successful on this journey called life.

PROLOGUE

My Journey

"If our joy is honest joy, it must somehow be congruous with human tragedy. This is the test of joy's integrity: Is it compatible with pain? Only the heart that hurts has a right to joy."
Lewis Smedes (1921-2001)

"Moving to Moscow? Moscow, Russia? Are you sure you want to do that?"

This was a fairly common reaction in 2002 when I stated that I had decided to live and work half-time in Moscow. No one expected that type of decision from a sixty-six year-old grandmother. But the resulting years have proven it to be wise choice and it has become a unique and rewarding adventure.

In Russia I teach health professionals (physicians, psychologists, psychiatrists, therapists, addictions counselors, social workers) as well as educators and clergy regarding the treatment of trauma, abuse, and deprivation, and their correlation with addictions.

I also have spent the past three decades studying how individuals survive painful events and the long-term effects upon their lives and families. Since difficult times are inevitable for all of us, how can we not just survive, but thrive, grow, and enjoy life to the fullest, despite our pain?

It has been a most interesting journey—one I would like to share with you.

~

The Story of a Family

"O God, how can we mortals grieve
When human eyes run dry of tears?"

—**Dr. Timothy Kloberdanz (1949 -)**

In 1767, the Volga River area of Russia is wild and unsettled, and a young immigrant couple, Johannes and Anna Reh, are excited about the possibility of raising their family in this new wilderness. But, unfortunately, life is harsh and the land is barren—cruel winters, gnawing hunger, and relentless diseases render a heavy toll. They suffer the loss of three of their six children and of their fourteen grandchildren, only two live to adulthood. Dealing with grief becomes a daily occurrence. Despite this veil of sadness, the families make Russia their home and develop a deep love for this land.

In the late 1800s, one of the Reh sons, Johannes, makes a hard decision—he takes his wife, Catharina and small daughter and travels to America hoping to find a better life. However, Catharina is unhappy there, and they return to Russia. In their Volga village, two more children are born, with one dying in infancy. Then, once again, tragedy visits the family.

It is an icy November day in 1891, and Johannes and Catharina are traveling near their village in a horse-drawn buggy. As Johannes has not been well, he holds their toddler while Catharina drives. Suddenly, a movement in the nearby field startles their horse, and the animal bolts with such a jerk that the reins become inextricably tangled around Catharina's wrists. As the runaway gallops wildly down the rough dirt road, the reins pull tighter and tighter until Catharina loses all control over the fugitive horse.

With one strong arm wrapped protectively around their child, Johannes frantically struggles to reach the reins and help his beloved wife but the wagon crashes violently over the

ruts and rocks, nearly throwing him from the seat and mak-
ing it impossible to intervene. As she takes one last glance at
her husband and her son, Catharina pleads, "Jump, jump!"
She is killed at age thirty; Johannes and their son survive only
to have the little one die within the year.

At age thirty-two Johannes already has experienced the death of his wife and three children (his first son died at birth).

Shortly after Catharina's death, Johannes marries Anna Simon from a neighboring village and takes her with him on yet another voyage to America where they settle in Brooklyn, New York. Johannes and Anna have eight children; their first daughter and a son die at birth.

Tragically, their remaining families in Russia are impacted deeply by the Revolution, the Civil War, and the violent upheaval as the Soviet system shatters their countryside. In the early years, some contact is allowed and news of horrific famines and Stalin's Great Terror reaches across the ocean. Even though Johannes and Anna are exceedingly poor, they struggle to save enough money to send to their families who are starving in the devastated villages. But their gifts and words of love never reach their destination.

Johannes weeps as he reads the final letters from his family thousands of miles away, "Why do you abandon us? We are starving to death. Don't you love us? Please, please help us!" Gradually their written words cease as the Soviets terminate all communication with the outside world. Johannes and Anna no longer are allowed to return to Russia and never again will touch the faces of their loved ones or the land of their birth.

Back in their village, one of Johannes's brothers leaves one day to walk to a neighboring village and never returns—rumor says he was beaten to death. One sister starves in the catastrophic famine in 1922 caused by the unrelenting confiscation of the farmer's grain by the Soviets. The eldest brother, who is the village mayor, refuses to hand over all of the village's grain, knowing that to do so would condemn the villagers to starvation. He is buried alive. Both his sons are killed, and his two daughters are sent to Siberia.

Every member of the Reh family still living in Russia is either murdered by the Soviets, starves, or is forced into a railway cattle car that delivers its battered human cargo to a Gulag in the far East. Not one survives untouched. News of their fates becomes obliterated by the fall of the Iron Curtain.

Johannes's faith is the one constant in his turbulent life and he makes a major decision to dedicate his life to becoming a pastor. He and Anna move their family across the country to the prairies of Kansas that often remind them of the distant billowing fields near their Russian village. He now is the Reverend John Reh and is the founding minister of a small church where the majority of the congregation is from the Volga region of Russia. Because the pastor's salary is small, John and Anna also become farmers to support their growing family.

June in Kansas is beautiful with wild roses and peonies in full bloom. The flowers brighten up the small farmhouse as Anna stands peeling potatoes in the kitchen. Gazing out the window she sees her youngest son Abraham, whom they call Abe, now almost seven, playing in the yard.

Shading his eyes with a tanned hand, the boy speaks to his older brother, Bill.

"Looks like there's a storm cloud a-comin'. You think it's gonna rain?"

"Nah," Bill replies. "There's only one little cloud."

But as the cloud moves above the prairie, it seems to stop and hover over the home of the Reh family. The blue sky begins to darken and suddenly unleashes a torrent of rain causing Abe and Bill to scurry for the cover of the porch.

But moisture was not the only cargo carried in the cloud this day. From within its depths a deadly bolt of lightning explodes with a blinding flash and a thunderous crack that numbs the senses. It drives its fatal thrust down the chimney, across the sink, and directly into the water in which Anna's hands rest as she prepares her family's dinner. And then, as quickly as it appeared, the cloud moves on, while the blue sky once again unfolds, allowing the sun to shine on the two little boys huddled together on the porch.

Anna is killed at 49, leaving children ages seven, nine, & twelve still at home. Wild roses and peonies cover her coffin as little Abe walks up the steps of the small church with voices echoing over and over in his head: "Be strong, don't cry, be brave."

At age 56, Johannes has lost two wives and five children. Within sixteen months, he remarries a woman who, unfortunately, is not a loving stepmother to Abe and his siblings.

After the death of their mother, Abe, Bill, and their sister Lydia cling together to survive. Their father buries himself in his ministry, his work, and his new wife and has little contact with his children except to issue orders in his typically rigid manner. Sundays are spent in church with no playing allowed throughout the entire day; the children are to sit on a stool and read the Bible and must obey at all costs.

Abe misses his mother and often is hurt by the lack of love from his father and the coldness of his new stepmother. His resentment of the time his father spends away from his children festers and grows. But feelings are not allowed for a male in his family, so young Abe comforts himself by keeping busy with farm work and school.

A quick learner, his curiosity for how things are made make him a favorite of the teachers. Unfortunately, his father insists that Abe's education ends at grade six and sends the twelve-year-old boy to work in the wheat fields of western Kansas. Abe's pay is sent to his father, and Abe never again returns home to live.

During these years, America is facing its own hardships as World War I and then the Great Depression unleash despair over nearly every family, young and old. At age sixteen, Abe travels alone across the country looking for work, but jobs are exceedingly scarce, especially for a teenager, and eventually he returns to Kansas when he is in his early twenties.

In his hometown of Marion, he meets a pretty young woman named Velma who has her own difficult past. She is the youngest child of John and Mata Byram who live on a small Kansas farm with their five children. Mata's sister Maude, her husband, and six children live nearby, and Velma loves playing with her cousins. In 1919, when Velma is age five, heartbreak befalls their family. During a severe flu epidemic, Maude's two-year-old twins and six month old baby all die within two weeks. She becomes so distraught she is placed in a mental institution and remains there until her death many years later.

Maude's husband cannot—will not—deal with the pain and abandons their remaining three children: Leota, age four, and two boys, ages six and seven. Velma's mother and father become foster parents, adding the little ones to their family.

The cousins soon become like siblings to Velma, and she enjoys having Leota as a sister and regular playmate. However, the addition of three more children to an already struggling farm family of seven creates many stressors, especially since the entire family is still reeling from the loss of five members within the space of a few weeks.

Twelve years later, Velma's older brother and two sisters are married, leaving Velma, one brother, and the three siblings/cousins still at home.

> *It is September, a prime month in Kansas, as the state brings forth a spectacular parade of fall leaves with occasional wisps of cool air floating through the waning, warm days. John is working in the fields with his son and two nephews/sons—now all fine young men.*
>
> *Mata, Velma, and Leota are ironing in the kitchen, enjoying the delightful breeze dancing through the open windows.*

They use two flatirons, alternating heating one while using the other until it cools. A glass globe of kerosene rests on top of the stove, slowly feeding fuel to the flames below. As it sputters dry, Mata asks seventeen-year-old Velma to go and refill the globe.

"Mom, I'm almost finished with Dad's Sunday shirt, and I don't want the starch to dry out. Can't Leota go and get it instead?"

Mata turns to the young girl. "Leota, do you know which one is the kerosene can?" The sixteen-year-old answers affirmatively as she skips out the door, happy for even a few moments to be immersed in the beautiful day. She goes to the shed where the fuel is kept, but in the dim light she does not read the label as she fills the globe to the brim: "GASOLINE. Danger—highly flammable."

Leota is bubbling about the smell of autumn in the air, and the curl in the edge of the rug goes unnoticed as she steps into the kitchen. With horror, Velma watches as Leota and the globe with its incendiary flood crash headlong into the hot stove.

John and the boys, bending over their rakes in the field, are startled upright by the violent explosion. As he whirls around, John is stunned by the sight of flames pouring from the kitchen windows and the women's tortured screams.

Within the house, a hellish scene blazes as Mata reacts instantly, throwing herself across the burning body of the child she has cherished as her own. Velma dashes to them but is pushed away by her mother whose clothing already is engulfed by the ravaging fire.

The teenager sobs hysterically as she watches her mother and sister burn to death in front of her in an inferno she thinks is her fault. "If only I had gone! If only I had not said, 'Can't Leota go instead?'"

Velma is allowed to grieve for only a few days, and after the funerals, the message is "Life must go on." Her guilt and

*pain hang about her shoulders like a shroud, but she con-
sciously represses her tears, allowing the overwhelming duty
of caring for her remaining family to engulf her.*

*She rises before dawn and faces the task of preparing
four meals per day for four hungry men; her young hands
are rubbed raw from scrubbing their dirt-encased overalls
on a washboard. All the while, she is surrounded by black,
smoke-covered walls that once created a kitchen resounding
with laughter and joy. It seems forever before the walls of the
house are restored—the laughter and joy never are.*

Velma and Abe marry two years later; both with fathers named
John and mothers who died sudden, violent deaths at age 49. It
is 1933, the height of the Depression, with scant job availability.
When their first child, a girl, is born in 1936 they move nine times
in twelve months looking for work. Abe finally obtains a new job
and often is gone several days at a time while driving a cross-
country produce truck.

*In a lonely room of a boarding house somewhere in Okla-
homa, Velma rocks her new baby and cries hour after hour.
But she makes certain she is smiling when her husband returns. Three years pass before she and Abe are able to return
to their hometown of Marion, Kansas, and both are eager to
again be with their extended families.*

*Velma and their small daughter travel ahead on the bus
while Abe loads their old pickup to the brim. Everything they
own and cherish materially is contained within its battered
sides: wedding gifts, baby clothes, family photos, and a few
pieces of furniture which have been a struggle to purchase.*

*At the home of relatives, Velma and her toddler anxious-
ly await Abe's appearance. But instead of the familiar pick-up
stacked with their possessions, a strange truck pulls into the
driveway. Abe gets out, thanking the driver profusely for the
ride. He turns to Velma and tries to speak, but the words won't*

come. Then slowly he begins to sob, "A fire, a fire in the truck, everything gone."

But, life must go on.

Although they settle in Marion, even there Abe is restless. Seeking to always better himself and his family, they move to a different home almost every year.

Velma's motto becomes "Peace at any price." To experience any intense feelings would endanger her precarious hold on her emotions and might release a floodgate of pain in which she would drown. But her fragile closed-mouth smile cannot hide the sorrow in her sad eyes. Her body reacts with severe migraine headaches and debilitating arthritis.

The year 1944 becomes significant; a new daughter is born and welcomed by her eight-year-old sister, and because WWII continues to rage, the family moves to the "big city of Wichita" so Abe can help win the war by working at the local airport. They live in one small home for three months and then move to a larger house where they have boarders who work in the aircraft factories or at the nearby military bases.

Thirty-year-old Velma is swamped, not only with emotional and physical pain, but with a new baby, four boarders, cooking with food rationing, one bathroom for eight people, and no car. When her eight-year-old asks to attend choir practice after school and ride alone on the city bus to the church, Velma is hesitant, but she trusts her little girl who is bright and independent and finally agrees. After all, in the small town of Marion where everyone knows everyone else, children are allowed to run about freely and nothing harmful ever happens, so Wichita must be safe, too.

Her young daughter is excited about riding the bus alone and the first few times is diligent in watching for the sign that signals her exit. But gradually she relaxes into the ride and one snowy afternoon picks up her schoolbook and begins to read. When she finally puts it down she is startled to see sky-scrapers directly in front of her, not where they usually are— far in the distance. She has missed her stop and gone deep in-to the center of the city.

As she attempts to find her way back to familiar streets, she experiences an event that changes her life. She is accosted by several young soldiers, with the ill-fated encounter evolv-ing into a sexual assault. But she is a survivor, and when her abusers leave, she cleans herself up and finds her way home, only telling her mother that she missed her bus.

In her family, painful issues are not discussed. No one has ever role-modeled how to deal with trauma and pain in a healthy way, and certainly no one ever has talked to her about such a thing as sexual abuse—and so, the child pushes down the feelings and the memories. But, the pain will not be de-nied; it seeps out in torturous nightmares and, like her moth-er before her, the child's emotional pain escapes through her physical body. A lifetime of asthma, headaches, and body pain emerges.

The child's name is Marilyn.

This is the story of my family.

~

Survival

"From our own despair comes wisdom through the grace of God.
—Aeschylus (525-456 B.C.)

Because my asthma continued to plague me though out my teens, I moved to the clear mountain air of northern Arizona upon gradua-tion from high school. This new climate relieved me of my asthma, but unfortunately, the asthma was replaced by headaches which gained in severity over the years. As an adult, unlike some people who use alcohol, drugs, nicotine, or food to cover their pain, I used work. I became a hard-driving, over-achieving, perfection-istic workaholic. In addition, I became an excessive caretaker of other people—what we now refer to as a classic codependent—someone who takes responsibility for the well being of others at the cost of her or his health.

Everyone who saw me thought I had a perfect life; I had a won-derful family and a successful career. I was active in my community of Scottsdale, AZ, and in my church. But others were not aware of my increasing physical problems which, by the time I reached age 44, had become resistant to all medication. I had been taking 25 Excedrin per day, 125 milligrams of Elavil per day, approximately twelve to fifteen Alka-Seltzer tablets per day, and about a bottle of Fiorinal (a strong pain reliever) per week—and still found no relief. Certainly, no one would have suspected that I was also be-coming suicidal because I could not escape the pain. That is, no one but my close friend Kay, who insisted I enter a center in California for intensive therapy.

I resisted vehemently because in 1980, no one from the con-servative community in Arizona in which I lived went to therapy unless he or she was certifiably psychotic. I kept saying, "Nothing is wrong with me—I don't need this. Nothing is wrong with my mind!" But I am a firm believer in God's timing, and I believe that He orchestrated my healing. My friend prevailed, and I finally en-tered what was intended to be two weeks of intensive therapy. Instead, I was gone seven months.

Uncovering the Pain

During my therapy, I began to realize that I was in a safe place where I could release years of unresolved pain. The memory of that snowy, late afternoon in Wichita when I had been reading on a bus and missed my stop came roaring to the surface. It was as though I was re-living being sexually assaulted by the soldiers at age eight. I was a child who had never known violence and was totally overwhelmed physically and emotionally. When my offenders left, I had no location in my conscious mind into which I could deposit this event. It did not fit into any familiar format, so I had to create a new place for it, deep in my unconscious. Then I cleaned myself up, found my way home, and told my mother I had missed my bus.

But, while my conscious mind refused to acknowledge my abuse, my body and my unconscious mind remembered. I immediately began having asthma attacks in which I was choking and couldn't breathe and felt pressure on my chest—all a replication of an oral rape. (Note: This is not meant to infer that all asthma has the same etiology as mine.) I also had terrifying dreams of being smothered and dying. My mother later told of her memories of my nightmares and screams, stating that when I awoke, I would cry and say I was "drowning in white glue" and had "sticky stuff" on my face (in 1944 sexual abuse would not have been in the realm my parents' thoughts.)

The power of the volcanic release of that event during therapy was so great that it left me in a quasi-eight-year-old state for six weeks. I could not read or write beyond the level of a third grader; I could not wear jewelry, makeup, or a bra; even the hair on my legs and under my arms stopped growing. I could "come-up" and be age 44 at will, if necessary, but it caused me so much stress that my therapist assured me it was okay to "just stay eight" for awhile if I needed to do so.

The Murray Method: Discovered by a Child

"If help and salvation are to come, they can only come from the children, for the children are the makers of men."
—Maria Montessori (1870–1952)

From the time I was very small, I have always had a very curious mind. My mother said that I drove her crazy with my constant questions of "What?" Why?" "Who?" and "How?" As I grew older, my interest expanded into many areas from how a bronze sculpture in our gallery had been created to why the women in our "More Than Friends" groups reacted differently to traumatic situations in their lives.

During those first six weeks in therapy, while I was still in a child-like state, I was connecting with, and bringing new insights to, my adult mind every day. When my therapist, Dr. Peter Danylchuk, asked what was happening to me, I struggled to explain the split I was experiencing. I said, "I think when I was created I was an Original Child, the person God designed me to be. Then when my abuse happened, I became a Sobbing Child, a child who carried all my pain. I didn't know what to do with her, so it felt like I put her in a 'box' and buried her, but when I did, my Original Child also disappeared into the 'box.' The child that buried them was my Controlling Child, my protector.

"In order to make certain that both my Original Child and my Sobbing Child stayed hidden, I had to always be my Controlling Child. She's the one other people know. She keeps busy, takes care of everyone else, and tries to keep a smile on her face. As long as she does those things, she doesn't have time to think about what she buried."

I had no way of foreseeing then that these childlike terms would one day become the basis of my theory—a theory written by a child.

As the days, weeks, and months passed, I was gradually able to become a functioning adult. But I had no idea how to balance and integrate all the inner parts of me. At first, I wanted to completely eliminate my Sobbing Child and Controlling Child, but I began to realize that they both had significant functions in my life. My Controlling Child gained a new job description, and I found that her main task was to remain my defense mechanism, to help me learn about boundaries, and to keep me responsible. My Sobbing Child, created from what I labeled as my Pool of Pain, embodied empathy and compassion and related to other people at the depths of their pain.

My Original Child—the person I was created to be, including all my innate capabilities, my personality, and my intelligence—played the most important role of all: she was the container of my soul, the part that sought to connect with God.

The Paradigm Shift

Similar concepts to the insights I discovered in therapy in 1980-81, were also brought into public awareness by the well-known author and speaker John Bradshaw in the late 1980s as he wrote and taught about the "inner child." Other theorists have also discussed the process of inner splitting, but, to my knowledge, they have not been from the viewpoint of the child itself.

As I discovered all three aspects of myself, I found they slowly began to integrate into what I termed a Healthy Balanced Person. This new adult was extremely fragile and appeared only fleetingly, but those precious fragments became embedded in my spirit. I knew I would never be satisfied until I genuinely understood her message.

Dr. Danylchuk gently guided me on a healing journey that not only dealt with my sexual abuse, but also helped to open my mind and heart to understanding my belief systems and the way I lived my life. God was creating a major paradigm shift that began to direct my spirit with a new intensity and direction.

As I lanced the deeply infected wound that had occupied my body and spirit for so many years, I became acutely aware of my need to allow a healing balm to come into that wound to fill the gaping void. To leave it as a raw, open wound would encourage future infections. Gradually I realized that only God and I could enable that healing to take place.

I was astounded by the interaction between my emotions and my physical being. As I released my emotional pain, my body began to change and heal. One day in April, 1981 is forever imprinted in my brain. I awoke sensing something was different. For decades I had lived with severe headaches caused by the enormous stress of holding down a lifetime of painful emotions regarding not only my sexual abuse, but also the fact that I had always repressed my feelings during any conflict. Over the years, as my physical pain grew more intense and debilitating, I tried every type of treatment— both traditional and non-traditional— without success. I remembered the words of several medical doctors in the years prior to my therapy: "We have no cure for your pain. You will simply have to learn how to tolerate and manage it." But on this day in April, I awoke to a sunny, beautiful spring day with *no headache*. It was the first time in over 25 years.

Not only did my headaches and asthma disappear, but my entire body became healthier. I began walking three miles a day over the San Francisco hills (sometimes eight miles on the weekends) on legs that previously had difficulty walking short distances and never up inclines without aching. I lost thirty pounds and began to look and feel more alive. I was ecstatic as I began to grasp what it meant to be a Healthy Balanced Person.

I began to comprehend that we are created as physical, intellectual, emotional, and spiritual beings, and that these strands make up the cord that is every human individual. When one strand is weakened, it weakens the entire cord; conversely, when one strand is strengthened, it strengthens the whole.

While I was feeling much improved, being away from loved ones for seven months was very difficult. I missed my family greatly, but I also knew this was a confusing, painful time for them. They did not know what to tell people who inquired about my whereabouts. I had gone from high visibility to no visibility overnight. Rumors spread of a "nervous breakdown" and other speculations. At that period in time, there were no explanations for what I was experiencing. I returned home in June, eager to see my loved ones and friends but extremely anxious concerning their reactions to me.

During my time at the therapy center, I also had the opportunity to listen to numerous stories of abuse from patients from throughout the world. The doctor who owned the clinic was well-known internationally, and I had the privilege of meeting patients from every continent during my stay. I arrived in Arizona wanting to shout, "Listen everyone, do you know what actually happens in the world? This is what children are enduring: sexual, physical, and emotional abuse." I found that most people had no knowledge of the extent of abuse happening daily in homes, schools, and streets across the globe. And, regrettably, very few wanted to hear about it.

I felt like I had left Kansas and Arizona to go to war and had been captured and placed into a prisoner of war camp. When I was finally liberated and returned home, people were delighted to have me back, but many really didn't want to know about where I'd been or what I'd experienced there.

Another World, Another War

Once you bring life into the world, you must protect it.
We must protect it by changing the world.
—*Elie Wiesel (1928 - 2016)*

I had been a prisoner of another war—a war that was just beginning to surface. I had no idea what my future would become, but I knew I wanted to be on the battlefield in this conflict. I prayed, "Lord, you open the door and I'll walk through it." As I said before, I am a firm believer in God's timing, and while I was experiencing my healing journey, many other people were beginning theirs as well. In 1981, abuse was at last becoming an open topic in the United States.

Within four months of my return home, I was asked to speak to a group of women regarding my experience, becoming one of the first people in America to speak publicly about sexual abuse. In the next two years, the issues of child abuse, especially sexual abuse, began to invade the media. I received requests to speak nationally: at universities, in churches, at other public presentations, and on television and radio. I was taken aback by the overwhelming response. After national television appearances, my mail arrived in huge sacks with most of the letter writers wanting to find trained therapists who understood abuse and could help them.

Dr. Danylchuk and my new therapist in Arizona, Dr. Ralph Earle, both encouraged me to return to college and study psychology. I went for two reasons: to become a therapist who could respond to the emerging urgent cries for help and to understand more about my own process. I wanted someone to explain what had happened to me when I "buried myself" at age eight.

The Scindo Syndrome

In the first year of my bachelor's program at Ottawa University in Phoenix, Arizona, I immediately began asking my professors and any clinician I met to explain the 'splitting' process to me— the process I had struggled to explain to Dr. Danylchuk when I first met my Sobbing Child, as well as my Controlling Child and My Original Child. I received many responses. Some thought I was talking about schizophrenia, since "schizoid" is the Greek word for "split." Others assumed I was referring to (what was then called) multiple personality disorder. I replied, "No, I am describing the natural phenomenon of dissociation (or splitting), which arises as a defense mechanism when a person experiences trauma or abuse." Some answered, "We know that experience happens, but because we ethically cannot replicate trauma in a laboratory—either with people or animals—we don't know much about it."

Several of my professors, as well as my therapists, urged me to write about my personal knowledge of this particular psychological process. As I began charting my seven months in therapy, I noticed a distinct pattern, which I assumed only applied to me. When I shared this information with Dr. Earle and one of my Ottawa University professors, they encouraged me to continue to expand my work, as they felt it was developing into a psychological theory that also would apply to others. I named my theory the Scindo Syndrome ("scindo" is Latin for "split," or "tear asunder," and is pronounced as *sin-doe*); I chose this term to differentiate this phenomenon of splitting from other psychological terminology such as schizophrenia or multiple personality disorder (today termed dissociative identity disorder.)

In addition to my other activities, I started working with incarcerated juvenile and adult rapists and child molesters in the Arizona prison system and became one of the first rape victims to do so. I found these violent offenders were most often victims who had become victimizers, and those who were willing to deal with their own pain made some powerful changes in their lives. It became a profoundly healing work, both for them and for me. I began to get an inkling of what grace and forgiveness were really all about.

Turmoil and Healing

Life must be understood backwards,
But it must be lived—forwards.
—Soren Kierkegaard (1813–1855)

I found that life is not perfect for any of us, no matter how sincere we are regarding transformation and growth in our own lives. We cannot change anyone else, only ourselves. Because I was struggling with numerous personal issues, I underwent another major life adjustment in 1984 and moved to California where I continued my education and professional work for the next thirteen years (If you are interested in further details, you may order my book, *Prisoner of Another War,* from our web site: www.murraymethod.com).

During that time in California, I felt like an Origami butterfly and remembered the first time I saw one of those unique creations. It is a most intricate work of art where paper is precisely folded, cut in the shape of a butterfly, and then put into a very tiny box. When you open the box and take out its precious contents, the infinite folds burst into a marvelous winged creature. Like its live counterpart, once opened, it can never be refolded and returned to its cocoon. My Original Child had been reclaimed and was maturing into a Healthy Balanced Person. I knew it was impossible ever to deny those aspects of myself and return to my box once again. I was created to fly.

Once I truly began to fly, I often felt as though my toes would never touch the ground again. The demand for help regarding the treatment of trauma and abuse was so great that I was constantly busy. But over the years, as the supply of qualified people and resources in the U.S. increased, God led me into the international field where the demand was still very large and the supply of help extremely small. When I was first invited to speak in the former USSR starting in Kiev, Ukraine, in 2001 and then in Moscow in 2002, I was very excited but had no idea it would develop into a permanent venture.

Russkaya!

In Russia, I begin each introductory class (Level I) by introducing myself with my *Story of a Family*. At the end, when I let them know the little girl in the story is me, my audience looks stunned; often many are in tears. Sexual abuse is not a common subject for discussion and certainly not in public. In addition, they are unaccustomed to sharing anything regarding painful family memories.

I also tell them about my cousin, Johannes, whom we found in Siberia, and who, at age 78, traveled four days and nights from Siberia to Moscow to meet with my nephew Tim Watson, who also lived and worked in Russia with his family, and me. From Johannes, we learned how he was sent to a Gulag concentration camp at age seventeen and how his fifteen-year-old brother and three-year-old sister died there and how not one member of our family survived the horrific brutality of Stalin.

I close my presentation by saying, "Ya ees Amerikee, nor na pa-lavino Russkaya," (I am from America, but I am half Russian), and am greeted by smiles, hugs, and cheers of "Russkaya! Russkaya!" Russians are normally very suspicious of outsiders, especially Americans, but God has taken the tragedies of my family and my own sexual abuse and used them to pay for my right to stand and speak in this place. During my seventeen years of working with more than 3,000 people from in the former USSR, no one has ever said to me, "You wouldn't understand."

A New Pathway—A Paradigm Shift

"Those who suffer deeply touch life at every point;
they drain the cup to the dregs while others sip
only the bubbles at the top.
Perhaps no man can touch the stars unless
he knows the depths of despair... and fought his way back."

—Anonymous

It is humbling to see how God has used these sessions to bring hope where there was none. Our participants consistently say, "At last, hope for healing is possible for me, and maybe also for Russia." A paradigm shift is beginning to happen. Each individual person who changes and becomes a healthy, balanced person transmits love and hope in a manner which is amazingly contagious.

The following are statements made by class participants that reflect their willingness to change and grow and their joy as they experience transformation in their lives:

- "I have always struggled with a deep desire and longing for freedom but also was restrained by my need for security and stability. I now understand that God and I together can provide freedom in my soul and security and stability in my spirit—no matter what happens around me. Today I am free and joyous for the first time in my life and I am fifty-five years old!"

- "I was a drug and alcohol addict for 15 years and for 10 years God has already been changing my life and I have been clean from drugs and alcohol. But these simple, easy-to-understand concepts showed me that I still have work to do because of the trauma and pain from my past."
- "It feels as though we are now on a pathway, walking toward the light. It is as though we have always been searching for this. I was raised as an atheist and had no concept of what my soul needed. Now I am finally am coming out of the darkness."
- "We were taught by the Soviet system that we were never to think for ourselves. They told us when to sit, when to stand, what to think, what to say, what to do. We had no minds of our own. We had no concept of how to make a healthy decision by ourselves. That system was our parent, our boss, and our God. Then when that dictatorial system fell, we were like little children, like three-year-olds being thrown out into the snow and told, 'Here, now you take care of yourselves!' We are not stupid, we are not lazy, we are not irresponsible—we just don't know how! Please teach us how to think, how to make good decisions, how to be responsible. We desperately need help and are eager to learn."
- "I had forgotten my joy. After these days, I feel like I am balanced along the road of life."

Passing the Baton

Never doubt that a small group of thoughtful, committed citizens can change the world. Indeed, it is the only thing that ever has.
—Margaret Mead (1901-1978)

I have been greatly inspired by these wonderful women and men whom I have learned to love deeply and to respect their incredible courage. They have experienced pain and hardship far beyond what most persons could ever begin to comprehend.

It is intensely rewarding for me to experience their excitement as they commit to applying their new wisdom to themselves, and also as they learn how to role-model this wisdom to their loved ones, clients, students, and parishioners in a healthy, respectful manner.

They are creating legacies of love.

No matter what your background or status in life, a healing journey is also possible for you. Please consider joining us...

GUIDEPOST ONE

PURPOSE AND PROCESS

Accepting the need for a personal healing journey in your life; *trusting* in the process of that healing, wherever it may lead you; and being *willing* to risk and actively participate with your *actions*

A journey can be a passage of a few hours undertaken spontaneously, simply as a relaxing way to spend a day. Or, it may be a major expedition which occupies much of your time, energy, and effort for a long duration. Many people approach life as though it were a casual, impulsive trip, allowing themselves to be tossed about by whatever crosses their path. They often reach the end of their lives feeling unfulfilled and empty. But if your purpose is to reclaim your soul and to reach your final earthly destination having lived a successful, worthwhile life, then you may want to slow down and contemplate if you honestly are on that path. Consider the stages that will prepare and enable you to begin a truly healthy, healing journey that will continue throughout your lifetime bringing healing, not only to yourself, but to countless others.

The stages of preparation are:

- **Accepting** the need for a personal healing journey in your life,
- **Trusting** in the process of that healing, wherever it may lead you, and being
- **Willing** to risk and actively participate with your actions.

Can you remember your last trip? You accepted the fact that taking this time to go away was something you genuinely wanted and needed. But what if you never stepped onto the plane or the bus or got into your car and allowed yourself to be carried to your destination? Unless you trust your transportation vehicle and are willing to risk taking action by stepping into it, your journey will never take place.

A healing journey is no different. It is somewhat like taking your first flight on an airplane. First, you must determine your purpose for the journey and whether or not it is a worthwhile endeavor and accept that it is something you need or want to do. A healing journey does not transpire in a vacuum; other people and your Higher Power are necessary companions. Allowing yourself to relax and trust in the process, even if it involves something or someone outside of your normal comfort zone, is essential. Finally, unless you decide to genuinely participate in this journey, it cannot take place. Once you are willing, you still have to step onto the plane. Without action, you will remain forever earth-bound and never fly. I encourage you to fly. Be everything you were created to be. Live a worthwhile life.

CHAPTER 1

Emotional Pain: Shock, Slivers, and Splits

*Pain—it seems to be the common
denominator of our human existence.
It's part of the life experience.
To avoid it is to detour the essence of life itself.*

—Tim Hansel (1941–2009)

Our Innate Protector

Of all the human experiences, pain is probably the most universal and perhaps least understood. Emotional pain, physical pain—who has been spared? Few people deny that pain exists. It is so obvious in the lives of other people, yet we often refuse to acknowledge it in our own lives. In discussing the expression of pain, many people differentiate between physical and emotional pain. But are they so different? Physical and emotional pain are inextricably intertwined. To understand how we respond to one gives insight into how we respond to the other.

The human body is a wondrous organism constructed to survive despite the fact that some pain is inevitable. The repression of pain is often not a conscious act but rather an unconscious instinctive reaction. We are fortunate to be created with an innate defense mechanism, generally referred to as shock, which helps us survive severe physical injury through a temporary deadening of pain.

The concept of physical shock is something most people understand. Many of us have experienced it at some time, to some degree. Have you ever had a bad accident in which you sustained a deep cut or a broken bone? How long did it take you to feel the pain? When I ask others this, they consistently reply, "I didn't feel any pain for quite a while." For some there was no pain for hours, or even for days. That delay is part of the shock response.

My friend Tim Hansel's story is a precise description of the concept of shock:

> It is the fall of 1974 and the air is crisp and cold. The reflection off the snow sparkles and dances as two men proceed carefully along the edge of a huge glacier. This incredibly beautiful place never fails to give Tim an exhilarating rush. At age 33, he looks forward to the day when he can bring his baby son, Zach, with him on one of these mountain climbs.
>
> Taking kids from all ranks of life on exciting outdoor adventures has captured his heart. As a graduate of Stanford, a top athlete and then high school coach in California, he finds that bringing together teenagers from the ghettos with others from higher social strata breaks down all racial and prejudicial barriers. Today, his mind is on an upcoming trip he is planning for a group in Los Angeles. Riots and racial strife have torn the area apart and he is anxious to help bring some healing to that portion of the city.
>
> Earlier in the day Tim and his partner were grateful the snow had formed a bridge across a deep crevasse. As they return, however, they are unaware that the sun has begun the devious task of melting the snow beneath their feet. Tim's foot hits what should be rock hard snow, but instead it gives way and sends him sailing in the air, upside down. It is as though he has been thrown off a six-story building. His partner looks on in horror—it takes so long for Tim's body to hit and when it does, it crashes into solid ice. His vertebrae crack, shatter, collapse.

As he slowly regains consciousness, Tim wonders if he is really alive or is actually dead and just looking at his body lying distorted on the snow. He is startled to find he can move his legs and feels only a slight amount of pain. With a great deal of effort he stands, and determines he will see his family again, he will stay alive.

After taking a six-story fall, Tim hiked 22 miles out to his car with a severely broken back and drove home, a trip of 350 miles. Later, Tim commented about his fall: "When I became conscious, to my surprise, I sat up. I didn't feel any pain; I just felt 'short.' I also felt very lucky. 48 hours later I awoke sweating profusely, delirious, in incredible pain, and not knowing where I was. I was coming out of shock."

Unfortunately, when the numbing effect of that physical shock wore off, Tim was left with agonizing, excruciating pain—sickening, perpetual pain that would not respond to any treatment or medication. That pain never diminished; it only increased. Yet Tim dedicated his life to helping others with disabilities and became a renowned speaker and author. His book, *You Gotta Keep Dancin',* is a profound account of his own healing journey. His death in December, 2009 brought an end to his physical pain, and I know for certain that he now is dancin' in heaven.

Shock

When we are hurt physically, our defense system activates automatically. Tim did not consciously will himself not to feel pain as he walked away from that glacier. The welcome relief of physical shock occurred unconsciously and instantaneously.

The delay of the sensation of pain allows the rest of the body to focus attention on the wounded part, to send energy where it is needed most. Although it protects us until we are able to deal with the enormity of the trauma, it is meant to be temporary. We eventually need to deal with the pain.

When the trauma occurs, the body is injured. Shock sets in temporarily and deadens the pain. Eventually, however, the shock wears off, followed by the experience of pain. Pain is necessary; it signals to our minds that our bodies are in trouble, that our injury requires care. This signal is essential in cases where the wound is not visible. Without pain, a person would not know to seek help until significant internal damage had occurred.

But what would happen if this shock defense mechanism remained active, if pain was never felt? Certainly the injured person would enjoy that respite for a time, but it would be harmful over the long term. If you were unable to feel physical pain, you might place your hand on a burning stove or step on a jagged piece of glass, unaware of the damage you had incurred. Certain diseases such as leprosy and advanced stages of diabetes cause damage to the body's nerve endings, especially in the extremities. It is not uncommon for people with these afflictions to severely injure their hands or feet from cuts or burns because they are deprived of pain. Both shock and pain are necessary components of healing from physical trauma.

We are also created with an innate psychological defense system, one that functions identically to the physiological one. It too activates spontaneously and is only meant to be temporary. Our emotional shock mechanism works in conjunction with physical shock at the time of a physical wound. Tim Hansel did not panic when he was hurt. Many people injured in severe accidents not only do not feel physical pain, but they also do not experience emotional hysteria at the time of the incident. We acknowledge this type of emotional shock as normal. This reaction is also common in times of war, terrorist activities, or catastrophic natural disasters such as earthquakes or hurricanes when many traumatic events are happening simultaneously.

In other situations, only emotional shock may be activated. For example, after suffering the loss of a loved one you may not feel the full impact of the loss for a lengthy period. Countless victims, families, and observers who related their reactions to the cataclysmic events of September 11, 2001, in New York City declared, "I was in shock." People were numb to their pain, and it lasted from minutes to months.

The ideal situation, after we have experienced a traumatic event, is one in which we are able to release our painful feelings as soon as the emotional shock begins to ease and we are able to talk about our experiences and feel the fear, helplessness, and grief within a supportive, caring environment.

If, however, we are unable to release our painful feelings shortly after a trauma has occurred, many different physical and emotional reactions may take place. In severe cases, new physical and emotional symptoms may appear. This phenomenon, originally documented and researched in regard to military veterans, was designated "post-traumatic stress disorder" (PTSD) in the American Psychiatric Association's Diagnostic and Statistical Manual IV. There are numerous manifestations of PTSD. Some of the more common include sleep disturbances, nightmares, night terrors, sleepwalking, recurrent intrusive recollections of the trauma, diminished ability to express emotions, an exaggerated startle response, difficulty concentrating, and memory impairment.

Our emotional shock defense mechanism is not confined to severe traumas, nor does it always end in PTSD. Painful events, which can vary widely, include verbal, emotional, physical, and sexual abuse; neglect and deprivation; and other traumas such as deaths, illnesses, accidents, natural disasters, criminal activity, prison experiences, and wartime tragedies. Each time a person, especially a child, experiences something painful and is unable to release the feelings connected with that event within a short period, then that person buries the pain, unconsciously repressing it. If that emotional shock continues indefinitely, it may cause severe emotional and/or physical damage.

The same universal laws that regulate physiological shock also regulate emotional shock. It too is meant to be *temporary*. If a person attends to a physical wound immediately, it leaves a scar relative to the size of the wound. But if the wound is allowed to fester and become infected, the infection will proliferate throughout the body, perhaps causing the loss of a limb or even death. The infection might even spread to other people upon contact.

In the same way, emotional pain that is denied because of chronic shock will take its toll some time, some place. An emotional wound, if ignored and left untended for years, will fester and grow. Then it will either erupt or be driven underground to emerge in other ways, with the resulting infection wreaking havoc on the person's psyche, physical body, and relationships. When repression of emotions and memories becomes long-term, the natural healing process is hindered. People in this state of chronic emotional shock—people for whom repression has become a lifelong pattern—endure injuries to their hearts, spirits, emotions, and egos that are often more damaging than the original events.

Pain inevitably demands its price. It refuses to be denied. Greater long-term damage is caused by the repression of feelings surrounding a trauma than by the trauma itself.

To Feel or Not to Feel? That Is the Question

Many factors determine whether emotional shock is temporary or becomes chronic, including age, personality type, ego strength, emotional health, and physical health. These additional factors also affect emotional shock:

- Has anyone modeled how to deal with painful feelings?
- Is it safe to tell, or will telling create more abuse?
- Is anyone available to listen and provide comfort?
- Do family, ethnic, and cultural mores dictate that feelings are not allowed?
- Is the source of the pain something not normally discussed?
- Will sharing the pain bring additional pain to a loved one?
- Is protecting others more important than healing oneself?

When I began processing my sexual abuse during therapy, it was as though that eight-year-old was re-experiencing that terrifying event; one of the first statements that child made was, "I can't go home and tell because this will make my momma cry." Because my mother had suffered the enormous loss of her mother and sister only a few years earlier, she was often very sad. I wanted to save her from any more sadness, at any cost.

Although my mother was sweet and loving and did not say, "Behave or you will make me sad," somehow that is the message I received. I never heard my parents argue, and painful, hurting issues were not addressed, so they could not be resolved in a healthy way. Consequently, I was poorly prepared to deal with the real world. My mother commented to me when I became an adult, "I wanted you to have only happy memories."

In 1944, no one discussed rape or child abuse. In fact, sex as a general issue was not a topic in the average household—certainly not in mine. The family history and tragedies of both of my parents solidified the idea that survival was the essence of existence. Consequently, their dictum became, "Do not feel; life must go on." All these factors combined to confirm my unconscious decision to bury the events of that fateful snowy afternoon when I was eight.

Splitting and Its Consequences

In an attempt to comprehend how I dealt with this painful experience in my life, I continued to expand my theory of the Scindo Syndrome (as described in the Prologue). I wanted to further understand the consequences of the emotional shock defense mechanism—especially when that protective response became permanent, not temporary, as it was originally intended.

I recognized that every human being:
- contains who they were created to be;
- has a Pool of Pain of some degree or intensity; and
- has a basic defense mechanism.

I also realized that how these aspects interact greatly determines how each person lives their life.

In order to clarify this concept during my therapy process, I assigned "names" to these various aspects. I hypothesized regarding the manner in which we split into different "children" during times of abuse and trauma, and that our goal, ultimately, is to unite these children and become a Healthy Balanced Person. I developed the following definitions to help explain my hypothesis:

Original Child

- is who you were created to be
- contains your soul, and your true spirituality, with its inherent desire to connect with God
- includes your innate intelligence, talent, personality, creativity, and physical appearance
- is an emotionally unfragmented child at conception with the capacity to feel all emotions—appropriately and inappropriately
- has free will and the capacity to choose good or evil

Sobbing Child

- contains all your painful feelings (fear, hurt, sadness, anger, loneliness, helplessness, shame, and so on)
- is created by outside negative influences, such as trauma, abuse, neglect, or illness
- is created from your Original Child
- contains a positive element in that it enables you to feel compassion and empathy, to be tender and caring

Controlling Child

- is necessary as your innate defense mechanism, including emotional shock
- is created out of your Original Child to protect your Sobbing Child
- is meant to be a temporary help in time of pain and distress, but can become unhealthy if it develops into a permanent status

- will use whatever is available in your environment or your innate abilities to manage pain
- uses several basic defenses:
  - repression
  - anesthetizers (such as nicotine, alcohol, drugs, or sex, and food in excess) and can become destructive when applying these defenses
  - diversionary tactics (such as relationships, work, reading, television, music, sports, school, church, or computers when they are used to avoid dealing with pain and difficult issues)
- when healthy, contains additional positive elements: it keeps you responsible and also helps you set appropriate boundaries (keeps others from victimizing you and you from victimizing others)

Healthy Balanced Person
- is your goal in your healing journey of recovery
- is integrated as a deeply feeling person who also is reasonable, thinking, and responsible
- is an effective synthesis of head (intellect) and gut (emotions)
- combines your Original Child with the positive strengths of your Sobbing Child and Controlling Child in a balanced, healthy way
- is capable of feeling all emotions appropriately
- generates maturity and therefore is part of a lifelong process

Fragmenting the Original Child

In my soul there is a treasure
And the key for it is given only to me
—*Alexander Blok (1880 - 1921)*

We each begin our life's journey as an Original Child, the core of which contains our soul and our true spirituality, with an inherent desire to connect with God. In this initial stage, the child is emotionally unfragmented and has an intact capacity for developing emotions.

We all are fashioned to be feeling creatures; our innate instincts urge us to experience our emotions. Unfortunately, the situations into which children are born are not always conducive to allowing that child to remain in its original state. At a very young age, we are conditioned as to whether or not it is safe to feel. As children, if we are allowed to cry and are comforted when we become frightened or hurt, we learn that it is okay to feel pain and that help will come, and, most importantly, that our pain will eventually diminish. If this is our experience, we develop a sense of the discomfort of pain, but we also learn that pain does not have to be overwhelming.

To understand that pain can be felt and expressed and to know we can survive is the beginning of healthy emotional growth. The crucial key is that when we are young, a caring person responds to our Original Child's pain, and that person values and respects the child as a feeling being. However, if, as children, help does not come when we cry out in fear, or if the person who comes punishes us or is perhaps the one who caused our fear in the first place, we then learn that expressing fear is not a safe thing to do.

To learn a healthy mode of expressing painful feelings, we not only need to feel safe to experience and express the pain; we also need a role model who shows us how to deal with the pain. Unfortunately, parental role modeling of beneficial, congruous expressions of painful emotions has been almost nonexistent. Many of today's adults were raised in an environment in which pain, fear, and anger were termed "negative" emotions. Our parents' pattern for dealing with those feelings was often learned from their parents' style of managing emotions: repression and denial. They handed down repressive admonitions to us with strong verbal and physical reinforcements: "Don't be a crybaby," or, "Be quiet or I'll give you something to cry about." Those remonstrances are still heard in many homes.

In some families, unpleasant emotions are expressed, but only by adults, and are not permitted by children. Adults are allowed angry outbursts that cause pain to others around them, while the children are forced to suffer in silence. In certain families and cultures, adults who wail and complain are tolerated. These expressions of distressing emotions, however, may create an aversion to histrionics in those unfortunate enough to have to listen. Statements such as, "If you don't behave, I'll go crazy and end up in an asylum, and then you'll be left all alone," or "You are going to make me kill myself!" are not uncommon in such households. Children and other family members, manipulated by the threat of impending disasters and illnesses, may become numb to the authenticity of true pain.

If a child lives in a home where physical, emotional, or verbal abuse is a daily fact of life, the child's instinctual repression of pain and its resulting emotions is eventually transformed into conditioned learning. An innate survival defense mechanism becomes an ingrained habit, one that is exceedingly difficult to break. The child gradually begins to discount and deny his or her own reality.

While the Original Child contains many positive aspects—our soul, natural talents and abilities, our physical, emotional, intellectual and spiritual aspects—it also has free will, so it also has the ability to be immature, selfish, irresponsible, demanding, reckless, impatient and other characteristics of a person who remains in a "childish," not a mature, state.

A Pool of Pain

I thought that I could not be hurt;
I thought that I must surely be impervious to suffering,
immune to mental pain or agony . . .
Then, suddenly my world turned gray,
and darkness wiped aside my joy.
A dull and aching void was left
 where careless hands had reached out to destroy.
—Sylvia Plath, (1932–1963)

Our painful experiences are uniquely our own. Each of us has a Pool of Pain that contains the hurt we have accumulated over the years, whether minor or major, occasional or chronic. The significance and intensity of each event and each person's reaction to painful events varies widely.

No one is the Original Child that he or she was created to be. Everyone has a Sobbing Child of some degree and intensity, and everyone has a Pool of Pain. Even if you had perfect parents (and I do not know anyone who did), painful things happen; you or a loved one becomes ill; a teacher at school yells at you; you are left alone while your parents work; your pet is accidentally killed; your beloved grandparents die; you see major tragedies regularly on the television news. As the late Scott Peck stated in his best-selling book, *The Road Less Traveled*, "Life is difficult."

Each time our Original Child experiences pain and we are unable to release and deal with our resulting feelings appropriately, a portion of whom we were created to be is transformed into a deeply hurting child. Imagine a potato peeler in one hand and an orange in the other; with the peeler, you could slice away a sliver of the peeling. However, with a paring knife you could cut off a slightly larger piece, including some pulp. With a butcher knife, you could sever a huge chunk of the orange. With a machete, you could chop the fruit in half. Your Original Child, which contains your soul, becomes fragmented in the same way. Sometimes the split is just a sliver; other times, it is a larger chunk. When this splitting occurs, it creates your Sobbing Child. Eventually, you are left with only a small fragment of your initial creation, your Original Child, who is now completely covered by your shredded, bleeding, Sobbing Child.

When this type of psychic rendering transpires, our innate psychological shock mechanism, the Controlling Child, is triggered also, and this child will do whatever is necessary to protect us from pain. As the emotional shock activator, this defense mechanism unconsciously represses and buries the majority of our emotions and in some cases a portion, or all, of our memories connected with an especially painful experience. Our Controlling Child admonishes, "Don't feel. Don't remember. To feel hurts."

But is our Controlling Child only a denier of feelings and a defender against pain? Or does that defender also become a captor of joy?

Unfortunately, we are unable to repress feelings selectively. How nice it would be to bury only fear, hurt, sadness, anger, loneliness, helplessness, shame, and so on in a box and close the lid, never having to face them again. But our emotions are connected, as if on a chain. When we bury our feelings of fear, hurt, and loneliness, we also greatly damage our ability to feel love, joy, and peace. As a result, our Original Child is also buried, becoming obscured by our Sobbing Child. Our Controlling Child then takes charge and becomes the stringent, sometimes tyrannical, regulator of feelings of any kind—positive or painful.

The Trauma Egg

I designed an exercise in 1983 which I call the Trauma Egg to demonstrate the concept of how psychological pain causes the Original Child to split into fragments, which creates the Sobbing Child and eventually the Controlling Child. The items inside the egg represent events that produce painful feelings with the various line widths expressing the intensity of an event. The lines around the outside of the egg denote long-term chronic events and stressors.

(Illustration 1: Trauma Egg)

I have my clients and students draw their own representation of this process, and it has proven to be a powerful instrument. Today, many international rehabilitation centers, counseling centers, and clinicians regularly use the Trauma Egg as part of their therapeutic programs. I continue to be surprised at its effectiveness across many cultures. In Russia, we use rolls of wallpaper, which are wonderful in that they do not limit the size of the drawings; many times they extend to more than 15 feet in length.

Because people often list events they have never discussed before, it becomes a painful but also tremendously healing experience. When done in a group setting such as our Murray Method classes, the Trauma Eggs are placed on the walls, and we usually spend several hours in complete silence while everyone reads these "pronouncements of pain" wallpapering the room. People are stunned as they read because they cannot begin to imagine that a room full of "normal-looking" people could possibly have endured such traumas. During our follow-up sharing time we hear comments like these:

- "This is a sacred place of sorrow—like being in a cathedral."
- "I feel like I am in a cemetery and these scrolls are the tombstones of our pasts."
- "I always thought my life was the most difficult, but now I see many others have experienced things far worse than me."
- "I am overwhelmed with sadness, but part of me wants to shout for joy and say, 'Thank you Lord! You saved us and we are still alive—we all survived!'"

(See Exercise 1: Trauma Egg)
(See Exercise 2: Wounds and Shock)

I encourage you to create your own Trauma Egg, as I know it will be a very enlightening experience. To assist you in this exercise, I am including examples of painful events that fall into three basic categories: specific trauma and/or abuse; chronic, long-term trauma and/or abuse; and deprivation.

Examples of specific trauma and/or abuse include:

- emotional, verbal, and/or physical abuse
- sexual assault or molestation
- being a victim of a crime
- losing a parent, child, sibling, significant other, or pet
- being in a critical accident
- witnessing a terrifying incident, especially if it involves a loved one
- torture
- being a victim of terrorist acts
- wartime experiences (specific or generalized)
- experiencing a natural disaster

Examples of chronic, long-term trauma and/or abuse include:

- alcohol or drug abuse by self and/or family members
- as a child, being left alone while a parent works or is otherwise engaged
- congenital or acquired mental or physical disabilities or deformities
- serious physical illness
- premature birth
- hospitalizations, especially if long-term and the parents were not allowed to stay with the child
- situations that cause one to feel different or like a misfit
- divorce
- long-term illness and/or impending death of a parent, child, sibling, or significant other
- financial crisis
- multiple moves (military, business, or other)
- self or family member involved in dangerous activities (such as soldier, police, or firefighter)

- excessive control, disrespect, and verbal and emotional abuse from parents, family members, peers, school officials, employers, or health professionals
- prejudice due to race, religion, culture, age, sex, or personal beliefs

Examples of deprivation include:

- long-term negative environment, the lack of nurturing and care essential to overall well-being
- lack of adequate food, clothing, or shelter
- physical neglect when parents could provide physical needs
- emotional neglect and "coldness"
- a lack of touch
- no positive affirmation
- an overly protective, smothering parent who refuses to accept the child as an individuated person in his/her own right, thus depriving the child of his/her original self

Many of my clients, upon completing their Trauma Egg exercise, simply stand back to contemplate the enormity of it all. They often react in amazement, with comments such as, "Wow, I've really come a long way!" They become more gracious with themselves as they begin to understand that multitudes of people with backgrounds like theirs have chosen a more destructive path, ending up addicted, in prison, or dead. Seeing your own life or another person's life this way is the beginning of developing empathy and compassion.

As you deliberate over and process what you learned from your own Trauma Egg exercise, various occurrences in your life that you previously deemed unimportant will now be seen as playing a more significant role. Also, numerous events and stressors, taken separately, will no longer seem monumental. However, when reflecting on the summation of your painful lifetime experiences, the evidence of such collective damage can provide you with important insights.

While not everyone will experience the same type of emotional release from the Trauma Egg exercise, it can enable you to have a profound awakening. By viewing your life in this manner, you can begin to recognize yourself, not as a victim, but as someone in the process of becoming a victor.

In Summary

One of the primary reasons that the defense mechanism of our Controlling Child exists is to take care of us in times of great distress, whether physical or emotional. We often respond to emotional pain, like physical pain, by entering a state of shock. This shock, however, is designed to be temporary and should eventually subside so the pain can be experienced and the wound can be cared for properly. However, long-term trauma or abuse, including neglect and deprivation, can cause us to remain in a state of chronic emotional shock, with the resulting feelings stored in a Pool of Pain which gives birth to our Sobbing Child. Our Controlling Child also buries our Original Child, which contains our soul and attempts to protect our Sobbing Child through anesthetizers and diversionary tactics, which can range from irresponsible drug addiction to overly-responsible workaholism. Ultimately, healthy emotional growth can begin when we accept the fact that we have a Pool of Pain and understand that it is okay to express and release our pain. We will not die by doing so, but instead we will set in motion our healing process, which will result in a healthy and balanced self.

CHAPTER 2

Roots and Patterns

Even a minor event in the life of a child is an event of that child's world and thus a world event.
—*Gaston Bachelard (1884–1962)*

Deprivation

There is no greater gift to give children than the feeling that they are valued as special people in their own right. Tragically, many children are left with only a legacy of pain rather than an endowment of self-worth.

My closest friend during my seven-month stay in therapy was a wonderful young woman named Toni who originally came from South Africa. Having earned a master's degree in social work, she had been a missionary in Hong Kong. In her early thirties, she was beautiful, though overweight. She wanted to have a healthy relationship with a man, but had never dated. During the intensity of our period in therapy, we often comforted each other as we wept for the deeply hurting child within each of us. Toni's pain was very real, very deep, and very different from mine in causation.

Toni was only ten months old when her mother gave birth to twin boys. It was a long, difficult labor, and her mother nearly lost her life. One of the twins was badly brain damaged at birth, leaving him with severe mental and physical motor impairment.

Toni was sent to live with an aunt, who was too busy to care for the baby girl. When Toni finally returned to her parents, the home was in chaos with her mother bedridden most of the time. During the short periods in which she was mobile, Toni's mother tended to the multitudinous needs of the newborn twins, especially the one who was physically and mentally impaired. Understandably, Toni's needs were largely ignored. Her mother was unable to give her the attention and love the toddler needed; her father was also physically and emotionally unavailable. Little Toni was cared for by a parade of nurses and household help.

Toni came from a fairly affluent family with parents who loved her. She had not been beaten or sexually abused, and her parents did not deliberately set out to ignore her. However, her childhood pain was extremely intense. She was a victim of deprivation and neglect.

Although most of us recognize what constitutes abuse, I still find that many people do not understand the concept of deprivation, except as it pertains to the absence of food, clothing, and/or shelter. Yet, depriving a child of nurturing is far more common and can be as devastating as other types of child abuse.

A deprived child may suffer from intense neglect, both physically and emotionally. In many homes, a child's physical needs may be met, but the parent may be too busy and distracted or too cold, non-nurturing, and uncaring to attend to the child. Either situation results in the child experiencing emotional abuse and deprivation.

A child who has a background of deprivation can be just as damaged as one subjected to physical and sexual abuse. However, deprivation can often be even more challenging to confront and overcome because the scars are far less evident. Consequently, the child thinks he or she has no right to feel badly since his or her pain is not as obvious as someone else's, such as visible evidence of abuse on the back of another child.

Therapeutically, dealing with deprivation is often like trying to chase the wind and hold it in your hand—wind that can vary from a moderate storm to a violent hurricane. You see the devastating results, but you cannot get a solid grasp on the situation.

Lack of nurturing, especially during infancy, is one of the primary forces which cause the early fragmentation of the Original Child. As I have listened to many clients re-experience their childhood pain, I have learned how little it takes to traumatize a child. Experiences that adults would normally regard as insignificant often have a lifelong effect on a child—usually a negative one. That is why virtually everyone has a Sobbing Child of some degree and intensity.

Rene Spitz, an Austrian psychoanalytic physician, reported that in a foundling home in Germany where the infants received no physical or emotional nurturing and no intellectual stimulation, the mortality rate was higher than 70 percent for infants less than one year of age. In 1915, James H. Knox, Jr., noted that, in spite of adequate physical care, 90 percent of the infants in Baltimore orphanages and foundling homes died within a year of admission (These statistics are from the book *Human Development*, by James VanderZanden, 1981.).

One of an infant's most basic needs is for loving touch. In his book *Caring, Feeling, Touching* (1976), Dr. Sidney Simon states, "No amount of food can satisfy this human hunger for touch. It cannot be permanently dulled by drugs, nor diverted for long by busy-work, frenetic entertainment, or any of the varieties of ways in which people seek to escape. It is a hunger for the touch, the feel, the concrete reality of our shared being. . . Loving touch delivers the most assuring message that can be exchanged between people: 'I am here, you are here, and we care.'"

Touch stimulates the Original Child. An infant cannot understand your words, only your touch. By and large, children determine whether the world is a safe place by the amount of loving touch, or lack thereof, that they receive. When a child has been starved by lack of touch, the effects are far-reaching.. Dr. Ashley Montagu's extensively researched and documented book *Touching* (1971, 1978) states that lack of touch affects all behavior: physical, sexual, emotional, and relational.

Lack of touch is only one aspect of deprivation. Dr. Conrad Baars and Dr. Anna Terruwe, in their excellent book *Healing the Unaffirmed* (1972), document cases observed during their combined clinical experience of more than 60 years. They confirm that deprivation consistently creates feelings of abandonment, rejection, insecurity, and inadequacy. A person who has not been nurtured as a child often has an insatiable need for affection, yet withdraws from intimacy, which causes major difficulties with relationships. The patterns of abandonment and rejection will probably continue for these children throughout childhood, imprinting their destructive etchings on impressionable minds and hearts. Without intervention, children who are imprinted in this way will find it difficult to create a new image for themselves that includes a happy landscape.

Alone

One of the issues that has troubled me most since I began teaching in Russia did not surface in my classes until more than a year had passed. When students discussed feelings they experienced as children, the words, "fear" and "loneliness" were mentioned consistently. During one session, I asked a psychologist if she could remember when she first felt fear. She responded by saying, "I think it was probably when I was left alone for twelve hours when I was ten months old." I knew her parents were alcoholics and I surmised she meant they had gone out one day, became intoxicated, and didn't come home for a long time. But I was shocked when I learned that it was not a one-time event, but rather, it happened every weekday because her mother was required to work by the government, and the infant had to be left alone. I could not contain my tears.

Turning to the rest of the class, I asked if this had ever happened to any of them. Over one-third of my class raised their hands, and several women tearfully admitted they also had to resort to this option with their own children during Soviet times. I learned that women were only allowed to stay with their babies for 56 days or less and then were required to return to work, even if they, or their newborn, were sick. It was expected that the baby would be cared for by an elderly family member (who was often alcoholic); it was also not uncommon that the little one was sent to live with someone far away from the child's parents.

If a family member was not available (which was frequently the case, as they were also required to work), then the child was placed in a government childcare facility where the infants were kept clean and fed, but the attendants rarely had time to pick up and nurture the babies. If this type of facility was not readily accessible, the child was left alone. In the wintertime, the heat was sometimes turned off in the apartments so toddlers would not burn themselves; the children would be bundled up, given some food, and left alone for ten to twelve hours. I could not begin to fathom what it would be like to be those little ones, or their parents.

Since that time I have continued to ask this question in my classes and consistently find that one-third to one-half experienced this bleak trauma sometime in their childhood. Many stories have been told in our classes regarding this issue. I especially remember one man who choked on his tears as he shared his story of being three years old and spending many long hours curled up in a ball with his one-year-old brother, trying to keep warm, as they scrunched up against the front door of their tiny apartment waiting for their mother to come home. He said they would sob until they ran out of tears, and eventually they learned that crying was useless. He never cried again until that day when he shared his story with us for the first time.

Almost all of these people saw the issue of being left alone as a small child to be such a common occurrence that they hadn't even put it on their Trauma Eggs. I began to understand why, as adults, they were so enmeshed with their parents and their adult children. It seemed as if everyone was trying to make up for what they lost as children and as parents. These parents were not bad people; they were simply characters in a drama staged by the Soviet system and had no choice in the roles they were assigned to play.

Unfortunately, I am aware that the practice of leaving children alone still happens today even though the former reason for it no longer exists. It has become "normal." Until this phenomenon is recognized as very destructive to the emotional health and growth of children, the country will continue to be inhabited by multitudes of people who suffer from being deprived of nurturing as children, and it will affect their relationships throughout their entire lives.

When children cry and their needs are not met by a loving caregiver, they then learn not to trust, and rage develops, which eventually takes its toll by exploding or imploding. This serious issue is starting to be addressed today in Russia and elsewhere by many young couples as they seek to be attentive, loving parents and to break the old cycle of neglect and disregard.

I am Bad

Actions that deprive children of being who they were originally created to be are destructive. Children perceive such behavior as an indication that they are not acceptable as they are. Gradually, children internalize the belief, "I am not loved for who I am, so I must be bad." Then they interject the concept, "I am defective; something is wrong with me."

Besides having internalized feelings of "being bad," the deprived child can also become attached to "nothingness." A friend, who was also one of my psychology professors, told me, "Marilyn, I almost envy the attack you experienced. At least you have something to go back to—something definite to work on in therapy. My childhood of emotional abuse and deprivation leaves me so frustrated. When I try to go down into my childhood pain, I feel as though I am drowning in a vast ocean, swamped by giant waves of unending pain. There is nothing for me to hold onto. I can't see any landmarks. I'm drowning in a sea of nothingness." For individuals who drown in that sea, intimacy in future relationships is almost impossible without extensive therapeutic help. My friend is an example of someone who persevered on his own healing journey and is now married and in a wonderful relationship.

Many individuals with backgrounds of deprivation and/or abuse spend their entire lives hoping that "maybe, just maybe, one day Mom and Dad will change and be the good parents they were intended to be." Unfortunately, that seldom happens. When I have clients with these expectations, I share one of my favorite quotes with them from a master verbal artist, Charles Swindoll, in his book *Killing Giants, Pulling Thorns*: "The chains of expectations, forged with the links of obligation, bind us forever in the dungeon of disappointment."

These people expect their parents to be good parents—after all, aren't they obligated to do so as mothers and fathers? If changes do not occur over the years, however, and these individuals are unable to release their parental expectations, they will remain forever in the "dungeon of disappointment," never proceeding on with their own lives.

Narcissism

Our children are not individuals whose rights and tastes are casually respected from infancy, as they are in some primitive societies... They are fundamentally extensions of our own egos and give a special opportunity for the display of authority.
—*Ruth Fulton Benedict (1887–1948)*

One of the most destructive parenting styles I have observed is that of the narcissistic parent, who has no personal boundaries and is the antithesis of a healthy parent. The following attributes illustrate the contrast between the healthy and unhealthy parent.

The Healthy Parent:

- supplies the child's physical needs
- sees the child as a separate, individuated person, worthy of love and respect
- provides safety, security, stability, and consistency
- gives love and gentle touch in a warm, nurturing environment
- role-models how to combine positive feelings such as joy and peace during difficult, painful times
- is not always negative and pessimistic
- provides encouragement and support
- role-models emotions and actions with respect and caring
- introduces a spiritual component into the family through a healthy personal belief in God and by sincere altruistic actions
- teaches the child how to make decisions based upon values and teaches responsibility for the consequences of those decisions
- encourages and role-models play and creativity
- helps the child discover and become skilled in his or her natural talents
- teaches the child how to live without the parent, so the child reaches the edge of the nest, wanting and knowing how to fly
- is willing to give up control and allow the child to become an adult and be a separate person with his or her own family and activities

- has a life of his or her own and does not expect adult children to be the sole source of emotional and physical support

While this is not an exhaustive list of parental responsibilities, it contains the major tenets. I know of no perfect parents who do it all correctly, but many parents genuinely seek to provide a healthy environment for their children. Unfortunately, the narcissistic parent does exactly the opposite.

The Unhealthy Parent:
- views the child as an object—a disposable possession
- sees the child as extension of the parent and, as such, can treat the child well or poorly
- believes the child exists simply to serve and care for the parent as long as the parent lives and shames the child when she or he does not live up to expectations
- treats the child like a miniature adult who is expected to already know how to do whatever the parent asks without instruction
- believes the child has no rights or opinions worthy of discussion
- resents having to take time and effort to teach or provide help to the child
- begrudges having to work to provide the basic necessities for the family
- does not like giving gifts or money; consequently, gifts usually have strings attached—making the child feel obligated to take care of the parent or so the parent looks good to the world
- believes that when the children become adults, the parent should be the adult child's first priority regarding love, time, attention and finances, over and above the adult child's spouse and children (and uses phrases such as, "Mothers are forever, wives are temporary.")
- feels like a victim and wants others to feel sorry for him or her; (also refuses to recognize how she or he victimize others)

You may notice that some of the listed traits for narcissistic parents were and still are common in many cultures. But these parents may or may not be narcissistic, as they believe they are only following cultural mores that have been established for centuries. If that is the case, it still does not alter the fact that these unhealthy beliefs create abusive, dysfunctional relationships and should be addressed.

In addition, some parents may have healthy traits combined with unhealthy narcissistic traits. If this is the case for you, those destructive traits must be dealt with. If left unchanged, narcissistic actions and attitudes will become like a rotten apple that eventually destroys the entire barrel.

"I Want to Do What I Want to Do"

Frequently, in a narcissistic household, one or both parents are addicted to alcohol, drugs, nicotine, sex, money, power, or religion. For any person who is an addict, the addiction becomes more important than anyone or anything else, and so the addict becomes narcissistic in his or her actions and beliefs.

While many people may have some of the narcissistic traits listed above, they do not necessarily qualify as full-blown narcissists and would not be diagnosed as having Narcissistic Personality Disorder. Nevertheless, it is useful to know the distinguishing characteristics of a narcissistic individual, and traits include:

- entitlement: expects special favors without assuming reciprocal responsibilities; believes, "I have the right to do whatever I want, whenever I want"
- interpersonal exploitativeness: takes advantage of others to indulge own desires or for self-aggrandizement; always gives their needs priority over everyone else's needs
- disregard for the personal integrity and rights of others: has no boundaries; has no respect for anyone but themselves
- lack of empathy: is unable to recognize how others feel, unable to appreciate the distress of others
- self-centeredness: sees every interaction as it affects themselves ("The world revolves around me.")

- superiority: is arrogant and egotistic ("I always know more/am more qualified than...")
- domination: has a controlling, demanding attitude
- exclusivity: feels that rules do not apply to them ("I am above the law.")
- grandiosity: regards others as lesser, "beneath me"
- hypersensitivity: responds excessively to any slights or imagined insults

Because narcissists view others as being there only to meet their needs, sexual and emotional incest are not uncommon. Although many people understand the concept of sexual incest and its connection to narcissistic characteristics, emotional incest is often not recognized as also being extremely destructive. Since the child is seen to exist only to care for the parent, the child often becomes a surrogate spouse with whom the parent shares intimate details and feelings that should be shared only with his or her partner. This "chosen child" will experience many of the same problems as a child of sexual incest, especially in relationships.

While the term narcissism relates to "self-love," most narcissists actually have an exceedingly poor concept of self-worth and can only feel "up" if everyone else is "down." To treat another as an equal or to concede on any point is tantamount to failure. It is all or nothing.

It's Always About Me

The following are some typical examples of narcissistic responses I have heard from clients:

- from a woman who just found out her unmarried daughter was pregnant, "How could she do that to me? What will my friends and family think?"
- from a pastor whose daughter was getting a divorce, "This will ruin my 'perfect' family—how could God let this happen to me?"
- from a woman who just learned her husband had to have double cataract surgery, "What if this leaves him blind? That would be terrible because then I would have to take care of him!"

For a narcissist, without exception, everything is about "me." They are unable to be empathetic and set aside their own feelings long enough to try to understand how events affect anyone but themselves. Most narcissists feel deeply resentful and "imposed upon" if required to give of themselves in any way to help another person, even in times of illness or crisis. To have a healthy, mutually rewarding relationship with such a person is impossible unless the narcissist is willing to seek intervening therapy.

You are probably realizing that the narcissistic traits of being self-centered and wanting "to do what I want to do when I want to do it!" are also common characteristics of small children. Some people, unfortunately, continue through life with these same childish traits and never become mature adults. They are usually people who have not had healthy adult role-models as caretakers.

Regrettably, I have seen an increase in narcissism in adults, teens, and children. In response to questions concerning the genesis of a narcissist, I have developed a list of factors that I consistently see with this type of client. This list is not meant to be a diagnostic tool, but rather it is designed to create awareness of the many factors that can contribute to narcissistic behavior. I have found that the greater the number of these factors in a person's life, the greater the problem.

The Possible Creators of a Narcissist

- narcissistic parents
- emotional neglect
- history of sexual, physical and/or emotional abuse
- gender (if a certain sex is more favored in a specific culture)
- race (if a certain race is more favored in a specific culture)
- favorite or chosen child (emotional incest)
- birth order (first born, last born, only child, first grandchild, "replacement" child— e.g., born shortly after the death of the previous sibling)

- gender order (e.g., first of a gender in a family full of children of the opposite gender)
- special talents and abilities (e.g., musical, artistic, athletic)
- exceptional intelligence
- personal or family wealth
- family name (e.g., Kennedy)
- historical lineage (e.g., Mayflower descendant)
- prominent local lineage (e.g., family well known in town or city)
- ethnic pride
- accomplishments and awards (self and/or parents)
- prestigious profession
- fame (e.g., entertainer, athlete, politician, musician)
- sense of personal privilege ("Don't you know who I am?!")
- sense of entitlement
- sense of grandiosity
- sense of emptiness

The Survival Narcissist

In addition to the conditions listed above, there also are several other major causative factors that could lead to a person becoming what I call a "survival narcissist." These factors include:

- being deprived of food, clothing, and shelter
- having personal safety and security violated

Under these circumstances, the person is in a "survival only" mode and therefore becomes self-centered and driven simply to stay alive. They push and shove to get to the head of the line in order to survive. If they do not, they and their families will starve. Their children will not have shoes in the frozen winters. However, if and when the deprivation or safety crisis ceases, these aggressive actions often continue because they have become conditioned, long-term habits. We see the Survival Narcissist every day in Russia. Even though people may not be physically pushing and shoving, the underlying attitude often has not changed. This aggression is palpable on the streets, in the metro, and especially on the roadways. Those who remain in a "survival only" mode find it sabotages personal growth and becomes an obvious hindrance in relationships.

Narcissism by Proxy

There are some people who develop what I term "narcissism by proxy." This usually develops when a person has been told and shown that they have no worth as a person and only exist to support a larger entity or system (family, government, ethnic group, political party, religious organization). Their personal value only exists as a result of their ties to this system.

While this type of system may have many good qualities for which its populace can be justifiably proud, the system also has many narcissistic traits. People who develop this kind of narcissism:

- state that they are the very best in the world—stronger and superior in everything
- feel that others are beneath them
- role-model that they do not respect anyone but themselves;
- will exploit others for their own purposes
- believe others have no personal worth and exist only to care for them
- disregard the personal integrity and needs of others
- are domineering and controlling (and share many of the other characteristics of a narcissist).

When a person dwells within such an entity or system, he can also absorb those characteristics and attitudes towards himself and others.

Unfortunately, if the larger entity collapses, then the persons whose personal value depended upon this association often find themselves in a "worthless wasteland." This descriptor was given by one of my Russian students trying to explain how devastating it was to so many Russians when the USSR fell because all of their personal pride and worth was inextricably woven into the Soviet System.

The Entitled Narcissist

Another type of narcissist—the Entitled Narcissist—is a person who has lived a life of privilege and always expects to be treated as someone special. He or she has never known what it is like not to be "on top," and therefore has no regard or empathy for those who are deemed to be less worthy. Despite coming from a privileged lifestyle, this child often has been raised by a succession of nannies and other caretakers and has no loving connection with his or her parents and is incapable of true intimacy.

I have had numerous clients like this. One handsome young man sat in my office and arrogantly bragged that he had never been held responsible for anything he had ever done. He smirked as he said, "My father is one of the most prominent businessmen in this country and he always bailed me out of any trouble I got into. I drove drunk, wrecked cars, got into fights, even hit my wife—but I always knew I would never have to be accountable. Even today, I can do anything I want. My wife won't leave me because she loves the lifestyle my money provides."

Tragically, his evaluation of her was correct.

The Power Narcissist

Unlike the Entitled Narcissist who has always had everything, the Power Narcissist usually comes from a deprived childhood where he/she had little or nothing. Consequently, these individuals feel they deserve to have everything as adults to make up for what they lost in childhood. He or she will charm, claw, climb, manipulate and ruthlessly step on and over family, friends, acquaintances, etc., to accomplish his or her goals of power, influence, and control and feel fully justified in doing so. We often see this destructive pattern in high level business and politics. However, because they do know what it is like to be "on the bottom," these types of narcissists are capable of occasionally having empathy and compassion for others (for example, John Travolta's character in the movie, *Primary Colors*).

I have had numerous clients who were extremely powerful men. They were successful financially and in their careers, but their personal lives were trainwrecks. They had consumed so many loved ones, friends, and colleagues in their ceaseless drive for power that when they finally reached the top, often the only people left around them were either "leeches" or persons waiting for them to fall and to eagerly take their place. In addition to power, many times they also have acquired other destructive addictions—sex, gambling, drugs, and/or alcohol.

The Victim Narcissist

This person has genuinely been traumatized, abused, and/or neglected as a child and also perhaps as an adult. He or she has a right to feel victimized. However, when his or her identity becomes entwined with "I am a victim and thus deserve special treatment," then this entitlement begins to move toward narcissism. He or she feels (even after they become adults) they warrant having others be responsible for their wellbeing; they resist become healthy, mature women and men and justify their actions by their "victim status."

Even if they start into therapy or join a 12-Step Program, sometimes this victim-state does not abate but can even become more intense. I have had students who were learning about boundaries and how to protect themselves—which definitely are good and necessary skills—but they were often not applied with balance.

It is imperative to understand that a boundary exists for two reasons: so you do not victimize me and, I do not victimize you. However, the Victim Narcissist usually only recognizes the first aspect. Like other narcissists, he or she interprets many actions of others as being "about me." When this occurs, the Victim Narcissist then steps up to confront others with the fact that they "abused" or "offended" him or her and states that he or she is setting a boundary with them to be protected from their behavior.

Unfortunately, this can be used to excess and the majority of the time the issues either do not concern the narcissist at all—or are a minor matter that has been exploited into a major conflict. As a result, other people are forced to "walk on eggshells" to avoid being accused of becoming an offending victimizer to this perpetual victim.

The Caretaker Narcissist

While many narcissists are very obvious, others are not. Sometimes narcissistic traits are difficult to distinguish because they can be hidden beneath an exterior that shows a loving, caring, and giving person who does not appear to be self-centered and selfish. I have had numerous clients who are in educational or helping professions (teachers, professors, therapists, psychologists, doctors, nurses, pastors) who spent their lives giving to other people but always felt somehow that they were not appreciated or valued for their work and usually had conflicted personal and professional relationships. When we delved into their pasts, I found that they almost all came from homes of emotional deprivation and neglect. Their parents gave them little love, if any, rarely spoke kindly to them, and often did not protect them from abuse. Frequently, there was a role reversal in which the children acted more like adults than their parents and had to be the responsible caregivers in the family. Many times, one or both parents were alcoholics or addicted to other substances or activities.

Children from this type of family are left with huge emotional "holes" that were supposed to be filled by their mothers and fathers, and when that did not happen, they spent the rest of their lives trying to fill those holes. As a consequence, these people stay stuck in that childhood state trying to get their needs filled. Unfortunately, those holes are bottomless pits which no amount of love, attention, and praise from others can ever fill.

Like all narcissists, they continually need a "narcissistic supply" of people around them. Caretaker narcissists feel more worthy if they are greatly needed by this supply, while other narcissists feel whole by having a supply of people adoring or serving them. Some of the narcissists try to fill their emotional holes with people or their work, others use alcohol, drugs, nicotine, sex, food, and so forth; however, regardless of the remedy, it is "never, never enough."

For Caretaker narcissists, their narcissism does not spring from arrogance or entitlement, but from neediness, a need to feel loved and valued. As a result, this person responds to every incident by asking "How does this affect me?" But, when confronted about this narcissistic trait, they are offended as they only see themselves as loving, giving people.

The Caretaker narcissist may be told: "Only God and you can fill those holes now, nothing, or no one else can. Even if your parents miraculously became perfect parents today, they could not go back and fill in the holes that they neglected when you were a child. Please give up your expectations of ever finding someone, or something else to fill those holes—only God and you can do it." Upon hearing these statements, the person is always very sad, and often quite angry. Some will say, "That's not fair! I deserve to have someone else give to me and to take care of me. I've given and given to others all my life, it's not fair!" I have to agree, it is not fair. Unfortunately, it is reality, and unless these people can allow God to help them be a good parent to themselves, they will remain in that deep pit of loneliness and emptiness forever. And their narcissism will increase.

Neediness is not unique only to the narcissist who is a caregiver, it is a strong characteristic of all narcissistic individuals, as all have vast emptiness in regard to childhood love and nurturing.

The Spoiled Narcissist
While some children suffer from deprivation because their

mothers and fathers cannot be bothered with parenting and are so self-centered they cannot give anything to their families, other children at the opposite end of the spectrum would probably welcome a brief respite from being the object of a parent's caretaking. These children are the victims of smothering, intrusive parents. These parents (often having poor self-worth and having had background of deprivation themselves) endeavor to give their children everything they never had. They have no lives of their own, and if their children happens to have a special talent or ability (especially in academics, sports, music, or acting), these parents will attempt to gain their own worth through the child's success. As a result, a child who is overindulged and doted upon may become a pampered narcissist who, as an adult, seeks a spouse that can continue to care for him or her in the same fashion, or who becomes so fiercely independent that no personal relationship is possible with anyone.

Narcissism can stem from other circumstances as well. I had a client who was adopted by older parents; he was the son they always wanted, and he also had incredible talents. My client commented, "I could have come home from school with an F, and I think they would have drawn a line on the right side and turned it into an A. I could do no wrong in their eyes. They never disciplined me." After relating a history of affairs and distorted personal relationships, he said to me, "I really need a course in 'How To Do Life 101.' "

A Rebel without a Cause

A characteristic often associated with a narcissist is rebellion against anyone or anything in authority. The dissenter never matures or grows beyond the mind-set of a spoiled child or a rebellious teenager. An attitude of "How dare you tell me what to do" keeps them always at odds with parents, teachers, employers, spouses, and the government. They resent being asked to do what is normally required of someone in the role of child, student, employee, partner, or citizen, feeling they are "above all that," even refusing to adhere to being on time for personal and professional engagements. They are oppositional and defiant and will deliberately argue any point, no matter how insignificant, just to win. They never ever want to lose or feel they are "giving in."

Dr. Sam Vaknin, who has written extensively regarding narcissism, states:

> *The narcissist occupies an eternal and timeless present. He/ she is a fossil caught in the frozen lava of a volcanic childhood. The narcissist does not keep agreements, does not adhere to laws, regards consistency and predictability as demeaning traits. . . . The narcissist is never whole without an adoring, submissive, available, self-denigrating partner (or child). . . . One remains bafflingly obscured by the giant shadows cast by the intensive interaction with the narcissist. . . . One merges with the narcissist to the point of oblivion. . . . The narcissist exploits, lies, insults, demeans, ignores, manipulates, and controls.*

Narcissism is Not Always Inevitable

Some people may have many of the narcissistic characteristics listed on the previous pages as the basis for this self-serving attitude—yet they are still able to become loving, caring people who are not selfish, egotistical narcissists. The major difference between these people and narcissists are that they had good, loving role-models vis-à-vis balanced care, concern, and respect for others and themselves, plus a healthy concept of God in their lives. They may also have been exposed to other cultures and have gained respect for those who differ from their own beliefs. However, when there is a lack of emotional and spiritual support, healthy modeling, and openness to others, and when there is an abundance of the etiological factors—a narcissist is almost certain to develop.

Change—Is It Possible?

Unfortunately, most narcissists do not feel they need to change as they like being set apart and above the pack. Their arrogance assures them that they are fully entitled to do exactly what they want to do. Unfortunately, those people rarely change because, even if they lose a spouse, they can usually use their charm, intelligence, or talents to weave someone else into their web to care for them and support their self-serving actions.

The only narcissists I have observed who made a genuine turn-around in their lives are ones who have gained a deep spiritual dimension and realized their incredible selfishness and immaturity. They then became open to working on those issues in therapy, in addition to facing the root causes and patterns of their behaviors. As they actually began to feel their own pain concerning their lack of healthy love, nurturing, and respect as a child, they finally were able to start to develop the all-important qualities of empathy and compassion.

(See Exercise 3: Narcissism, a Generational Affair)

In Summary

Trauma and abuse are not the only destroyers of children. Deprivation, defined by emotional neglect, abuse, and the absence of loving actions, can also cause damage as great and far-reaching as physical cruelty. It is especially painful when parents, care-givers, or family members have narcissistic tendencies and are especially self-centered.

Whether our parents' lives were too full of conflict, or busy-ness, or they were too self-absorbed to pay attention to us, emotional deprivation leaves us feeling devalued and undeserving of love. Other entities, such as governments or ethnic groups may also leave us with a legacy of feeling that we are unworthy of respect and care. As a result, we may become narcissistic and self-centered in an attempt to fill the "holes" left by such experiences.

We can, though, with the help of God, learn to be a healthy caregiver to ourselves—loving, responsible, creative, altruistic, and joyful. When we do so, we leave our narcissism behind and truly begin a healing journey toward becoming a healthy, balanced, giving adult.

GUIDEPOST TWO

BALANCE & HEALTH

You: becoming Balanced and Healthy—Physically,
Emot-ionally, Intellectually and Spiritually with an
Integrated Original Child, Sobbing Child, and Controlling
Child; and with **God** as your primary relationship

If you have accepted that you have a Pool of Pain, are trusting in this process, are willing to accept help from your Higher Power, and are now allowing your actions to reflect those decisions, you have already traveled a considerable distance on your healing journey. Congratulations—you are now ready for Guidepost Two: Balance and Health

The goal imbedded within this foundational guidepost consists of:

- being balanced and healthy physically, intellectually, emotionally, and spiritually
- integrating your Original Child, Sobbing Child, and Controlling Child
- having a faith in God—your Higher Power, as the primary relationship in your life; as you reclaim your soul, you will find yourself connecting with your innate desire to have an intimate relationship with God

Our goal is to become balanced and healthy—physically, intellectually, emotionally, and spiritually; this is accomplished as we unite our Original Child, our Sobbing Child, and our Controlling Child. Then we are able to start on the path toward becoming who we were designed to be: a healthy, mature feeling person. This integration process however, can become a daunting task if attempted alone. Asking and depending upon God to assist and comfort you in the process is a vital factor that will determine your success, or failure, on your healing journey.

CHAPTER 3

Cleansing the Pool of Pain:
Releasing Your Sobbing Child

A child's cry contains a universal translation; it sounds the same in any language.
—**Marilyn Murray**

Pain is No Respecter of People

I first heard the following poem when Dr. Marion Wright Edelman read it at the annual conference for the American Association for Marriage and Family Therapy in 1990 in Washington, D.C. Dr. Ralph Earle was national president at that time, and we were presenting a workshop together regarding the effects of trauma on individuals and families. I never will forget, "And we pray for those ... who live in an X-rated world ... and whose nightmares come in the daytime."

A Prayer for Children

We pray for children: Who sneak Popsicles before supper.
Who erase holes in math workbooks.
Who can never find their shoes. And we pray for those
Who stare at photographers from behind barbed wire,
Who can't bound down the street in a new pair of sneakers,
Who never "counted potatoes,"
Who are born in places we wouldn't be caught dead in,

Who never saw a circus,
Who live in an X-rated world. We pray for children
Who bring us sticky kisses and fistfuls of dandelions,
Who hug us in a hurry and forget their lunch money.
And we pray for those
Who never get dessert,
Who have no security blanket to drag behind them,
Who watch their parents watch them die,
Who can't find any bread to steal,
Who don't have any rooms to clean up,
Whose pictures aren't on anybody's dresser,
Whose monsters are real. We pray for children
Who spend all their allowance before Tuesday,
Who throw tantrums in the grocery store and pick at their food,
Who like ghost stories,
Who shove their dirty clothes under the bed
and never rinse out the tub,
Who get visits from the tooth fairy,
Who don't like to be kissed in front of the carpool,
Who squirm in church or temple and scream into the phone,
Whose tears we sometimes laugh at
And whose smiles can make us cry. And we pray for those
Whose nightmares come in the daytime,
Who will eat anything,
Who have never seen a dentist,
Who aren't spoiled by anybody,
Who go to bed hungry and cry themselves to sleep,
Who live and move, but have no being.
We pray for children who want to be carried,
And for those who must be.
For those we never give up on, and
For those who never get a second chance.
For those we smother
And for those who will grab the hand of
anybody kind enough to offer it.

—Ina J. Hughs

With the encouragement of my former therapists, Drs. Earle and Danylchuk, I became a specialist in intensive outpatient psychotherapy focusing on the treatment of trauma, abuse and deprivation. The majority of my intensive clients were referred to me by their primary therapists throughout the United States and numerous foreign countries.

As Dr. Earle and I began giving workshops, he often referred to me as an "emotional open-heart surgeon." Many times I have remarked, "If for one week, I wrote word-for-word what I hear in my office from clients regarding their childhoods, people never would believe it—especially if they saw those clients walking out the door—because they look and act so normal, on the surface."

Awareness or Apathy

Pain is a great leveler, a great humbler.
It knocks you down and stomps on you,
and when you struggle to your feet,
it knocks you down and stomps on you again.
Excruciating pain, physical or emotional,
pain from which you cannot escape, strips you of all reason.
It short-circuits the brain.

—Marilyn Murray

Child abuse in all its configurations—emotional, physical, sexual— has affected millions of us. Even with all of today's media attention to the subject, it remains a very thorny topic to discuss. In the 1980s and 1990s I wrote, taught, and gave presentations on abuse and its consequences, especially sexual abuse. As I traveled throughout the country on speaking engagements, I heard stories from a wide cross-section of cultures and backgrounds. People came from far distances, sometimes in horrible weather, and stood when we ran out of seats.

After a presentation, I remained and listened while people stood in line to share their stories with me: "I've never told anyone this before," "I told my parents (teacher, pastor, doctor), and they said it was no big deal and I should just forget about it," and "You're the first person I've known that I think could understand." I held them while they sobbed—female and male, young and old, Caucasian, Hispanic, African-American, Native American, and Asian. The lines ran down the aisle and often out the door as I listened for hours.

I remained in each city for an additional three or four days after my presentation and counseled for free, fifteen hours a day; it seemed as though they slid my meals under the door. Because I did not want to leave "bleeding bodies" behind me, I always spent considerable time and effort attempting to locate therapists in each area to whom I could refer these deeply hurting people. While these clinicians were competent, caring people, they usually had no specific training regarding abuse issues.

In those decades, it was important to raise a new awareness of the enormity and frequency of child abuse of all kinds and sexual assault of children and adults. We also needed to rattle countless cages concerning domestic violence and physical, emotional and verbal abuse. Raising consciousness was the first step: "See, this is the disease, a highly contagious infection that affects everyone it touches. Beware!"

Along with abuse, neglect and personal trauma, people worldwide certainly have become aware of pain caused by other tragedies. Even those who have lived fairly comfortable, sheltered lives have been violently ejected from their naivety by events such as the fall of the World Trade Center on September 11, 2001, and other horrors such as the killing of more than 300 Russians—half of them children—in the Beslan, school massacre.

As we face the traumas of today with terrorism and wars, where do we, as citizens of the world, go from here? Even if we do not always agree with decisions made by politicians, remember, change and healing must begin in each person. Just as it takes two healthy people to make a healthy couple, it takes individual people who are healthy—physically, intellectually, emotionally, and spiritually—to make a strong, healthy country and world.

A New Land

If there is anything that we wish to change in the child, we should first examine it and see whether it is not something that could better be changed in ourselves.

—Carl Gustav Jung (1875-1961)

You cannot change anyone else, only yourself. How often have you heard that phrase? For me, the concept of changing myself not only meant a major paradigm shift in how I discerned what constituted a healthy system of values and behaviors, it also meant being willing to truthfully look at my own issues, past and present. In addition, it meant widening my worldview and removing my traditional, Kansas/Arizona, conservative monocle. I felt vulnerable, afraid, and not in control. I was traversing totally foreign territory, and, in 1980, I didn't have a map.

Part of my fear of change stemmed from my cultural and religious beliefs regarding therapy. I did not trust psychology and the mental health profession. I thought, "I run a very successful business—nothing is wrong with me mentally. I don't want any shrink messing with my mind!"

When I speak at professional psychological conferences, I often ask, "How many of you work with people who are psychotic, truly mentally ill?" The response is usually about five percent and that number comes from psychiatrists, psych techs, and psych nurses, and a few other therapists. I feel the remainder of us are not mental health professionals, but rather are emotional health care professionals; at least, that is how I view myself. We care for people who have been wounded emotionally.

Hopefully, as you begin to acknowledge your own emotional wounds, you are now open to the idea of changing yourself, but you may be confused regarding how to determine where you are in that process. I have found the following concepts about the stages of recovery to be especially helpful in evaluating the phases of a healing journey.

The Stages of Emotional and Spiritual Recovery

In 1969, Dr. Elisabeth Kubler-Ross, a physician who worked with terminally ill patients, wrote a book, which has become a classic, entitled, *On Death and Dying*. In that book, she identified the five stages of grief: denial, anger, bargaining, depression, and acceptance. Dr. Kubler-Ross's research revealed that acknowledging and working through painful emotions is beneficial not only to the person who is terminally ill but also to their survivors. These stages of grief have also been recognized as being applicable to any major loss or trauma. For individuals suffering from bereavement or other loss, working though these stages is essential for healing and future peace of mind.

In addition to providing closure and acceptance regarding loss, I have found these stages to be relevant to therapeutic recovery. Instead of addressing loss, however, here the focus is upon recovery and restoration—of personal health and of relationships. In adapting and re-configuring the stages of grief into the "Stages of Recovery," it is important to note that Dr. Kubler-Ross's fourth stage—depression—is expanded and labeled as "Grieving." In addition, the term and concept of "Forgiveness" is added to the fifth stage.

In order for an individual to become an emotionally healthy person, I feel it is necessary for him or her to work through all of these stages.

Five Stages of Recovery

1. **Denial**—acknowledging that pain and the resulting consequences have happened in one's life and should be addressed.
2. **Anger**—recognizing and releasing this emotion appropriately; however—staying stuck in this stage, and allowing oneself to become a victimizer when expressing anger (either aggressively or passive-aggressively) is abusive and unhealthy.
3. **Bargaining**—feeling that when stages 1 and 2 are completed, one's work is finished; a predictable phase that can last from

minutes to months; this person often stays "in their head" and talks about their pain, but never allows themselves to actually feel and experience it.

4. **Grieving**—sadness from the depth of your soul; profound sadness for the loss of "what could have been, what should have been," not only for one's own experiences, but for parents, grandparents, and others who have also known pain (realizing they were not born as abusive people and that they also had been wounded, is a fundamental insight needed to begin developing empathy and compassion).

5. **Acceptance and Forgiveness**—accepting those who have caused harm and pain by separating the person from the deed; being able to forgive the person (even if he or she has not changed or asked for forgiveness) while still acknowledging the deeds as destructive; then turning the issue and the person over to God, letting it go and moving on (but with boundaries so abuse does not continue).

Addressing all these stages is an essential element of every healing journey. It is important to know that:

- the stages do not necessarily flow in order
- an individual may be at separate stages with different people and situations (for example, a person may be at stage one with mother, stage four with father, and stage two with an ex-spouse)
- earlier stages may be revisited, accompanied by decreasing intensity with each visit

Many people stay "stuck" at a particular stage, especially stages 1, 2, and 3. For some, the first stage of Denial may be the only stage ever role-modeled as appropriate by their family and culture. It simply may seem easier to continue to maintain the façade, rather than making the effort to continue through the healing process. Others may stay firmly entrenched in the second stage of Anger because they feel it gives them power and control—to lessen it in any manner feels as though they are denying the enormity of their pain.

This type of person goes from being a victim to a victimizer and feels justified for doing so. The third or middle stage of Bargaining is what I often refer to as an "escape into health" in which a person wants to immediately "jump over" the pain and quickly get on with her or his life. I remember telling Dr. Danylchuk, "I fully believe that in the future I can be a whole, healthy person if I persist on this healing journey, but getting there is just so difficult. Isn't there an easier way?" I still can hear his answer, "I'm sorry, but pain isn't something you can jump over, you have to walk through it."

Once you give yourself permission to continue on that arduous walk, you step into the Grieving process of stage 4. This differs from the sadness and pain you probably have felt numerous times over the years or have experienced when you started working through stage 1 of Denial. Stage 4 grief is much deeper, it is that profound realization that everyone has experienced pain and no one has escaped totally from the consequences of those encounters. You begin to see your parents with new eyes and feel empathy for what they experienced as children. As you look at all the people who have contributed to the pain in your life, you will also begin to see the wounded child in them and have compassion instead of hate. Allowing yourself to authentically grieve, not only for the pain in your life, but for the wounds in the lives of others will greatly contribute to the cleansing of your own Pool of Pain.

A note of caution here—the same as with Anger, it is extremely important not to become stuck in the Grieving stage and to move on to the final stage. For example when I do my work in Russia, I find that it is common for people to remain in stage 4, and stay in a depressed, negative, "woe is me," "the world is a horrible place," victim stance for years, or a lifetime. Such behavior occurs in the U.S., as well, and can be seen, for example in adult children of alcoholics or others who confront their childhood victimization but do not move on past the Grieving stage. They remain stuck in a child-like, victim mode and never grow into mature adults.

Forgiveness: the Ultimate Test

Forgive us our sins as we forgive those who sin against us.
—Luke 11:4

Acceptance and Forgiveness, stage 5, is the culmination of the process. However, my clients often have a great deal of confusion and conflict regarding this issue. They either forgive too quickly or refuse to forgive at all.

Some feel they must forgive first, before dealing with anger and sadness. They have often been pressured to forgive immediately, either by the person seeking forgiveness, a concerned family member or friend, or a religious counselor or pastor. No one, especially children, should be pressured into pre-mature forgiveness.

However, if a person does try to forgive before proceeding through stages 1 to 4, not only will it delay the healing process, but it will also increase the psychic damage. The other stages will eventually surface, leaving the person feeling bad and guilty and wondering whether he or she had not been honestly forgiving the first time around.

When someone asks for forgiveness, it is appropriate to say: "I am willing to be willing to forgive you, and I am actively working toward that end; however, I need time to deal my anger and grief first, before I address forgiveness. Do not pressure me to hurry the process."

Other people will not even consider forgiveness for various reasons: they feel the deed done to them was so horrendous, it does not merit forgiveness; they feel the power of their anger and believe that forgiving lets the offender off too easily; they want to get even, and they withhold anything that might help the victimizer; or they fear that forgiveness will give the offender free license to re-offend. But anger, bitterness, resentment, and unwillingness to forgive destroy the person who carries these emotions—such negative emotions gnaw at the spirit, the soul. Forgiveness does not mean accepting the victimizing deeds; it does mean separating the person from the deed and forgiving the person though still abhorring the deed.

The final step of giving the person, the deed, and your feelings of anger and bitterness over to God allows your psyche to be cleansed. (This is especially important if the offender has not changed or asked for forgiveness.) If you choose not to forgive or to prayerfully turn the person and deed over to God, you not only victimize others, you victimize yourself. You were not created to carry these burdens; that is one of the reasons God is in your life— to carry them for you.

Equally important, you must set firm boundaries to protect yourself from becoming either a future victim or a victimizer. When discussing forgiveness, I do not mean to intimate that I do not feel that victimizers should not be made accountable for their deeds. I absolutely agreed they should be held responsible and the victims protected. However, allowing God and/or the law, not you, to seek retribution is essential.

(See Exercise 4: The Stages of Recovery)

If you have never kept a journal, I encourage you to consider starting one. In addition to writing your feelings and thoughts in a traditionally organized or chronological manner, try recording your thoughts free-form. One of the most effective ways to cleanse your Pool of Pain by accessing your Sobbing Child is to write with your non-dominant hand while not correcting for spelling, grammar, or punctuation, thus bypassing your conscious mind. After using this technique personally for years, I am amazed still as to what appears under my pen. You might also experiment with writing in this manner on a large pad of easel paper, or on the backside of a roll of wallpaper (using your non-dominant hand and a felt-tip pen), writing under the headings "I hate it!" and "Not fair!" Allow your words to flow and fill as much paper as needed. This free-form exercise always results in new insights.

Writing poetry and prose can also be helpful exercises. Or, you might compose "dump" letters (dumping your feelings) to people who have hurt you, but without mailing the letters. These are all excellent ways of tapping into your Sobbing Child. Since this is a part of you that you may have neglected for a long period, give yourself the gift of time and patience with these exercises. That child deserves to be heard.

When you have finished, share your work with someone you trust, and then prepare a ritual in which you destroy these remnants of your pain. I feel this is an exceptionally important aspect of healing as I know many people who "dump" and exhale their pain, only to inhale it back in again—never really letting it go. It is important to allow yourself a genuine release of your painful feelings, but this is often a very daunting task to accomplish without help from your Higher Power. I often encourage my clients to burn the pages representing their painful wounds and allow God to receive the ashes. As they do so, they also open their hearts and find they have traveled a surprising distance on their healing journey.

(Exercise 5: Cleansing the Pool—Listening to Your Sobbing Child)

My Parent's Garbage

Even from a bad family—good, precious recollections may be preserved if your soul is able to find something precious.
—*Fyodor Dostoevsky (1821-1881), Brothers Karamazov*

When working with clients on their anger issues I often ask them to do the writing and drawing exercises I have described to you. When finished, they either tear the pages into pieces or sometimes, they will use a tennis racket or plastic bat to hit a pillow covered by the pages until they have annihilated the remnants of their pain. During this process they also give their voices the freedom to speak what has been unspeakable. They now are safe and strong enough to defend themselves and release years of anger and pain (without becoming a victimizer to someone else in the process of venting their rage). It becomes an exhilarating release and they end up feeling joyful and victorious. They are no longer carrying the burden of someone else's shameful deeds and are liberated to begin to truly live, at last.

The remaining ritual of burning the shredded pages has often brought out unusual creativity in my clients. One of my favorite stories is about a courageous woman in her thirties who had survived years of horrific abuse by both her parents. After their deaths, she finally felt free to seek therapy and her therapist referred her to me for a three-week intensive session specifically to enable her to release her pain, and her anger.

During this intensive session she spent many hours working through the exercises I have described concerning the release of the Sobbing Child, including drawing and writing on reams of paper. In her last session, she used a tennis racquet to shred the paper until the floor of the therapy room was literally covered with bits, pieces, and scraps of her anger and pain. When she finished, I handed her one of the extra large plastic bags I keep in my office just for the purpose of containing the results of such a session. She couldn't stop smiling as she shoved every last piece of paper into the bag, filling it to the top and creating a huge bundle which she gingerly swung over her shoulder as she departed on that final day.

Two and a half weeks later I received a phone call from her saying she had something very interesting she wanted to share with me and wondered if I could see her over my lunch hour that day. She sounded so eager I agreed.

She arrived exactly on time and the words tumbled from her mouth, "Remember I told you my husband had planned a special vacation for me and we were to fly to Kona, Hawaii the day after I finished my intensive? Well, I decided I would take the bag containing my parents garbage' with me—I put it in a garment bag and stuffed it into the overhead compartment on the plane. Luckily it wasn't very heavy.

"The next day I hired a helicopter and my husband and I, along with the bag of my parents 'garbage,' took off from the Kona airport to fly over the famous volcano of Mauna Loa. I'm certain the pilot wondered what I was doing with that huge plastic garbage bag. But I knew he probably would not understand that I wanted to rid myself of the pain I had carried for over thirty years by burning that 'garbage' in the most intense heat possible. I wanted to drop that poisonous sack directly into the mouth of the roaring inferno of Mauna Loa.

"But—the volcano was erupting and the pilot said he could not get us near it. I was so disappointed! But, our money wasn't totally wasted as we did enjoy seeing the magnificent display created by the eruption.

"So, for the rest of the two weeks, all I could think of was trying to find some other way in which to burn my parents 'garbage' that would be as powerful as the volcano. My husband had a great time—he went swimming, he went fishing, he went scuba diving, he went snorkeling, he went surfing, he went hiking, he relaxed on the beach. And all the while he was playing and enjoying a wonderful vacation, I was going up and down the island every day carrying that damn bag trying to find the perfect place to incinerate it!

"Finally, the last day of our vacation arrived and we were at the Kona airport, getting ready to board our plane. In that airport, you have to walk from the terminal out across the tarmac to the plane because the plane doesn't come right up to terminal. And would you believe it? There I was, standing in my colorful Hawaiian dress and beautiful lei with a huge battered plastic garbage bag slung over my shoulder! I still had that stupid container of my parents 'garbage.' The loud speakers were calling for all passengers to board the plane and just then I spied a big dumpster that sits right outside the terminal, on the edge of the tarmac. I simply walked over to it and very unceremoniously threw that infamous bag into that messy, stinky container. Then I gave my hands a 'that's that' brush off, put my head up and my shoulders back, and boarded the plane.

"All the way back across the ocean on that long flight I kept thinking about those two weeks and I couldn't believe I had messed up so badly! I kept saying to myself, 'Well, you did it again—you allowed your parents 'garbage' to consume your life—you even let it ruin your much-needed vacation in Hawaii!' And I did it to myself. My parents didn't do it; they've been dead for a long time. I just picked up where my parents left off—I became the victimizer to myself."

I heard from her again about six months later when she came in for a two-hour session. This time she was smiling and relaxed as she began to talk, "I've been seeing my primary therapist every week since we returned from Hawaii and we've been working through the rest of those Stages of Recovery. I keep remembering what you taught about those stages and that unless I finished working through them I never would be genuinely free.

"I know I needed to do the pain and anger work with you and I thought after I completed it, that I was finished and was 'well.' I guess I just fell into the Bargaining stage instead, the part you call the 'escape into health.'

"But, that only lasted a few hours because I went on that crazy trip to Hawaii and found I was right back into being obsessed and angry with my parents again. I didn't really let them go until that final day at the airport dumpster.

"Then, on the flight back from Kona I began to think about what you said about the last two stages and how I needed to allow myself to genuinely grieve, not only for my own childhood but also to give myself permission to grieve for my parents and their lives.

"So, about a week after I got home from that fateful trip, I went to my closet and pulled an old box off the top shelf—I hadn't looked in that box for many years. When my parents died it was one of the few things I kept when I sold their house and furnishings. It was full of old photos, of them and of me.

"I sat in the middle of the living room floor surrounded by images of my family and began to recall what I had been told about my grandparents. I never knew any of them, my parents rarely talked about them except for a few nasty comments. My mom's father was a violent alcoholic who regularly beat her mother, but her mother would never leave—and she didn't protect her children either, so they also became recipients of her husband's rage. My mom ran away from home when she was sixteen. My dad never knew his father; he abandoned his family when my dad was two. His mother dumped all her anger toward her husband onto her kids, especially my dad because he looked so much like his father. My dad got out of there as soon as he was old enough to get a job.

"As I shuffled through the photos I saw so many sad eyes. Almost every childhood picture of my mom or my dad revealed little pinched faces with such hollow eyes. Even in the few prints in which they were smiling, the smiles looked forced and not real. There were only a couple of snapshots of them with their parents and, in those old black and white photos you could see stress etched on every face.

"I just sat there in the midst of those tattered long-forgotten pieces of memories and began to cry. My parents weren't born monsters. They had no role-models for parents—they just parented me the same way they were parented. I kept looking at their little innocent faces when they were about age two or three and felt deep sorrow for them. They looked so much like the photos of me that also occupied that small box—all those school pictures in which my eyes were bleeding with pain.

"Then I happened to pick up a photo I had never seen before—it was my mother and father as young adults. They were both smiling and looked truly happy. They were hugging each other as they held a tiny baby—it was me. My tears came in a torrent. They were looking at me with love. They actually loved me, and each other, many years ago. I don't know what happened to that love, all I ever remember was them raging at each other and at me. But, I know now, that at one time, they did love me and looked as though they were delighted to have me.

"I took that photo and also found the best ones of my mom, of my dad and of me (and that wasn't an easy task) and bought some nice frames for them and now I have them on my bedroom dresser where I see them every day. I can't tell you how freeing that has been. I feel I have not only reclaimed my Original Child, but also, she now has a family.

"Today, I do understand what stages 4 and 5 are about. I feel sincere compassion and empathy for my parents, and for their parents, on back through the generations. I allowed myself to profoundly grieve for all of them and when I did, I began to see and accept them as people of worth and value, separate from their horribly abusive actions.

"The greatest thing about all this was that when I accepted them, I found I had forgiven them! I never wanted to do that before. Now I know that one of the reasons I've obsessed about them so long, even doing that crazy garbage bag thing in Kona, was because I was resisting leaving the anger stage. I felt that if I ever let that go, and moved on to compassion and empathy, I somehow would be saying that what they did to me was OK. And as for forgiveness, forget that—I had sworn it would be a cold day in hell before that ever happened!

"But now I see that by carrying all that hate and bitterness, I wasn't hurting them, I was only hurting myself. I feel a hundred pounds lighter now that I have honestly allowed God to take away those terribly destructive emotions. I feel I am, at last, fully on the road to recovery and feel free and healthy for the first time in my life. I know that God and I will be the healthy parents to that hurting little girl inside of me—it's like re-parenting her and giving her the loving parents she never had.

"Oh, by the way, remember I told you my husband always wanted to have children and I never did because I did not want to carry on that horrible legacy of abuse? Well, now I know I can be a good mother (as I am learning to be a good mother to myself) and we are excited about starting a family—I will certainly let you know when that happens."

Within a year I received a wonderful photo of my client, her husband and a delightful baby girl named "Joy." All three were smiling.

In Summary

One of the major stumbling blocks on our healing journey is the fear of change. A major step in that journey is facing our beliefs and memories and determining what in our life needs to change. That will happen as we begin to alter our view of ourselves and of our place in our world. The journey to becoming a Healthy Balanced Person is not about changing others; it is about changing ourselves and our relationships with others.

We not only need to cleanse our Pool of Pain, but it is essential that we also work through the Five Stages of Recovery regarding the people who created that pain—especially the final stage in which we forgive and hand the victimizer over to God, and allow Him to pass judgment upon them, rather than us seeking retribution ourselves. It is this process that revolutionizes our attitude toward others and frees us from our past, thus transforming ourselves and our actions. As we do this work, we will clear our pathway and travel far on our healing journey, without stumbling.

CHAPTER 4

Memories and Medicine: Cleansing the Filters and Lancing the Wounds

The longest journey is the journey inward.
—Dag Hammarskjold (1905–1961)

Burial Grounds

A book that was very helpful to me in my healing journey was a narrative on reflective thinking and commitment, written by Daniel Taylor and entitled *The Myth of Certainty*. Taylor states:

> The reflective person is, first and foremost, a question asker—one who finds in every experience and assertion something that requires further investigation. He or she is a stone-turner, attracted to the creepy-crawly things that live under rocks and behind human pronouncements. To be reflective is to be sensitive to and fascinated by the complexity of things. It entails an openness to the nuances and grace notes of life, and it implies an eye for hidden beauties and whitewashed sepulchers. The reflective person seeks demarcation in the indivisible and finds unity in diversity, discovering likeness in seemingly unlike things.

To understand the human psyche means looking under rocks, and, unfortunately, finding large, frightening, creepy-crawly things sometimes. It takes courage, not only to glance into the camouflaged burial ground, but to be willing to walk into it and look around—especially if it happens to be your own. But the search for understanding and wholeness also reveals hidden beauties and songs, if we are committed to opening our eyes and ears to those subtle nuances that often escape our hurried lives.

Remember, one of the primary goals of this healing journey is to reclaim your Original Child, the person you were created to be. But, this cannot be done until you are able to restructure your defense mechanisms— your Controlling Child—and release the pain of your Sobbing Child who has kept your Original Child buried and inaccessible for years. For many people however, the process of accessing and releasing the Sobbing Child seems impossible. I have many clients who make comments like, "I can't remember my childhood at all," or "I have spattered bits of memory but it all seems so foggy and unclear."

Knowing Just the Facts is Not Enough

Oh, memory of my heart
You are stronger than the sad memory of my mind

—*Constantine Botushkov (1787-1855)*

Much has been written regarding the reliability and the unreliability of memory. We have all had experiences when we have disagreed with others over the facts of a particular incident. Several years ago for instance, I was driving in my car with two friends and was waiting in a left turn lane when two cars collided in front of us, the flying debris damaging my car. We immediately got out, and, within minutes, the three of us and the three occupants of the other cars reported what we had observed to the police. There were six diverse versions of that accident. Each one of us had been focusing on something different when the accident occurred, so we had a variety of views on the particulars of the event.

I sometimes work with entire families, and I always find it

interesting to hear the often oppositional opinions as to what went on in that family when the children lived at home. Each adult child—depending upon birth order, personality, gender, abilities, parental favor or disfavor, and so on—experienced the family in a different way. Additionally, parents often stridently disagree with their children's viewpoints of their childhood experiences. Trying to decide whose memory is most accurate is futile.

It is essential to understand that children are damaged internally by what they perceive happened, not by what actually occurred. I therefore encourage a family to set aside their evaluations of who is right or wrong, and instead I have them listen to what each person perceived and what each one felt.

Because memory can definitely be tarnished and tainted, I choose to have my clients focus on what they felt as children rather than asking them to try to untangle the web of facts and perceptions. Often clients will ask that I help them know for sure whether a certain event happened in their childhoods. I always explain that I cannot do so, but I also assure them that they can find healing and peace in their lives even if they never know exactly who did what, when, where, and why.

The most important task for these clients is that they need to listen to themselves as they voice feelings they should have released back in childhood—but were unable to do so because it was not safe. Recovery of memory is not the focus, but rather the validation of feelings. Having a caring clinician, family member, or friend hear and confirm their feelings adds greatly to the individual's sense of validity.

When training therapists, I insist that they never encourage a client to confront or accuse someone else of abuse based only on perceptions. I have my clients work on what they know as absolute facts, rather than attempting to determine the truth of perceptions or intuition regarding their past. Without definite evidence, it is unfair and damaging to accuse someone of something they may not have done. Let me share a story from my own family to illustrate this point:

My daughter Missy was born with a low-functioning immune system and, as a child, was often very ill. As an adult, she addressed that issue in therapy, and, in one session, she re-experienced being age three and hospitalized with convulsions and a fever of 105 degrees. While held down by several nurses, she was packed in ice, and, as she screamed in pain and terror, she looked and saw her father and me standing outside a window watching, doing nothing to help her. She felt she was being killed; not only were we not helping her, she also believed we had handed her over to them so they could torture her. At that moment, she unconsciously made the decision never to trust us again.

Missy felt terror, pain, confusion, anger, and total helplessness. She also felt betrayed and abandoned. But while all those feelings were real for her, the source of her feelings was not valid; rather than being betrayed and abandoned, in actuality she was being cared for by nurses and loving, concerned parents.

In this case I was able to corroborate what she remembered, and I deeply empathized with her feelings, sharing how sorry I was that she had to endure something so horrific. I shared how powerless her father and I felt, and that the sound of her terrified screams tormented us because we could do nothing to help her. I was fortunate that she readily realized that we had not intentionally planned to give her over to anyone to hurt her, yet in therapy she still had to deal with the issue of not trusting us. Many parents have not been able to explain a situation so easily, and some have indeed been guilty of what the child believed happened.

The therapeutic process should always aim toward restoration of the individual, and of the family—and toward a healthy, respectful resolution, if at all possible. As such it is imperative to avoid becoming caught up in trying to sort through the facts (with a potentially irresolvable conflict of opinions) and instead focus on validating the reality of each person's feelings.

Separating the Person from the Deed

Some clients feel they are betraying their mothers and fathers if they look clearly and deeply at their childhood issues. I remember the day my therapist suggested that maybe, just maybe, my mother wasn't perfect. I was so offended.

In dealing with past or current events, it is essential to separate the individual from the deed. Being able to acknowledge that each person was created as an Original Child with the capacity to choose to do right or wrong, is a major tenet in this process. Though it can be difficult, it is possible to love a person while continuing to experience conflicting emotions about his or her misdeeds.

Many people are also unable to look at how they have injured others because doing so swamps them in guilt. Being able to love and respect yourself while acknowledging culpability is a basic step on the healing journey.

Filtering Life's Experiences

To understand why we react to the actions of others in ways that are unhealthy, it is often helpful to perceive the Trauma Egg which you created in Chapter One as a filter through which you experience life. Imagine your Trauma Egg being held in front of you and observing that everything you receive from other people and from your environment has to pass through that filter before it reaches your psyche. As a consequence, all your perceptions about other people and events are greatly colored and influenced by your past experiences. The reverse situation also follows the identical pattern. Each time you act or react, your actions also have to pass out through that same filter, so they, too, are stained by your past. Our actions and reactions are in direct response to the painful events that have accumulated in our Pool of Pain. Understanding this concept helps explain why abusive and dysfunctional actions proceed from generation to generation.

Cleansing this filter—both of the abuse done to us and of the pain we have caused others—is a crucial aspect of this healing journey.

When we have acted or reacted in a way that is injurious to others, we should feel healthy guilt. We need to be able to acknowledge our fault, learn how it happened and correct the situation so it does not occur again. We further need to make amends, ask for forgiveness from the injured party and from God, forgive ourselves—and then let it go. Some people cannot forgive themselves and continue to beat themselves up ad infinitum. Instead of saying, with healthy guilt, "I am a good person who has done a bad thing," the guilt turns into shame that says, "I am a bad thing."

Some people will not admit their own liability and continue to blame others or situations, or they say "I'm sorry" but continue to repeat the same harmful action over and over. They never learn how to course-correct, as their actions continue to be projected through the filter of their past experiences. As long as their filter remains full and uncleansed, their actions cannot change.

Before I began therapy and was in severe physical pain, I was told by some well-meaning but misguided people, "You aren't getting well because you must have unconfessed sin in your life." So I scraped my soul daily, repenting of any sin I could find, no matter how insignificant, asking God to please forgive me. I became panicked as I sought to make certain I was in God's will every moment, but this did not bring healing to my spirit or my body. Although I was taught how to confess sins that I did to others, no one ever taught me how to rid myself of sins that others did to me. For decades, I carried the guilt and shame that belonged to someone else—not to me.

In order to rid yourself of the demons of someone else's shame and to deal with your own behaviors in a responsible manner so you do not continue to repeat the same dysfunctional actions over and over, you need to be willing to cleanse the filter of your past— to be honest, open, and willing to look at what you have done and what was done to you.

Two's and Three's, or Nine's and Ten's?

Good emotional health is when you deal with today's feelings, as only today's feelings—and you do it today.
—*Marilyn Murray*

In order to deal with today's feelings today it is essential to cleanse the filter of your past pain through which you view your current life. In relationship counseling, the majority of problems emerge because one or more people are overreacting to a situation. They dump garbage from old issues between them that should have been resolved years ago, or they transfer feelings and attitudes upon their loved one that someone else (such as a parent, sibling, or ex-spouse) actually created.

I believe most of life's everyday challenges can be rated—on a scale of one to ten— as "ones", "twos", and "threes". While there are many "tens"—such as abuse, severe illnesses, death, wars, natural disasters, and other traumas—they account for a smaller percentage of events in the average life of the majority of people today. Sometimes people react strongly—at an "eight", "nine", or "ten"—to an issue that seems to merit less than a "five". These strong reactions occur as they filter the issue through past pain, either from childhood or adult situations. Such high scoring can also result when someone stockpiles current smaller issues— stacking up the "ones" and "twos"—until they become a "ten" and the person erupts. (This is a case of "the straw that broke the camel's back.")

To establish and maintain good emotional health, you must:

- cleanse your old filter—allow God to help you wash away the stains of past hurts and resentments
- commit to making amends for prior overreactions and blaming others
- learn healthy communication skills in order to deal appropriately with today's feelings today

I have used many metaphors and phrases to help myself, and eventually my clients and students, understand the importance of liberating oneself from the pains of the past—whether it is called "Emptying the Pool of Pain," "Cleansing the Filter," "Releasing the Sobbing Child," or "Lancing the Wound." All of these techniques are effective in assisting us to better comprehend this sometimes confusing and illusive process which is so necessary in our healing journey.

The Operating Room

The truth will set you free, but first it will make you miserable.

—Anonymous

Lancing a psychic wound is akin to a surgical process. Whether it be emotional or physical, surgery can be a painful, difficult event. A person who has cancer surgery may walk unaided into the hospital, actually feeling fairly good. The morning after the operation, however, the patient feels terrible, has a huge wound, and can't walk or go to the bathroom alone. Later the doctor may say, "You'll be better in a few weeks, and when you are strong enough we'll start chemotherapy treatments. During that time your hair will probably fall out, and you will be very ill. But I'm confident that in the end you will be cancer-free and have a good prognosis for a healthy life."

A similar scenario may seem true when dealing with emotional injuries. While we would like to think of progress as forward and up, in reality, progress is forward and down before it starts going back up—things often get worse before they get better.

For many people, fear of the downward cycle restricts them from attempting the healing process at all. The long-term damage from refusing to address and care for either a physical or an emotional wound however, far outweighs the temporary relief one gains from that refusal. As I tell my students, "I have never known anyone who died because he or she expressed feelings appropriately; however, I know of numerous people who died early deaths because they did not allow themselves to feel."

Whenever I have doubted the validity of addressing my emotional wounds, I would remember the protocols for properly caring for a physical wound. Please review the following regarding the treatment of a physical wound.

Physical Wound Treatment

- Your wound is acknowledged—it does exist. Even if you attempt to cover it with clothing and ignore the wound, it will not go away, it cannot be denied without adverse results. If the wound becomes infected and is not lanced, it will eventually burst creating more dire problems or spreading the infection throughout your entire body causing severe, even fatal consequences.
- It is treated correctly. Perhaps you would like to simply spray a little medication on it and apply a small band-aid, but that is not sufficient for a major wound.
- If the wound is serious or infected, a professional is contacted who knows when and how it should be cleansed. You allow the professional to treat the wound, even if it is painful. This professional will not continue to scrape the wound ad infinitum.
- Medication is placed in the wound and it is sutured shut.
- The wound is properly bandaged and you are taught how to continue to keep the wound clean and apply new bandages.
- You are encouraged to find out what caused the initial wound so the damage will not be repeated.
- Finally, you learn all the things needed to enable healthy flesh to regenerate and fill in the cleansed wound (for example, eating well, getting plenty of sleep and rest, taking medication and vitamins, and exercising when the doctor states the time is appropriate)

Each one of the above steps is crucial in caring for a physical wound. In addition, hospitalization may be required, depending upon the severity of the injury. Addressing and caring for an emotional wound follows a very similar procedure.

(Exercise 6: Acknowledging the Wounds)

You may already be feeling discomfort as a result of doing the Trauma Egg exercise or from sharing your issues with others. There are many things you can do besides seeking therapy to help you lance the infected emotional wounds in your spirit. One of the most effective techniques is to draw. After they have completed their Trauma Eggs, I have my clients draw their Sobbing Child. This is a very powerful exercise, and I encourage you to try it. (While the Sobbing Child can represent early wounds, it can also denote pain from any age of your life; do not limit any of the exercises to childhood issues only.)

(Exercise 7: Releasing Your Sobbing Child)

When teaching my theory and treatment methods to health professionals and to clergy, we start with a basic Level I class taught over the course of five consecutive days. During this class, the participants do many of the exercises I present in this book. On the second day, they tape their Trauma Eggs and their Sobbing Child drawings to the classroom walls. When they view the sheets of pain that encircle the room, they comment: "We really are alike, at the depth of our pain." "I'm amazed—the drawings contain so many of the same things." "When I looked at all the put-together, competent professionals at the start of this class, I had no idea all this pain actually existed underneath those polished exteriors."

Remember that pain is subjective. Whether your pain has its genesis in abuse—verbal, emotional, physical, or sexual; or whether you are a child of neglect and deprivation; or whether you have experienced the trauma of illnesses, war, or natural disaster—your pain is your own, and it matters. Do not compare your pain to others; that invalidates your reality. Every person's pain is maximum to them. Acknowledge your pain and treat it gently.

A Legacy of Pain

Myriads of people world-wide have inherited lives filled with pain. I have students from thirty-seven countries and have listened to incredible stories of abuse and neglect, and of survival. During my time in Moscow, however, as multitudes of Russians have shared their hearts in our classes, I have gained a greater level of understanding regarding the enormity of the unique, harsh issues they have endured.

One of the most profound unspoken tenets that formed the Soviet system was: *human life has no value*—except for the lives of the rulers and authorities. This dogma forms a tragic legacy inherited from the former USSR where the citizenry was repressed, oppressed, used and sacrificed in whatever manner the leaders deemed appropriate in order to accomplish their goals. It derives not only from that oppressive system, but also from centuries of being subject to autocratic rulers who often regarded citizens as property and unworthy of respect.

For most people raised under the Soviet system, this dogma is reinforced by "tapes," internal messages which still play in their heads, rebuking them in endless ways that deny all personal worth. Today, this ruinous conviction is reflected by the fact that being careless regarding one's safety and health is considered normal. People drive recklessly and often think it is unnecessary to follow the rules of safe driving. Some ridicule anyone who is careful regarding their personal wellbeing. Many males and females of all ages drink, smoke, or do drugs to excess without being concerned whether or not they will die in the process. In the past, life was often so problematic that people did not care if they lived to see another day; their depression and hopelessness were drowned by alcohol or other addictions.

While disregard for personal wellbeing, depression, and addictions are also common in the United States and other countries, Russia is unfortunately overwhelmed with these destructive issues, as is exemplified by this startling information:

- United Nations' studies show Russia to have one of the highest abortion rates in the world. Abortions peaked in 1965 when there were 5.4 million reported abortions—2.74 abortions for every 1 live birth. Not until 2007 did live births and abortions in Russia reach near equal figures. While the government is presently addressing this issue, I have found that many of my female students have had one or more such procedures and their mothers and grandmothers far more—some with as many as 12-18 abortions.
- The World Health Organization in 2006 reported that Russia is #2 in the world in male suicide; 9 of the top 11 in this category are from the former USSR and other communist countries.
- When I arrived in Russia in 2002, the average Russian male life expectancy was age 57. It has risen to age 64 in the past decade, but still remains 10-20 years under other developed countries in Europe and the Americas.
- There has been a significant population decline in past years. In 2010 the annual death rate was 14.3 per 1000 persons vs. birth rates of 12.6/1000.
- Alcohol: the statistics of Russia's current alcohol problems are staggering:
    a. The per capita consumption of alcohol in Russia is now approximately 18 liters. However, if you remove infants, non-drinkers, and the elderly, then the figure reaches 30 liters per capita (almost eight times more than in the US). "In the opinion of World Health Organization experts, consumption of more than 8 liters per year poses a real threat to the health of the nation. Russia has long exceeded this level at 18 - 30 liters," Russian Interior Minister, Rashid Nurgaliyev (RIA Novosti; 24/09/2009).

b. Between 600,000 and 700,000 Russians die each year from alcohol-related causes (physical illness, homicide, suicide, vehicle accidents, drowning, work negligence) (Roundtable conducted in the Russian State Duma, 23/22/07).

c. Alcohol is blamed for 52 percent of all deaths last decade, versus 4 percent average for the rest of the world (Moscow Times; 26 June 2009; from research done by Russian, English, and French medical doctors and reported in medical journal, Lancet, 2009).

d. In Russia, approximately 75 percent of individuals arrested for homicide had consumed alcohol shortly before the incident (World Health Association, 2006).

During my Russian classes, I have heard scores of incredible statements which echo the cry, "I am worth nothing!" Mothers and fathers who do not love themselves, do not know how to love their children. Abuse and neglect flourish in these painful environments. These pronouncements remain in my mind and heart as an aide-mémoire of the malevolent power created from the rejection of valuing human life and spirit:

- "I had a ringside seat on the edge of hell."
- "When I would cry as a baby, my father would set me outside alone in a box."
- "My father was an alcoholic who beat both my mother and me. My mother raged at me and humiliated me often....but I think my parents did love me. Even though I am now a pastor, it is really hard to deal with God as a 'father' and to try not imagining him as abusive."
- "I awoke to loneliness, I spent my days in loneliness, I went to sleep in loneliness."
- "We were taught, 'Never, never feel.' My father was a political prisoner and was in Gulag for six years and my mother almost starved to death in the Great War. Yet they would never, ever talk about this. We lived in stoic silence."

- "Left alone?? Of course, that was normal! I was alone from age four months on."
- "During the war, we had to hide - the bombs came so close - everyone was terrified. My father and brother were both killed in the military and my mother and I had to survive alone - we nearly starved to death."
- "I was sick and put in a sanatorium from age four to six and only saw my parents a few times. I cried every day from loneliness and learned that I was not valued by anyone."
- "My mother and brother died in one day (my father had abandoned us) and I was put in an orphanage at age three where I was treated very harshly by the staff and sexually abused by the older kids. I was finally adopted at age seven but my new parents constantly threatened to throw me back to the orphanage if I was not perfectly behaved. I lived in constant fear of that. Today my daughter asks me why I can't hug or kiss her - I don't know how - no parent ever did that to me. "
- "I think Russia became the largest prison in the world."
- "My mother screamed in a whisper...a deadly whisper."
- "I was the middle child of five girls in our family and when I was about age six, we all became critically ill – we were starving and were so cold. Then my two older and my two younger sisters all died within one week – they expected me to die too but I survived - I don't know how because I was so sick and so hungry."
- "There were volumes of atrocities."

I have been deeply affected by all I have heard from these courageous people as they began to open the pools of pain that have been buried for so many years – pain from families, illnesses, war, government, schools and so forth. They have not remained immersed in that anguish, however, but are now moving forward to becoming healthy people, at last. They, and you, certainly deserve this healing time.

Abraham Lincoln once commented, "Love is a chain whereby to bind a child to his parents." Tragically, many parents bind their children with chains of abuse, not of love. I encourage you to break this chain, if it still binds you, and to commit yourself to ensuring that it does not bind your loved ones who follow you.

In Summary

One of the primary goals in our healing journey is to give our pain a voice and allow unexpressed feelings (past and present), the freedom to surface—but in a manner that does not victimize others. Validation of feelings is more important than validation of memories, as memories are not always reliable.

The residue of unprocessed painful issues can create a distorted filter through which we perceive our world and relationships. It is vital that we cleanse that filter so we are able to view others with clear eyes, not ones covered by the film of pain. Another metaphor regarding this issue is to perceive our pain as an infected wound which needs to be lanced, cleansed, and healed. Understanding that treating an emotional wound requires steps similar to physical surgery, and that it is common to "feel worse before we get better," helps ease the stress during our healing journey. Be gentle with yourself and your emotions, and remember—every person's pain is uniquely their own and is maximum to them.

CHAPTER 5

The Eleventh Commandment: "Thou Shall Not Feel"

Smile though your heart is breaking
Smile even though it's aching . . .
Everything will be worthwhile
If you just smile
—Charlie Chaplin, Johnny Turner, and Geoffrey Parsons,
Excerpts from the song, Smile

Strong and Silent

Until recent years, the majority of the United States and Canada was populated by people with Northern European backgrounds and for these populations stoicism has been the optimum standard regarding emotions. Keeping a stiff upper lip, and being strong and silent, were considered virtues. Generations of Americans idolized the movie star, John Wayne and Jacqueline Kennedy, wife of President John F. Kennedy, for their ability to contain their emotions. In a television interview of the Kennedy brothers, one stated, "We were taught that a Kennedy never cries." When President Kennedy was killed, newspapers featured photos of Mrs. Kennedy and her children standing stoically, with headlines touting her courage. Rigid self-control equated courage.

When children are small they have natural waves of feelings; they can cry and laugh almost in the same breath. I remember seeing two little girls, age two, hugging and loving one another until one reached up and pulled the other's hair and screams erupted; within minutes, they were hugging again. Most American children are allowed to express feelings openly for a few years, but that freedom changes over time as expectations increase for them to grow up and fit in.

My father's ancestors lived in Russia since 1767, and all faced life-long quests for survival. Several years ago I prepared a story of our family history for a first-time presentation at the national conference of a historical society. Since then I have given this lecture to several psychological conferences in the United States and to multitudes of other groups internationally, especially in the former USSR. When I began my research for this project, I created a questionnaire that I gave to colleagues, students, and friends. In it, they were asked to list what came to mind when they thought of someone who is Northern European, both the positive and negative qualities. The following attributes were listed most often:

Positive qualities:

- strong
- responsible
- intelligent
- determined
- courageous
- orderly
- God fearing
- loyal
- perfectionist
- protective
- hardworking
- tough
- persistent
- industrious
- leaders
- clean
- ethnically proud
- punctual
- dependable
- family oriented
- resourceful
- survivors
- quality workers
- resilient
- honest
- self-sufficient
- thrifty
- traditionalists
- sturdy

Negative qualities:

- inflexible
- strong willed
- compulsive
- unyielding
- stern
- harsh
- stubborn
- rigid
- argumentative
- forceful
- critical
- demanding
- controlling
- narrow-minded
- autocratic
- cold
- aloof
- begrudging

- aggressive
- stoic
- domineering
- arrogant
- unemotional
- workaholics
- overpowering
- secretive
- hard-driving

These attributes do not apply only to people of Northern European heritage; they are universal qualities. Do any of them look familiar to you or your family?

One of the truths I have affirmed over the years is that people, who possess great strengths, also have the capacity for great weaknesses. We can confirm that truth by looking at the lives of many of our worldwide heads of state who have shown great skills in leadership, but who also have awesome personal flaws. Remember, positive and negative qualities reside in all of us, but each type can vary greatly in degree.

I have shown the lists of Northern European traits to many people, and a few said they didn't think the negative characteristics were necessarily bad. However, spouses and children have described living with someone with these attributes like this: "He is very inflexible and so, it's tough to be with him." "She's a hard-liner." "We have no intimacy at all." "If I displease him, he won't talk to me for weeks, sometime months." "She is cold and withdrawn; there is little warmth in our home." "He's very domineering; everything has to be done his way." Such descriptions deal not only with issues of commission but of omission.

For anyone—child or adult—living in abusive or difficult circumstances (including my ancestors living in Russia during extremely harsh times), suppressing emotions as a way of life is necessary and expedient. What was once necessary and expedient, however, can become an exasperating liability later when attempting to be intimate and fully in touch with yourself. When you repress fear, hurt, anger, and loneliness, you also retard love, spontaneity, joy, and peace.

You may stifle emotions for many reasons: cultural mores, family role modeling, personality type, and/or as a survival defense mechanism. Whatever the reason, when you engage in this repression (whether you realize it or not), your Controlling Child is put in charge of your life.

Obviously, the characteristics of any given culture (American, European, Russian, Asian, Latin, African, or other) are not the only factors that influence our character. Our innate personalities, families, and experiences all contribute greatly to our own personal strengths and weakness. It will be helpful, however, if you keep these lists in mind as you contemplate your own positive and negative traits. Please start to analyze the constructive qualities of your character that have enabled you to survive and also note those aspects that have been destructive and need to be eliminated. You have a right to claim all your own marvelous attributes. Do not allow yourself to be influenced by antagonists who would rob you of your birthright.

Emotionally Disabled and Disadvantaged

My mother was a wonderful, loving woman who was beloved by many people. But when it came to emotions, she kept a very narrow line. You didn't go below the line and express anger or act out in any way. But neither did you go far above the line. "Behave," "Don't be silly," and "Act like a lady" were constant admonitions for me as a child. She gave me the same rules for living that were given to her.

When I was thirteen, I was very excited about my first "long-dress" occasion, our school's Seventh-Eighth Grade Banquet. I received my first corsage (white carnations whose fragrance I still remember) from my boyfriend and sat with him at the dinner in the basement of the City Building in our little town. A local minister was our speaker, a delightfully funny man who kept us entertained. My mother was in the kitchen with the other moms, preparing and then cleaning up after our meal.

After my boyfriend walked me home, I was eager to talk to my mother about what a wonderful evening I had experienced. Before I could begin, she sat me down and told me she was very embarrassed because, while she worked in the kitchen, she could hear me laughing during the minister's speech and then admonished me with, "Ladies do not laugh out loud." Until I was forty-four, I never again laughed aloud unless I placed my hand over my mouth. When my daughters, Jinger and Missy, were teenagers, I loved to hear them laugh uproariously while watching television or talking with friends. I genuinely envied them.

Mother often told me I should never do anything that would make anyone upset with me. In other words, "Be all things to all people." So I became a chameleon: you want me to be red, I can be red; you want me to be blue, I can be blue. When I met someone new, I would ask many questions regarding the things they liked or did not like. I even went so far as to keep a list of those preferences in my billfold so I could peruse it the next time I met with them to make certain I remembered them. If they came to my home for dinner, I knew whether they liked lemon pie or brownies without nuts. I became so other-focused that I lost myself. I don't think I ever really knew her.

When I started therapy, Dr. Danylchuk often asked me what I was feeling. At first I replied, "What do you think I should feel?" Needless to say, he didn't let that continue. As he pressed me on this issue, I'm certain he became weary of me just shrugging my shoulders and saying over and over, "I don't know." And I truly did not know. For me to be able to feel, I first had to learn what I did that kept me from feeling. What were the techniques my Controlling Child had used over the years to keep my emotions so contained?

The Controlling Child will use whatever natural talents or environmental elements are available to keep you from looking inside at your Pool of Pain. Toward this end, in addition to repression, most people use anesthetizers and diversionary tactics. For children, anesthetizers may be cookies, cake or ice cream. For adults, it may be food, nicotine, alcohol, drugs, or sex. For children, diversionary tactics may be school, computers, video games, television, reading, sports, music, texting or talking to their friends. For adults, it may include those same diversions as well as their work, spouse or significant other, children, grandchildren, exercise, caretaking, church, and keeping busy in general. Anger is also a major diversion—it keeps the focus off you.

I have my clients list what their Controlling Child did as a child, and now does as an adult, to keep their Sobbing Child suppressed. I also have clients use a large easel pad to draw the younger version of their Controlling Child and the adult version. I encourage you to do the same. When I drew mine, my child had a lopsided halo and was carrying an armload of books. My adult image of the Controlling Child showed her halo shattering. She wore a strained smile and had ten pairs of arms and legs all running frantically while trying to take care of the rest of the world. I was totally drained.

(Exercise 8: *Controlling Child Past and Present*)

Exhausted Body and Spirit

If on this earth one moment's peace could I find,
then unto it would I say,
"Stay with me awhile, so fair thou art."
—Johann Wolfgang von Goethe (1749–1832)

It takes a great deal of physical strength to hold down emotional pain. When a person's energy is focused in this area, it becomes diverted from its original intention. Energy that should be committed to keeping the physical body intact (e.g., the immune, histamine, neurological, and endocrine systems), is sidetracked in the effort to restrain emotional pain. Consequently, the person is left with reduced resources to resist diseases and communicable illnesses. I know this certainly happened to me.

Fortunately, our bodies are amazing instruments. When I took the lid off my box to release my emotional pain, my Controlling Child was finally able to return to her appropriate occupation as my temporary defense system, which released energy for keeping my body healthy. I have not had any asthma attacks, very few allergy problems, and almost no headaches since 1981. I have taken no prescription pain medication since that time (except after surgery). However, my immune system had been damaged—I was diagnosed with discoid lupus in 1986.

I now see having lupus as a positive circumstance. Since it does not have any cure, there is no medical treatment, and it can only be controlled by diet, sleep, and lifestyle, it forced me to make radical changes in how I lived my life. I keep firm boundaries around my sleep habits, eat healthy, exercise regularly, and have reduced my stress level drastically. Unfortunately, it also meant giving up my Ph.D. program. Today, however, I am in good health, as long as I make certain I reduce my stress and get plenty of rest.

In the early 1980s I hypothesized about psychological and physiological connections, based upon my own experience. I consulted with many professors, psychologists, psychiatrists, and medical doctors who said research into the mind-body connection was undeveloped. I am pleased that what I hypothesized many years ago, is now being proven to be accurate. Information regarding the relationship between mind and body is now more widespread, such as the work by Dr. Bessel van der Kolk, a psychiatrist and professor at Harvard Medical Institute. He is one of the foremost authorities regarding the effects of trauma upon the body, and writes and teaches extensively on this subject. (See his website, www.traumacenter.org.)

Perfectionism

A strong Controlling Child defense mechanism may not only damage emotions and the physical body, it also can affect the intellect's ability to function appropriately. Because its main job is to protect a person from feeling pain, it is capable of going to extremes to do so, possibly resulting in perfectionism, obsessive-compulsive disorders, or addictions.

A child who is punished each time he or she makes the slightest error, including mistakes common to all children (such as spilling milk), becomes very afraid to risk. Children who come from alcoholic homes where drunken rages can occur without warning feel as though they are walking in a minefield and become hyper-vigilant.

Other children may try to please a demanding mom or dad or try to live up to a highly successful parent, feeling they always fall short. These people either drive themselves excessively to be perfect in every detail, or go the opposite direction and become fearful of trying anything at all, believing that their efforts will not be good enough. At the extreme, their fear may develop into agoraphobia, where they become housebound and unable to function in society.

I know people who are highly intelligent, gifted, and very capable, but who have allowed their fear of risk to keep them incapacitated. Some become eternal students so they never have to leave the safety of the academic realm and venture into the frightening world of independence and responsibility, and they continue living with their parents. Still others marry someone who will take care of them and tolerate their behaviors. For these people, it is very scary to grow up.

I became such a perfectionist that it was absurd. I arose earlier than my husband and made my half of the bed with him in the other half. After we had dinner parties for families and friends, I stayed up all night (even though I had to work at the gallery the next morning), washing all the dishes, completely straightening up the house and even waxing my floors so the next morning it would not appear that twenty or more people had been there a few hours earlier. Although I could see the insanity of it all, I did not know how to change and do things differently.

Distorted Thinking and Becoming "Stuck"

My Controlling Child, in addition to keeping me busy so I would not have time to address my painful issues, was trying to prove to God, the world, and myself that I was not a bad person. As a child, I had been taught that God loves little children and sends guardian angels to protect them. When I was attacked at eight years old, I was praying for God to send someone—anyone—to rescue me. When that did not happen, it seemed that God had turned and walked away from me and said, "You've been a bad girl today, not bad enough to go to hell, but bad enough to never go to heaven. So the kindest thing I can do is just erase you, your emotions, and your soul." I felt rejection and abandonment at the deepest level.

Children have distorted thinking—they think, "Good things happen to good people and bad things happen to bad people." As a consequence, children assume the blame for the negative things that occur. Even when they become old enough to know and understand that something was not their fault—that they were the victims of abuse, that Mom or Dad was drunk or neglectful, or that they didn't cause their parents divorce—at an unconscious level they still feel responsible.

In addition to the issue of children carrying the burden of blame, they are also dealing with feelings of fear, shame, pain, and abandonment. If they did not possess a defense mechanism, and were compelled to feel the full intensity of those burdens and emotions, their small, undeveloped systems would not be able to handle the enormity of it al. Being too vulnerable and fragile, they could possibly become psychotic or die.

Fortunately, children have the special gift of their Controlling Child, their innate emotional defense mechanism, who puts their painful feelings in a box and says, "Don't feel; if you do, you will die!" This defense is necessary and appropriate for the child's survival; however, when it becomes a lifelong practice rather than a temporary safety mechanism, it creates a multitude of problems. Because the choice genuinely feels like a matter of life or death, a person can become emotionally stuck in this childhood mindset.

You may be thinking that this sounds a bit dramatic and drastic. I did too when I first grasped this concept. After years of listening to numerous clients as well as my own inner dialogs however, I know that a traumatized person can stay emotionally stuck at the age of their victimization, and can be overwhelmed by the concept of releasing the feelings connected with their abuse, even when, physically they become adults. This inability to let go and feel explains why people hold so tenaciously to certain behaviors, addictions, and other Controlling Child defenses, even though doing so could cost them their relationships, careers, children, and future happiness.

At age forty-four, my Controlling Child was still functioning as though I was eight years old and just coming out of a sexual assault. She was unable to comprehend that I was now an adult, fully capable of caring for and protecting myself. Being able to gradually take responsibility for myself, as an adult, became a major goal on my healing journey.

Your Controlling Child may also be stuck at eight, or two, or ten, or fourteen. If so, it is vital that you connect with the reality of your physiological age. I often have my clients take an indelible pen and write the present year and their actual age on the palm of their hands. They also write this information on a batch of sticky notes and place them all over their houses, in their desks at work, and in their wallets or purses as they reprogram their unconscious minds to recognize their correct age.

Many clients have come back to sessions saying how startled they were to realize that their Controlling Child had been acting as if they were still trapped in those overwhelming childhood events. Once they began to genuinely look at themselves and understand they were fully competent and capable adults, things began to change rapidly.

(Exercise 9: Affirming Your Actual Age)

The Ultimate Risk: Letting Go of Control

RISK

To laugh is to risk appearing the fool
To weep is to risk appearing sentimental
To reach out to another is to risk involvement
To expose your feelings is to risk exposing your true self
To place your ideas, your dreams before a crowd
is to risk their loss
To love is to risk not being loved in return
To live is to risk dying
To hope is to risk failure
But risk must be taken because
the greatest hazard is to risk nothing
If you risk nothing you dull your spirit
You may avoid suffering and sorrow
but you cannot learn, feel, change, grow, love, and live
Chained by your attitude you are a slave
You have forfeited your freedom
Only if you risk are you free
—Anonymous

Risking and letting go of control is nearly impossible for some people. Their Controlling Child has invested years in focusing on others, either in caretaking or managing another's addiction. Today, people who exhibit this behavior are referred to as codependents. I was raised to be a codependent when I was told it was my job to fill others' needs and make them happy. As a result, I "kissed it and made it well" for multitudes. In therapy, I worked longer on understanding this aspect of myself and learning about boundaries than on any other issue, even my sexual abuse.

Unfortunately, in 1980-81, the term "codependency" was not well known and I knew nothing about it or its destructive aspects. When Dr. Danylchuk began to challenge me regarding my excessive caretaking I adamantly argued with him that to not do so would be selfish and non-Christian. He would listen quietly to my disputes and then softly say, "But, does it work? Does it produce healthy individuals and families?" It took months of his consistent, wise questioning before I began to waver.

Today, my definition of a codependent is someone who sacrifices her or his self-worth by submitting to and taking responsibility for another person, which enables the other person to engage in destructive behavior. Codependence is doing something for someone else that they should be doing for themselves. It also means being focused on others, not only in caretaking but in blaming. It is attempting to manage the behavior of others rather than your own.

God made it clear to me that I was in the way when I covered up, protected, and kept others from facing the consequences of their actions—God wanted me to move so divine influence could work in their lives. That's extremely difficult to do if the person you are trying to protect is a family member or someone else you love, or if allowing them to fall will also have a detrimental effect on you. Oliver Wendell Holmes put it very aptly when he said, "The great act of faith is when man decides that he is not God."

One of my clients, an executive with a worldwide mission organization, arrived one day with his wife for therapy. She came from a very abusive background and had suffered long bouts of depression. As a hard-core Controlling Child, he was used to "fixing" people and therefore was frustrated and resentful that—despite his love, care, and advice—he had been unable to "fix" his wife. Several years before, a counselor had told him that he had a messiah complex, but it hadn't changed his attitude.

Fortunately, he allowed his heart to be open, took off his imaginary "I'm with Her" sign and started to look at himself. As he realized that he had his own issues to confront—especially his excessive control and codependency— he actively worked on changing those unhealthy behaviors. Later he shared, "Up until this time I had always been so sure of everything: who I was, what I believed, what needed to be done, how God worked, how to minister to people, and on and on. This is going to sound crazy and incredibly prideful, but in some ways over the years I think I began to confuse myself with God. At times I can remember thinking, 'If God would have done it my way, things would have worked out better.'"

His wife addressed her Pool of Pain with a long-term commitment to the process of becoming a Healthy Balanced Person. Today this couple experiences intimacy because he has genuinely stopped his controlling behavior and she is taking responsibility for her own emotional health. But since life isn't perfect, he still becomes frustrated sometimes when things don't go the way he expected, and he can't automatically jump in and fix it. But they are growing and healing.

The Changing of the Guard

During my intensive therapy, I thought my Controlling Child had no feelings, that she had buried them all—but I was wrong. She became angry and hurt, and felt discounted and displaced when she learned that she needed to come down off her throne. She said to me, "Why are you listening to Dr. Danylchuk? I'm the one who has been taking care of you since you were eight!" She thought I was throwing her away.

My Controlling Child knew her job was to protect me and keep me healthy. Gradually, however, she began to realize that what she had been doing when I was a child had been necessary for my survival, but now it was detrimental, and she did a 180-degree turnaround. But in typical Controlling Child manner, she still wanted to manage my time in therapy.

One night when I went back to the home where I was staying, I sat on my bed and wrote out a list of feelings and scheduled when I would address each one. I really wanted to hurry and get through all this so I could go home to my family in Arizona. My list read: "Monday I will do sadness; Tuesday I will do pain; Wednesday I will do fear; Thursday I will do abandonment; Friday I will do anger; etc." I proudly took my list to Dr. Danylchuk the next morning. Since he is a gentle, kind man, he tried hard not to laugh as he commented, "Well, I'm not certain you can program your feelings quite like that." He was so right; it took me weeks just to work through the first one.

My Controlling Child needed to be restructured and to receive a new job description: boundary setter. And learning about boundaries was a topic I certainly needed to address. I found that a boundary exists for two purposes: so you do not victimize me, and so I do not victimize you.

I had no idea how to begin. It felt selfish for me to think of caring for myself. Then I remembered what a flight attendant on an airplane says before takeoff: "If you are traveling with small children and an emergency arises, always put the oxygen mask on yourself first before helping them." I was finally beginning to realize the necessity of ensuring one's own health first as a wise, rather than a selfish choice; and that the ability to genuinely assist others emerges out of that healthy state.

But I didn't have the faintest clue how to respond to requests from other people and how to know when it was appropriate to say "Yes" or "No." The following outline given to me by Dr. Danylchuk became very helpful for me in this area.

Five Ways to Say "Yes" or "No"

1. Healthy Yes: You ask me, it feels good for me, I say "Yes."
2. Unhealthy Yes: You ask me, it doesn't feel good for me, I say "Yes," but I resent it.
3. Healthy No: You ask me, it doesn't feel good for me, I say "No," and I feel okay about it.
4. Unhealthy No: You ask me, it doesn't feel good for me, I say "No," and I feel guilty. (Codependents and people who are unaware of healthy boundaries usually are stuck at #2 and #4.)
5. Healthy Yes (concession with boundaries): You ask me, it doesn't feel good for me, but, out of love and concern for you, I say "Yes," and I do not resent it. The key is, this must be temporary assistance—if it is not, I am back at #2—or I may set a proper boundary at #3.

Any time you choose #3, you are setting a healthy boundary. You may also want to be gracious and offer another option to the person or propose doing the activity at another time. People who chose #4, an unhealthy "No," usually beat themselves up endlessly and feel they are selfish and uncaring.

Number 5, which involves a compromise, is the tricky one and often causes distress. Please note, if you cannot say "Yes" without resentment, you are acting at #2, an unhealthy "Yes." The most important factor here is, your assistance must be temporary. Here's an example: Because I have lupus, I need strong boundaries around my sleeping habits and I let my clients know that I do not take phone calls at night. However, should a client become suicidal and need to call me at 3:00 a.m., out of concern for that client I would take the call and plan on getting extra sleep the next night. But if the client called me several nights in a row, I would either be saying "Yes" and resenting it (#2, an unhealthy "Yes"), or I would need to move to #3 (a healthy "No"), and say, "No, I am sorry I cannot take your calls here anymore. You need to be hospitalized; this is no longer helpful for you or for me."

Anyone who is married or has children has experienced #5 many times, for example, when you sit up all night with a sick child or spouse. People who care for their elderly parents or a child with a disability or chronic illness face the enormous challenge of living at #5 daily—not in a temporary situation but in one that is permanent. For those people, it is essential that they carve out time for themselves and obtain additional care support for the patient, even though the patient may protest. I have seen caregivers die before their patients because they have not set boundaries for their own health.

I kept this *Five Ways to Say "Yes" or "No"* list on my mirror, refrigerator, sink, desk, and car dashboard for years. I urge you to begin to use these responses in your life and to discuss them with your family and friends.

(Exercise 10: How to Say "Yes" and "No")

Lifting the Veil

The real voyage of discovery lies not in seeking new landscapes, but in having new eyes. —
Marcel Proust (1871–1922)

When your Controlling Child steps down, it is as though a veil is lifted or a curtain is raised. You begin to view the world through new eyes, eyes no longer veiled in tears or covered with control, but eyes sparkling with wonder and with love—the way they were designed to be. It is a very special gift to view people with the eyes of God.

In Summary

Many children worldwide laugh and cry at will. However, many of us are taught early on to refrain from being too emotional and to present a calm "adult" face. Our Controlling Child (which is designed to be a temporary internal defense mechanism) learns to use anesthetizers and diversionary tactics to distract us from painful feelings. If our Controlling Child becomes a "king or queen on a throne," however, and therefore a permanent fixture in our lives, we will never deal with our emotional issues. As a result of this repression of feelings, we may develop physical problems, re-lationship issues and codependency, or addictions. Relieving our Controlling Child of total control and learning to feel safe with our feelings—good and bad—opens us up to all the wonders of the world, helping us become the person we were designed to be.

In addition, our Controlling Child (who probably has grown weary of trying to be in charge of everything), will now have time and energy to devote to the tasks for which it was originally in-tended—of being our healthy defense mechanism; of setting boundaries so we are not victimized, or become victimizers; and of keeping us responsible. As this restructuring takes place, these new skills will be available to support and keep us safe as we prog-ress on a journey that may seem to be filled with risky road-blocks and dangerous detours.

CHAPTER 6

Finding the Prize: Reclaiming Your Original Feeling Child

"A great man is he who does not lose his child's-heart."
—Mencius (372-289 B.C.)

Discovery

Pain is reality—maybe the only earthly reality, while joy and love are relative.

The proportion to which we face our pain determines the extent to which we experience joy and love. Your willingness to face your own Pool of Pain with honesty, despite what you may see in its reflection, greatly determines your ability to truly reclaim who you were created to be. Such effort helps revive your Original Child, bringing you not only empathy and compassion, but a depth and breadth to what could otherwise become a shallow existence.

During my time in therapy, I spent hours convincing my Controlling Child to stand aside while I lanced the wounds of my Sobbing Child, but I did not have the slightest conception of how to go about finding my Original Child. I realized she had been buried under a painful heap of memories and emotions. Then, one day it was as though I heard her cry: "Hey, let me out! I've been buried down here just as long as she (my Sobbing Child) has; I want equal time and attention."

As I slowly lifted her out of that dark hiding place, I found she wanted to go out into the sunshine. I began taking long walks (on legs that formerly could not do so without pain) and I stopped to smell the magnificent roses along the way. The San Francisco Bay area in the spring of 1981 was in full bloom, and I felt as though I were seeing each flower and tree for the first time.

Sensual - Sensuous

I believe we are created with physical, emotional, intellectual, and spiritual components that are like four strands making up the cord that is every individual. When any one strand is weakened, the whole cord is weakened. Conversely, when any strand is strengthened, the whole cord is strengthened.

When emotions are repressed or buried, it also damages a person's capacity to be healthy physically, intellectually and spiritually. This is especially true in the physical realm, as your ability to use your five senses—taste, touch, sight, scent, and sound— becomes hampered.

As I became more in touch with my own senses, I studied the words "sensuous" and "sensual" and found that sensuous pertains to the five senses, while sensual refers to sexuality. The effect of the five senses on sexuality and upon emotions is common knowledge. It is appropriate then to conjecture that when emotions are suppressed, physical responses (especially those consisting of the five senses and sexuality) would also be hindered. However, the converse is true—when a person releases emotions, his or her ability to fully experience the richness of taste, touch, sight, scent, and sound as well as healthy sexuality is liberated as well. For me, when my emotions became unhampered, my senses became alive and vibrant. I felt good about being female and realized that femininity and strength were compatible. It was an incredible revelation.

In the old story of The Velveteen Rabbit, the little stuffed rabbit wished he could become real without having uncomfortable things happen to him. But he found that once he became real, he couldn't become unreal again, even though he wanted to. Ultimately, he discovered that being real was worth the discomfort and he had no wish to change back. Once upon a time, I was that little velveteen rabbit and I too found that once I genuinely tapped into the Original Child I was created to be, I was unwilling to be without that child ever again.

The Prize

You must carry the chaos within you in
order to give birth to the dancing star."
—Friedrich Nietzsche (1844-1900)

I believe one of the main purposes of the healing journey is to reclaim your Original Child and the soul that dwells therein. I often draw a rough sketch for my clients showing the Controlling Child, with hands on hips and a stern face standing firmly on top of the ground, looking totally in charge. Buried deep down in the dirt underneath that commander's feet, however, lies a fragile Sobbing Child. Then, below that wounded child, hidden deeper still in the black soil, rests a beautiful box containing a marvelous gift: The Prize—the Original Child, the child you were created to be— and that Prize is like a wondrous shell containing a magnificent pearl—your soul.

The Freedom Process

I feel the most effective manner in which to free those imprisoned children is to work first with your Controlling Child so this defensive mechanism begins to realize it is not helping, but hindering; and will therefore need to stand aside and allow the rescue to begin. The next step is to gently lift up your Sobbing Child and allow that child to release the painful feelings that were secreted away for so long. As this child is freed, you will also be clearing out mounds of dirt and mud so you can, at last, reach the concealed treasure, your Original Child. Raising that infinitely valuable part of you up to freedom will bring you a special joy you never will forget.

Some people feel a healing journey should only encourage a person to strengthen his/her defense mechanisms (having the Controlling Child in charge). This model promotes intellectualizing; usually negates past experiences and feelings as unimportant; or stresses behavior modification only. While I agree that learning how to modify behavior with new skills is a necessary part of healing, it is only one part.

Other people may emphasize the importance of dealing with emotions and the Sobbing Child's painful past. But, if only the past is addressed, a person may dig endlessly in the dirt, throwing mud balls at parents, siblings, extended families, ex-spouses, God, employers, and so on; taking little responsibility for actions as an adult, and remaining a victim. Yes, dealing with the reality and pain of the past is certainly an indispensable aspect of therapy; however, it is essential not to become stuck, swirling perpetually in the pain, and not progressing toward becoming a Healthy Balanced Person.

Remember, reclaiming The Prize, your Original Child, is one of the primary goals in your healing journey. No one has a right to that child but you. But in doing so, do not concentrate only on your Original Child and the resulting good feelings. If you do, any results will be temporary because you will have ignored your pain and it will eventually resurface. You need not delve endlessly in your Pool of Pain, but you do need to do so long enough to clear out the debris and make a passageway for you to reach and reclaim the unique, valuable child that is you.

Healthy Balance

I had the privilege in the 1990s to present numerous weeklong seminars at a retreat center operated by Robert Schuller's Crystal Cathedral in California. When presenting the concepts of the three "children," I always asked the participants to buy a special gift for their Original Child and then show the gift to the group and share why they chose it. Some of the gifts were funny, or outrageous or delightful; others brought tears to the eyes of everyone there.

During a couple's workshop on intimacy that Dr. Ralph Earle and I gave, I vividly remember a young man who had been born in Mexico and was married to a woman from California (they were expecting their first child). He stood before the group holding a large, yellow dump truck. Silent tears etched his cheeks as he told us it was the first toy he had ever owned. I encourage you to allow time for your Original Child to choose a special gift too.

I also ask my clients and students to detail how they take care of each aspect of their Original Child—physical, intellectual, emotional, and spiritual—and how they might create further growth in each of these areas. Please do the following exercise, making such a list for yourself and actively begin working on becoming balanced and healthy in all four areas:

(Exercise 11: Creating Healthy Balance)

Since your Original Child houses your soul - this unique aspect of yourself is also the creator of your passion, your creativity, and your talents. I have clients take their large sheets of paper and draw their Original Child as they would perceive that child to be if he or she had been raised in a healthy environment. I also ask them two questions about what they would truly like to be and to do. I encourage you to do both exercises, the drawing and the questions. Let your mind fly—what are all those things you've always wanted to do? What are you passionate about?

(Exercise 12: Reclaiming Your Original Child)

I struggled a great deal regarding devoting any of my time and energy to any activity that my Original Child might enjoy. Then one day I read a quote by the famous poet, Henry David Thoreau that was life-changing for me: "Alas for the bird that never sings, and dies with his song still in him." It was as though God was saying to me, "I designed and created you; never be ashamed of my creation. Just as I created the bird to sing and fly—I also gave you special gifts of unique talents and abilities—find them, use them!" That wasn't an easy task, but I knew I did not want to die without allowing my original child to sing—or to fly. I encourage you to come fly with me.

Physical Health:
"Dancing? Did someone mention 'dancing'?"

At age forty-four when I discovered my Original Child, I asked her what she really wanted to be and do. She replied, "I want to be free to learn to love and respect myself, God and other people. I want to do some fun things: take dancing lessons, play the guitar, and maybe take an interesting class or two."

Realizing I needed to pay attention to all the components of my Original Child, I knew I had neglected my physicality over the years. I was excited that after my intensive therapy I had strength in my legs for the first time in my adult life. As a result I began taking long walks and started aerobic dance classes and was delighted to discover I could keep up with my daughters, Jinger and Missy. Later, after I moved to California, I took dancing lessons from a professional and even won gold medals in international competitions over a period of several years (long before the television show, *Dancing With the Stars* became popular.)

While my therapy accessed my Sobbing Child, my dancing sessions helped me find my Original Child. Like most victims of sexual abuse, my body was rigid and inflexible and I had a poor body image with distorted feelings concerning sexuality. Dancing gave me a safe time and place to relax, release emotions, get in touch with my physical self and even be female and sensual in a healthy, appropriate way. I loved it.

I often recommend dancing lessons to my clients, especially for couples; it is a wonderful way to obtain healthy exercise, have fun and connect with your loved one. I encourage you to try it as it is a marvelous Original Child exercise. Watch any child who is old enough to walk when a lively song is played; they immediately become animated and dance to the music. They do not need to be taught—it is innate. Find the type of exercise you enjoy most and make a commitment to begin.

Today at age eighty I still love to dance, though, no longer in competition. I also exercise and spend time walking in the parks. When my grandson, B.J. was in high school, he thought it was cool to be the only person in his class who had a grandmother in her sixties who worked out with weights and who had also been interviewed on *Geraldo* and *Hard Copy*.

While I was aware that many of my clients did not take care of themselves with proper diet, exercise, vitamins, and so on, I have also been surprised to find how many people neglect having regular check-ups for their eyes and teeth—and how many women ignore having mammograms and pap smears while men ignore prostate tests when their age and sex indicate the importance of such evaluations. No one can make you healthy except you; even God cannot accomplish healing if you do not cooperate.

Intellectual Health: Back in Kindergarten

Toward the end of my intensive therapy in 1981, Dr. Danylchuk asked me one day whether I had ever considered returning to college. I answered that while I loved to learn, I had been very successful in business without a college degree and I only had twenty-five credits from night classes taken when I was a newlywed. Those few credits were not enough to complete even a freshman year in a bachelor's program which meant I'd have a long way to go in order to earn a degree.

He responded by describing a new type of learning experience especially geared toward adult learners and he strongly encouraged me to check it out. Because of his continued insistence, I did some research and found Ottawa University in Phoenix, Arizona which specialized in teaching adults. But my Original Child's desire to take an interesting class or two was entirely different from the possibility of embarking upon a whole new career. However, my Original Child became excited about going back to school with the prospect of obtaining degrees in psychology, and so I finally enrolled at Ottawa. The university and its staff became a beacon of hope for me through many difficult times during the next two years.

At first I was distressed by the thought of starting over in a new field, saying, "Here I am forty-five years old and nearly everyone else my age in the field of psychology has already had their graduate degrees for almost twenty years. I feel like I'm only in kindergarten!" I debated whether or not to continue. In one of my classes I read a speech given by an eloquent statesman in the 1950s to the graduating class of a woman's college. One sentence was so powerful I had it made into a plaque that still hangs over my desk: *"Never let the tyranny of the normal trample down the supreme contribution of the unique." —Adlai Stevenson (1900-1965)*

The wisdom of these words imprinted on my spirit the idea that each person is unique and does have a supreme contribution to give, even me. I did not want the "tyranny of the normal" to keep my Original Child buried in her box for the remainder of her life. I stayed in school. In the next three years, I earned both undergraduate and graduate degrees in psychology.

I was honored that Ottawa University asked me to come back to their campus in 1997, not as a student, but to develop and teach a specialty program entitled, " The Treatment of Trauma, Abuse, and Deprivation," for their graduate students in counseling psychology. For seven years I taught eight courses a year there using the Murray Method and I enjoyed it immensely.

Whether you take classes or not, keep your intellect sharp, hone your mental skills and stay connected outside your own private world. Since I am over sixty-five, I receive many articles addressing senior issues, especially concerning ways to keep one's mind healthy. The general consensus usually centers on keeping the brain active and challenged in order to maintain optimum health. The maxim, "Use it or lose it," also applies to the brain, not just the body. Continue to read, continue to learn.

Emotional Health: A Psychological Thermometer

"We should not pretend to understand the world only by the intellect; we apprehend it just as much by feeling."
—*Carl Gustav Jung (1875-1961)*

The majority of this book is dedicated to the encouragement of becoming emotionally healthy. A commitment to psychological health should be life-long, just as a commitment to physical health is not a short-term option. It means continuing to grow emotionally not only by taking time to read helpful materials, but also by sharing, perhaps receiving counseling, being in a group, attending workshops, and so on.

Please remember that just as different physical problems occur throughout our life time, so do psychological issues become apparent at different stages of our lives. Many times we are equipped to handle these problems without professional help, but I found that seeking a psychological professional was necessary for me.

When I started my therapy I thought that when I finished working on my sexual abuse issues that I would be done. Instead, God seemed to tap me on the shoulder and say, "Now it's time to work on codependency and boundary issues." Later on, just as I thought that work was completed, I had to address the issues of abandonment and loss, and so it went for several years.

When you are physically sick, you see your physician. The doctor takes your temperature, gives you an examination, and perhaps uses various tests including blood analysis to determine the severity of your illness. There is concrete, specific evidence of "wellness" such as a normalized temperature and blood count. Unfortunately, we do not have an emotional or mental health thermometer or blood test. No one is ever completely "well" or "cured;" we are always in process. Personal growth and maturity are what the journey of life is all about.

This does not mean going to therapy and staying there without end, but rather being sensitive to your own process. If you feel well physically, are healthy emotionally and your personal and professional relationships are going well, then you need not be concerned. If, however, you are depressed, are into addictions, are having relationship problems, or have suffered the loss of a loved one or job—then seeing a therapist or joining a helping group will be good medicine on your road to better emotional balance and well-being.

Different therapists, modalities and groups offer unique assistance on varied issues. Just as you don't go to one medical doctor for all your needs, please consult various psychological specialists and avail yourself of the appropriate resources when the need arises.

If a therapist or group is not available to you, please contemplate asking a small group of friends and acquaintances to share this book and ask each one to also considering doing the exercises within it—then commit to meet together on a regular basis to share the results of your work. If you do so, you will provide encouragement for each other as well as accountability. I can assure you that this type of endeavor will bring amazing and rewarding results to all participants (and to their families).

But, there is another major reward besides healthy relationships and internal well-being. As you address your emotional health, your physical health will also be affected. As I have already related, I was overjoyed when I found that as I released long-buried emotions, my physical body was able then to divert the energy that I had formerly used to restrain those painful feelings, and instead to use that energy as it was intended—to maintain my immune system. As a result, my physical health improved dramatically.

In Summary

Our Original Child has been buried for as long as our Sobbing Child, and certainly deserves our attention and nurturing. Allowing this part of ourselves to develop, grow, and eventually fly, becomes the heart of the therapeutic process—it is Finding the Prize. Reclaiming our Original Child and discovering what this child really wants to do and to be, is not only essential, but also a delightful part of this healing journey and one we cannot neglect. In addition, it is *de rigueur* that we become willing to care for and listen to this original part and respond with actions, not just thoughts and wishes. Being committed to a healthy balance—emotionally, spiritually, physically, and intellectually— will create a safe, stable base from which our Original Child is able to traverse on the journey toward becoming a Healthy Balanced Person.

CHAPTER 7

Spiritual Health: Intimacy with God, Is It Possible?

Of all the needs ... a lonely child has,
the one that must be satisfied,
if there is going to be hope and a hope of wholeness,
is the unshaking need for an unshakable God.
—Maya Angelou (1928–)

Angry with God

They That Sow in Tears Shall Reap in Joy[1]

"My God, my God, why hast Thou forsaken me?"[2]
Are You blind? Can't you see?
"No, no, not me!" I screamed, pleaded, cried
But no one listened, no one cared ... and so, that small child died.

Years of pain, then deepest agony
You turned your back, abandoned me.
In my black pit, no trace of light,
Dear God, this has been such a long, long night

My heart is breaking, in such great need
But, yours is too...my tears you did heed.
Twas not your will, on that day long ago
When evil men went against you, hurting me so.

---

1   Psalm 126:5
2   Psalm 22: 1; Matthew 27:46

You began then to prepare one special man
To be the fulfillment of your healing plan
You brought him to me, for a time...such as this
The arms with which you held me were his.

Doctor, family, friends, all loving, concerned, caring
And even when I could not, they continued praying.
Your love Lord, shown through them
Brought the matchless new dawning,

"Weeping only lasts for the night
Joy comes with the morning"[3]
—Marilyn Murray

This poem, written five days following my return home to Arizona after being away for seven months in therapy, reflects my inner spiritual struggle at that crucial period in my life. Prior to my time at the center, my relationship with God had been the single most important aspect of my life. I believed in an all-loving God who cared about everyone, especially children.

The most painful issue from my childhood attack was feeling that He had turned and walked away from me. I felt betrayed by the one I had trusted most. I was angry.

But allowing feelings of betrayal and anger to surface was not an option for me. Not only was anger never allowed in my family, anger at God would be absolute blasphemy. Nevertheless my therapist, Dr. Danylchuk (who was also an ordained pastor), gently persisted and urged me to deal with this issue, saying I would never become healthy until I did.

I still remember his words: "I think your relationship with God is very important to you and that you want it re-established. But you cannot mend a relationship until you acknowledge that it's broken. God already knows your heart and knows how angry you are. *You* are the one who needs to recognize that fact. Besides, I think God is big enough to handle your anger. In the Psalms, King

---

3   Psalm 30:5

David rants and raves at God many times, yet God also said David was 'a man after my own heart.' God gave you the emotion of anger and wants you to accept it as a gift, not a burden." Although Dr. Danylchuk delivered this message to me repeatedly, I still rejected it.

As the days passed I listened to my Sobbing Child's painful feelings, but I was terrified at the thought of really hearing her anger. Week after week, as I peeled back layer after layer of feelings—fear, pain, shame, ugliness, abandonment, rejection—I felt like I was falling into a giant black pit. When I finally hit the bottom, I released what I feared: a violent explosion of rage at God. Years of anger and rejection came pouring out with unmitigated ferocity. The intensity was so great my body exploded upward, causing my head and shoulders to break the tiles of the low, sloping ceiling above me. I fully expected to be struck dead immediately. But I did not die. In fact, that moment was the turning point that enabled me to really begin to live. Now, thirty years later, I see that day as the day when God and I began to relate on a genuinely intimate basis.

I now know that I can only be intimate with someone else—even God—to the level and degree that I am intimate with, and know and understand myself. Until I learned how to listen honestly to myself and my feelings—including my anger—at a very deep level, my relationships were on a surface plane. Even though I had spent years praying and reading my Bible daily, I knew something was amiss. I certainly did not understand intimacy with God and did not comprehend the simplicity and effect of an intimate relationship with God.

In the weeks and months following my explosion of rage, I began to feel cleansed. It was as though the core of a long-festering boil had been purged from my soul. Finally, restorative healing could replace the toxic infection that had plagued my spirit for thirty-six years.

As I released my Sobbing Child's feelings, including her rage, at last I could touch my Original Child. Buried under years of

unreleased emotions, she felt she had been in solitary confinement for nearly a lifetime. I began to understand that the heart
of my Original Child contained my soul, my spirit, and I could not
connect with God until I rescued her from her place of captivity.
But I found I could not do this alone; I had to ask God for help.

This was difficult because I was still angry; however, I found
God to have inestimable patience. I felt as though we both were
standing in a big room with me saying, "You stand in that corner,
and I'll stand in this one, and I'll wave to you once in awhile; but
don't come too close." Gradually, I moved closer to the center of
the room and, when I did, God did too.

I had to be quiet and listen to my Original Child, allowing her
to connect with God, rather than relating to God as I had been
through my Controlling Child. As I relaxed, I began to grasp the
concept of an unfragmented child created in the womb of God—in
an infinitely safe, secure place—and to comprehend the reality of
that child's pure spiritual intuition and true wisdom. I also started
to understand that this child could become fragmented (when on
an earthly plane), while continuing to seek the eternal safety of
that original parent.

Gradually, God began to lift up my Original Child, revealing who
she was created to be with all her creativity and talents. I came to
know her soul—my soul. God began the renewing, healing part
of our journey—a journey of reclamation and restoration. I read
Scripture with new eyes. I had read and quoted the Twenty-third
Psalm hundreds of times but never fully understood it before.
Now the phrase, "He restoreth my soul" gained a powerful new
meaning for me.

This time was like a new birth for me—an inspiring, invigo-
rating time, but also a tenuous, somewhat fearful time. Not only
did I feel like a fragile infant, there were few guideposts for this
part of my journey.

I know that many of you, also, are probably really struggling
with anger at God as a result of the abuse, trauma and neglect

that has happened in your life and in the lives of your loved ones. Please give yourself permission to do the following exercise and truly process any feelings that arise.

(Exercise 13: Anger at God?)

Choosing Spiritual Health

We are not human beings having a spiritual experience. We are spiritual beings having a human experience.

—Pierre Teilhard de Chardin, (1881-1955)

Each person's spiritual journey is unique; yours is different from mine. Though I was a Christian, I still had not connected with God on a deeply intimate level. I have many clients with backgrounds similar to mine; we seek God in our lives but find that intimacy is frustratingly illusive.

Many people do not trust God and question why God allows excessive abuse and pain to occur in the world, especially to innocent children. All the answers seem confusing and evasive, as nothing seems congruent with their concept of a loving, caring God.

I believe that we are created with free will and have the capacity to choose between right and wrong, good and bad. Unfortunately, when people choose to go against God's will for their lives, many painful things happen—to them, and to others. Regrettably, those others are often children. Six of the Ten Commandments, when broken, create an innocent victim—someone else pays the price for another's transgression. Realizing that God's will for us is to keep us safe and healthy, and that commandments are given for that purpose (rather than to control us), is essential in our healing process.

Although I believe God has the power to modify or stop any of our actions—because God has chosen to give human beings free will—we are allowed to continue our actions unhindered.

I also believe God looks at innocent victims and says, "I can make something good come out of this terrible circumstance, and

I will arrange for your healing someday." The reality of this statement has been proven over and over, not only in my own life, but in the lives of numerous others.

Grace, Amazing Grace

Grace: accepting and seeing yourself and others as God does; not for what you or others have done, or not done; but because you exist as creations of God, and thus are worthy of love and respect.
—Marilyn Murray

From the time I was a child, I have been aware of the concept of grace. While I believed in it and even taught it during the 1970s in my *More Than Friends* support groups for women, I did not fully comprehend that unique concept of love, acceptance and forgiveness called grace. And I certainly knew that I did not feel grace deep down inside. Until I was able to become intimate with myself—accepting myself, including all the painful things done to me and all my own mistakes and failures—I could not accept the gift of grace. Not only did I have to offer it to myself, I subsequently had to receive grace from God, the most difficult step of all.

The mental mantras, like tapes being played in my head, kept repeating the words of my old Controlling Child who admonished me by saying "You have to be perfect, you can't make any mistakes." That voice was difficult to silence. I found that although I believed in "salvation by faith," I lived "salvation by works." At first, I found it easier to extend grace to others than to myself.

Over the years as I have worked with clients and students, not only from the majority of Christian denominations, but also from Jewish, Muslim, Hindu, Buddhist, Taoist, and other religious groups, I've learned new lessons in grace and understanding. As a psychological professional and university instructor, I need to respect each individual's personal beliefs and enable them to balance the spiritual dimension of themselves in a way that is right for them, although it may differ from my own belief system. But even if it was not a professional and ethical requirement, I would still respond in the same manner. I have not changed my own personal beliefs; I have simply become more respectful and nonjudgmental of others. Although I feel I have remained conservative in doctrine, I am now more liberal in unconditional love and acceptance.

This shift did not come quickly or effortlessly. As a child in Sunday school, I heard stories about Jesus who was often criticized for associating with people not accepted by His faith. When I remember that, hearing my old mental tape of "What will other people think?" doesn't seem to matter so much anymore. God confirms to me daily that unconditional love and acceptance of each person is the foundation upon which all relationships are formed. It does not mean accepting unhealthy or harmful actions, but rather accepting who each person was created to be. Learning to separate the person from the deed is essential before we see others as God sees them.

Religion and Spirituality

Religion can be one of the greatest blessings or one of the greatest curses in a person's life. I have worked with many people who have backgrounds of spiritual abuse because the families and religions in which they were raised were unhealthy systems that provided a distorted sense of values. Most of these people still desire a relationship with God, but they do not know how to separate God from the destructive systems in which they grew up. Others may come from religious systems that were not as destructive, yet they, too, have some old mental tapes playing which need to be cleansed and reevaluated.

Despite the fact that religion can be destructive in the wrong hands, it can also be our strongest asset. For many of us, our strength comes from not only having a personal relationship with God in our lives, but also from acknowledging that some of our most cherished memories revolve around church activities. In my small Kansas hometown of 2,500 people, eleven churches formed the core of the community. I am deeply grateful for the support and comfort I received from my strong heritage of faith and for the many people, especially my parents, who role-modeled honesty, responsibility, loyalty, love, and generosity of spirit and actions.

In the therapeutic process with clients, I find that people with a commitment to a relationship with their Higher Power always progress better than those without this support. It is a very scary thing to dip down into one's Pool of Pain alone. Knowing that God is there with you, holding your hand and guiding you, is a primary stabilizing factor.

As we recognize that a solid basis of faith is foundational, religiosity is gradually set aside and healthy spirituality is embraced. This concept is being addressed in a wide range of venues, not just in churches. The view of what it means to be a spiritual person is progressively changing. People of all faiths are incorporating their beliefs into all the areas of their everyday existence. Many intellectuals are no longer embarrassed to admit their belief in, and dependence upon, God.

This interest in God and in spirituality is reflected in numerous ways. One of the fastest growing spiritual movements in the world today is the Twelve-Step movement. Started in the 1930s by Bill Wilson with the inception of Alcoholics Anonymous, the Twelve-Step movement is based upon the concept of reliance upon a Higher Power and group support for conquering addictions and other problems. The magnitude of the impact of this concept is seen in scores of Twelve-Step programs now available for dealing with addictions of all types, as well as the issues of codependency for spouses and families. The resulting life changes of the millions of people world-wide who live by the Twelve-Step philosophy force even a skeptic to ponder the effectiveness of tapping into the strength of a Higher Power. While Twelve-Step programs have proven to be successful for many people, not everyone in the psychological community accepts them.

When I first developed many of the ideas in this manuscript in 1982, there were very few books available which addressed both psychology and spirituality. I researched psychological textbooks from a wide variety of sources looking for any connection between psychology and spirituality and found that any references to "religion," "spirituality," "Christianity," "religious faith," or "theology" were used only in conjunction with pathology. Further, listings regarding addictions or Twelve-Step programs were exceedingly rare. I am a firm believer in God's timing, and during this same period many others were researching and sharing views similar to mine. Within a short time, the concept of being healthy—physically, intellectually, emotionally, and spiritually—became a popular topic.

When the late Dr. Scott Peck (a psychiatrist) wrote *The Road Less Traveled*, it created a worldwide phenomenon, breaking records on the *New York Times* best-seller list in the 1980s. Advocating the primary role of spirituality in emotional healing and growth, his book has now been translated into many languages. Spirituality soon became the focus of many best-selling books in the market.

Love, Medicine and Miracles, by surgeon Dr. Bernie Seigel, emphasized the power of spirituality in physical healing. I was first introduced to his work by my friend, Virginia Satir (an internationally acclaimed therapist, teacher, and author who helped establish the concept of marriage and family therapy). In 1988, when she became terminally ill, I visited Virginia in the hospital just after the doctor had informed her that her cancer was incurable. She asked me to read to her from Dr. Seigel's *Love, Medicine and Miracles*, which was at her bedside. Several weeks later, I had the special privilege of being with her during the last few days of her wonderful life.

In 1989, at a national psychological conference at Stanford University dedicated to the memory of Virginia Satir, I was given the honor of being the opening plenary speaker and was asked to share my memories of her. Dr. Seigel was presenting also, and I told him how much his work had meant to Virginia. I attended his workshop which was liberally sprinkled with Scripture texts and comments on the healing power of prayer. I was delighted when, in closing, he had the whole audience stand, hold hands, and sing "Amazing Grace."

While living in San Francisco I became friends with many people who identified themselves as Humanists—a philosophy that views humankind as uniquely creative and controlled by its own values and choices. We learned a great deal from each other. I found that Humanists know how to live, but frequently do not know how to die, while Christians know how to die, but often do not know how to live. I determined to learn how, not only to die, but also how to really live.

Pragmatists, Professors, and Prayer

During the 1980s, people from many different religious backgrounds in the United States began challenging their own dogmas. They became pragmatic questioners, forcing their spiritual beliefs through the sieve of intellectual inquiry and emotional validation. To become truly whole, including a healthy concept of God, is a radically different experience for each person. Seeking God may mean: starting from scratch; thoroughly evaluating present beliefs and values, resulting either in changes or in affirmation; throwing out old beliefs all together and starting over; or reclaiming abandoned childhood teachings anew as personal values, not just as the values of one's heritage or culture.

In 1988, as national president of the American Association for Marriage and Family Therapy (AAMFT), Dr. Ralph Earle made a monumental decision: he chose to present a workshop regarding spirituality and emotional healing at the AAMFT National Conference. It was a courageous decision to present such a controversial topic in front of one of the largest psychological associations in existence, and especially as their president. He received rave reviews.

From that time forward the subject of spirituality has consistently been presented at each AAMFT National Conference. For many years now, workshops considering this subject have received the highest evaluations, and requests for additional AAMFT workshops on spirituality continue.

Even prestigious institutions, such as Harvard and Duke University in the U.S. are actively pursuing clinical research studies on the power of spirituality, religion, and prayer in physical and emotional healing. Dr. Harold Koenig, M.D., director of Duke University's Center for the Study of Religion/Spirituality and Health, states that "of the more than 1,200 studies on religion and healing . . . two-thirds to three-fourths of them find a link between religious practices and physical and emotional well-being." In addition, he notes that up to 90 percent of patients rely on religion during times of serious illness for either comfort or strength.[4]

As of 2008, Harvard Medical School has sponsored its annual Spirituality and Healing in Medicine conference for thirteen years with large audiences of health professionals attending each year. Religious practices worldwide and their effects upon healing are discussed, with empirical evidence presented that confirms the power of spirituality on physical and emotional health.

The Harvard staff has been researching the effects of spirituality on physical health for forty years and their research states: "When a person engages in prayer and when intrusive thoughts are passively disregarded, a specific set of physiologic changes ensue. These changes—decreased metabolism, heart rate, blood pressure and rate of breathing—are the opposite of those induced by stress...Spirituality was expressed as experiencing the presence of a power, a force, an energy, or what was perceived of as God, and this presence was close to the person. Furthermore, spirituality was associated with fewer medical symptoms."

---

4 (See *The Healing Power of Faith: How Belief and Prayer Can Help You Triumph over Disease* by Harold Koenig, 1999.)

In the last fifteen years, there has been a shift in medical education with increasing focus on the influence of spirituality in healthcare in the United States. The National Institutes of Health and Human Services, the Centers for Disease Control and Prevention and the National Center for Health Statistics reported that, in 2002, more than 50% of all Americans used mind/body approaches for better health. The most commonly used intervention is prayer.

To Survive or Thrive?

Our hearts, our hopes, our prayers, our tears, our faith triumphant o'er our fears.
—*Henry Wadsworth Longfellow (1807-1882)*

In his book, *The Psychology of Religion and Coping* (1997), Kenneth Pargament, Ph.D., states that coping is an active process involving difficult choices in trying circumstances. He goes on to explain that religions influence how we view and understand situations within our coping process. Religion doesn't necessarily change the facts of the world we live in, but it can change the way we see those facts.[5]

I continue to research my paternal and maternal family backgrounds, and as I do, I gain more understanding of how their concept of who God was in their lives greatly influenced their ability to survive. Life for them was harsh and hard; they lived through the enormous loss of loved ones and many other painful and difficult circumstances. My ancestors in Russia accepted that life would always be difficult and had little hope for anything better.

The only way my forebears, and others like them, were able to endure such hardship was by believing that life was transitory and they would soon meet their loved ones in heaven. They also

---

5   (See *Religion and Health: The Effects of Religious Faith and Practice on Physical and Emotional Health* by Suzann Schoonover, 2001.)

believed that living a life of pain and hardship increased spirituality. Religious martyrs were greatly esteemed and sacrificing one's life for others was often accepted without question. While I also believe that giving to others is an essential part of a healthy, worthwhile life, I am very aware of how destructive that can be when it is not in balance with also caring for one's own health.

In the culture of my childhood, I felt that the "world" was an unsafe place from which one should stay as separate as possible. As a youth I remember singing a chorus in church: "This world is not my home, I'm just a passin' through." The general message was that my main job on this earth was to stay pure and make certain I got from here to heaven in the shortest, most efficient time possible and to refrain from touching the "world" in the process. I was also taught that there was a small, narrow passageway for that journey, and I was to never look right or left; anything that was not spiritual was of the flesh, and therefore, part of the devil's doings. Consequently, I often discounted many of the wonderful gifts God was giving to me here in this lifetime.

I now believe that if God had not intended for us to enjoy this life, the earth would have been created like the surface of the moon and humans to look like ET; instead, I see a magnificent creation with incredible beauty, filled with colors, sights, sounds, fragrances, and loving, caring people. Yes, there is pain, ugliness, and cruelty, but God also gives us wisdom and creates incredible opportunities for healing.

God has provided many wonderful people in my life over the years as an extension of His divine love for me. I believe that since God cannot come and personally place arms around us when we are hurting, others are sent to do that instead. At the beginning of my therapy, Dr. Danylchuk, told me he had made a lifetime commitment to be a vessel of God's love to hurting people. His respectful, gentle hugs were often an oasis of safety and healing for my tearful, frightened eight-year-old Sobbing Child during the painful days of my treatment.

In the following years I began to comprehend that God genuinely wanted me not only to survive, but to thrive. And that meant taking care of all the parts of myself, not just listening to the powerful voice of my Controlling Child or the tears of my Sobbing Child, but also delighting in the person I was designed to be—my Original Child. When I am obedient to that concept, then God is able to use me to help bring healing to the lives of others.

(Exercise 14: Grace, Blessings, and Prayer)

In Summary

Most people, if they are truly honest, will admit to feeling angry at God during certain periods in their lives. If intimacy with God is something you desire, then processing that anger is a requisite on your healing journey. As you become genuinely honest with your feelings regarding your Higher Power, you will begin not only to experience intimacy, but also to feel and understand grace and love in a manner never before possible. Being open to all the aspects of God in your life will reveal many blessings heretofore not noticed. There still will be challenges, hardships, and loss, but God provides many ways to move beyond that pain into a life of healing and wholeness—prayer being one of the most powerful gifts available to us. Making a genuine spiritual connection with God in your life is a critical step in becoming the person you were created to be.

GUIDEPOST THREE

FAITH & VALUES

Love and respect of God, self, and others.

The third guidepost, resting upon the first and second, represents Faith and Values: your love and respect of God, self, and others.

Once we have developed confidence with the first two guideposts, we are ready to continue on our healing journey toward becoming a mature Healthy Balanced Person. When we have gained familiarity with all the inner aspects of ourselves, and have begun the process of achieving balance in our lives—physically, intellectually, emotionally, and spiritually—it is important to contemplate and develop our own ethical values as adults in an ever-changing world, and to acknowledge the role that faith plays in this process. The families and communities in which we were raised may, or may not have had a healthy sense of values; it is our challenge and opportunity to decide what values we genuinely desire to embrace at this stage of our lives. I found that a personal value system of faith—based upon the principle of mutual love and respect of God, ourselves, and others—was indispensable during this critical portion of my own healing journey. I encourage you to determine your own value system. No one can do that but you.

CHAPTER 8

Back to Basics

It is the heart which perceives God and not the reason.
That is what faith is: God perceived by the heart, Not by the reason.
—Blaise Pascal (1623–1662)

Foundation of Faith

Give me my staff of faith to walk upon.
—Sir Edward Coke (1552–1634)

When I work with clients, I explain that we are created to be physical, intellectual, emotional, and spiritual beings, and then they are asked to evaluate their personal health in each of these areas. Quite often, there is a void or a sense of confusion in the area of spiritual health. Some say they do not believe in God or a Higher Power, which may be the case with you.

In time, however, many of these people begin to open up and want to connect on an intimate level with a Higher Power. I often have them simply say, "I don't know if you exist, God— but if you do, please show yourself to me." When they take this step, God always answers in a very distinct manner that could not possibly be a coincidence. As a firm believer in God's timing, I know there are no coincidences or "accidents" where God is involved. I believe God definitely orchestrated my healing journey and will continue to do so throughout my life.

One of the ways in which many have ascertained the presence of God in their lives is through the next exercise. They are asked to look at their Trauma Egg and begin to determine how they endured painful events. We address what I call their Internal Positive Influences (IPIs), and External Positive Influences (EPIs). They look at their drawing of their Original Child and list all the internal strengths they were given as gifts at birth (such as intelligence, sense of humor, creativity), these are their IPIs and reflect many of the strengths that enabled them to survive. In addition, they start to reflect upon all the positive influences in their lives, their EPIs, including the people and events (special people, schools, activities, and so on) that have provided encouragement and support throughout their lifetimes.

After completing their lists, clients often say, "I now can see that God really has provided for me in ways of which I was not aware before—I don't think all these things happened, just 'by accident.' I thought God had forgotten me, but now I realize God truly has been loving and supportive all along." They also relate validating incidents that indicate God is present in their lives today. Gradually these individuals begin to establish a new, healthy basis of faith and gain a new sense of who God really is, unlike the distortion they have carried in their hearts and minds. Please join us in this meaningful exercise.

(Exercise 15: Accidental or Purposeful?)

The Basis of Faith: Love and Respect of God, Self, and Others

Eight words—love and respect of God, self, and others—are among the most essential facets of a healthy journey—those words form the basis of faith, which directs a person's path. Faith is the starting point for living a worthwhile life. Without faith, you can stumble in and out of detours and dead ends, be overwhelmed by roadblocks, and remain forever a wanderer. As a maxim, these words sound rather simple and uncomplicated, but they are filled with intricacies and often are difficult to implement.

(Illustration 2: The Circle of Love and Respect)

I see this concept as a filter with three holes—representing God, self, and others. If, as you place this filter in front of you, the words and actions directed toward you are respectful of God, self and others, then accept them into your mind, spirit, and heart—if not, leave them outside the door of your psyche.

Conversely, be sure that your words and deeds are respectful of God, yourself, and others. If your behaviors do not fit through this filter of love and respect—stop—do not practice behavior that will be harmful to yourself and others.

Love and Respect of God and Others, But Not of Self

He who undervalues himself is
justly undervalued by others.
—Ambrose Bierce (1842–1914)

As a child, growing up in the Bible Belt in Kansas, it was role-modeled to me that I should love and respect God and others, but, I also gained the impression that I was not to love and respect myself. I thought there were only two reflections of how a person could view themselves—either with arrogant pride or with humility. Obviously, the only acceptable choice was humility, and if I deviated from humility even one inch, it would be regarded as displaying arrogant pride. I was never aware of a balanced concept of healthy self-worth or respect.

Parents did not want their children to have a "big head" or be "too big for their britches." Consequently, parents generally did not praise their children or acknowledge a job well done. Some parents regularly used sarcasm and put-downs to keep their children from being egotistical.

I was fortunate in that my parents were loving and let me know they were proud of me for the things I accomplished. But I felt their words also contained an underlying message that said, "We can be proud of you, but *you* mustn't be proud of you." As a result, I began a lifelong habit of self-deprecation. I apologized for everything. A friend once told me, "Marilyn, you apologize for things that happened when you weren't even there!" I even said "I'm sorry" if I bumped into a chair.

I was also raised to believe that JOY is spelled "Jesus, Others, and You"—and "you" is always last. I felt it was selfish, and definitely not spiritual, to ever put myself over others. For me, there was no such thing as a balanced state where everyone's needs and feelings were considered. Things were seen as black and white, in polarized extremes. What we would now regard as balance was seen as fence-sitting, middle of the road, and wishy-washy behavior.

Love and Respect of God, But Not of Self and Others

In my private practice I have been privileged to work with Dr. Earle, his son, Dr. Marcus Earle, and their staff at Psychological Counseling Services in Scottsdale, Arizona. One of our specialties is working with clergy from throughout the world. Often these clients think they are being loving and respectful of God, but they do not love themselves or others. They serve God in a manner that denies their own needs and the needs of their families.

Some of the most deeply disturbed clients we have are children of missionaries and ministers. What a tragedy. People who genuinely think they are doing God's will, instead are creating chaos in the lives of the ones for whom they should care the most. A missionary stated, "We serve God and abandon our children—and ourselves."

One does not need to be clergy to be unbalanced in his or her love of God over self and others. Many people feel that denial of personal needs equates to godliness. Whether we realize it or not, our inner needs demand to be acknowledged, and they will be met, somehow, some way, often inappropriately. Sex, food and work addictions are among the most common issues for those who love and respect God to the exclusion of themselves and others.

Love and Respect of Self, But Not of God and Others

A narcissist is a good example of someone who loves and respects only him/herself, but not others, not even God.

I had a client who was from a prominent East coast family, was good looking, and was exceptionally bright. He was also narcissistic. Raised to believe he was better than others because of "who he was," he truly felt he was entitled to special treatment and that rules did not apply to him. His numerous affairs had finally caught up with him, and his wife insisted they come to couples counseling. During their counseling sessions, he actually stated that he viewed his wife as inferior to him. He had no empathy for her and could not genuinely apologize to her for his actions. She however, had finally begun to value herself and to set boundaries around his behavior. When he found out that in order for their marriage to continue, he would need to change, he left and the marriage ended. He loved himself, but not God or others.

Values and Behaviors: Congruency or Conflict?

In the 1980s I worked part-time over a period of eight years on a pro bono basis in the Arizona prison system with rapists and child molesters. The Sex Offender Treatment Program (SOTP) had two components: individual and group therapy, and an eighteen-month psycho-education program consisting of nine classes that taught healthy life skills and behavioral changes. One of the classes, "Values and Decisions," gave instructions on how to make decisions based upon one's own values. An inmate shook his head sadly as he said, "If I had been taught this as a child, I wouldn't be here today." Another commented wryly, "I thought a 'value' was a bargain in a grocery store."

For part of the homework assignment, each man was asked to list his personal values. I remember the first time I sat in on this group and heard the men read their lists. It sounded rather like, "Mom, The American Flag, and Apple Pie..." I responded, "Hey, you guys are here for rape—be honest!" The amazing thing was, they thought they were being honest. Fortunately, over the next several years, the majority of them made major commitments to changing both their values and their behaviors.

So many people think they have a particular set of values, yet their behavior consistently contradicts those values. Numerous people have so convinced themselves that they hold those values firmly that it usually takes a major wake-up call to recognize that their actions were not in any way consistent with what they believed their values to be.

Healthy Guilt and Homeostasis

One of the dynamics that has a high impact on how we make, or do not make, the choices which determine our behaviors is a concept most people recognize: healthy guilt. The idea of healthy guilt arises from our conscience, and is usually experienced as a thought pattern which says, "This is wrong, do not do this." Healthy guilt is a reflection of the spiritual, emotional, and intellectual aspects of ourselves.

Besides the dynamic of healthy guilt, our behavior is also determined by a physical mechanism as well: homeostasis. This term, homeostasis, refers to an organism's tendency to maintain a normal, internal stability and balance in order to sustain equilibrium. We all seek stability and equilibrium at our core; we share a natural drive to be congruent. When we are not, that drive activates and manipulates our psyche to get us back in line again. It's rather like water seeking its own level; you cannot deny your natural course without consequence. Have you ever told a lie, or did something you felt was wrong, and then immediately got a sick feeling in your stomach or a headache? If so, then you experienced the homeostatic process as your physical body gave evidence that your behaviors were not in line with your values.

If your individual value system is consistent with your behavior, then you have no reason to change. You feel congruent: your inner self is satisfied—emotionally, intellectually, spiritually and physically—you are living authentically.

When your behavior is contrary to your values, however, the conflict activates your conscience and homeostatic process, which in turn create a dissonance, a tug to try and bring your behavior back in line with your beliefs—to feel congruent again. This is a healthy process.

When Values and Behaviors Collide

While many people say they believe in love and respect of God, self, and others, their behaviors are inconsistent with that maxim. If their misaligned behaviors continue and they do not respond to the conflict created by their conscience and homeostasis, they will begin to depart from their original values.

The Justifiers

For some people, as the distance between personal values and actual behavior increases, the less guilt they feel. They may, however, continue to have a homeostatic response with a physical reaction. It is important to note that homeostasis will *not* allow them to stay incongruent without major physical consequences. As a result, whether they realize it or not, their values actually begin to change and to come in line with their behaviors. This shift is essential in order to become congruent once again—and to keep the homeostatic process in balance. Keeping their unhealthy behaviors becomes more important than maintaining their values.

These people learn to justify, rationalize, and make excuses for their behavior, until they begin to truly believe their actions are acceptable. Now they see no reason to change because they feel congruent; they are morally satisfactory in their own eyes.

They make excuses why it is okay to do many things—such as cheating on their spouses. I have had persons tell me: "Well, my wife never wants to have sex with me any more, so it's alright for me to look elsewhere." "The only thing important to my husband is his career—he is so focused on becoming the top salesman in his company that he acts as though I don't exist. I have been so hungry for attention that I was vulnerable and ready to respond when a guy at work told me I was beautiful." Their values had shifted to justify behavior that in the past, they would have rejected.

"Justifying" is especially true of people who have become addicted to sex, alcohol, drugs and gambling. They can always find a reason to justify why they do not need to quit: "I'm not really an addict and can stop any time I want." "I really enjoy this—it makes me feel good—I don't want to give it up!" "All my friend do this—if I stopped, I'd be isolated and alone."

This process of justification also explains why people and governments can commit atrocities—because they have convinced themselves that their behavior is acceptable and ethically correct. They often feel that they have been offended—or are in danger—or have a right to revenge some prior offense against them or their loved ones—and so they have a right to bring retribution with even worse violence than what they endured (in Russia they say, "You hit me with a feather, I will hit you with a tank!"). Unfortunately, this only perpetuates a cycle of hatred and revenge as victims then become justifying victimizers who create more victims who become...

The Privileged
Then there are those who believe that because of their gender, race, religion, social status, occupation, education, and so on, they

are superior to others. Attempting to get people with a sense of privilege to change is often futile because they believe their behavior has *always* been correct. Their actions are in line with what their culture and family have taught as acceptable and customary. These people, as well as the "justifiers" mentioned above, usually come to therapy only because they are forced to be there: a spouse has threatened to leave, a parent dragged them there, an employer threatened loss of their job, or the law mandated it. Consequently, any change will probably be temporary, and their behavior will eventually revert to match their value system.

I am deeply grateful that the United States underwent a major paradigm shift in the past fifty years regarding becoming more respectful of people despite their gender, race, age, religion, and so forth. I often am appalled however, when I watch old movies from the 1950-60s that were popular when I was a teen and a young adult (or the television series, *"Mad Men")*. I have to sadly admit, "Yes, it was truly that bad back then—and I am so thankful that now, values have changed dramatically, especially for the sake of my children and grandchildren."

Unfortunately, there still are people in the States who are stuck in the "Privileged" status and who continue to victimize multitudes with their "dark ages" beliefs and actions. And, as I work with many more cultures internationally, I regret to say that a vast multitude of people on our planet still live under great inequality with the "Privileged" in control of their countries and ideologies.

Honesty – a Painful Look at Reality

To permanently transform a lifestyle, an individual (not just a country) must first make a paradigm shift in their value system. As personal values begin to change, then behavior can begin to shift also. If the paradigm shift is genuine, the old opposing value system will no longer be negating personal progress, and healthy new behaviors can be learned, leading to lasting life changes.

Are you willing to address your own value system honestly? Are your behaviors congruent with your values? If you asked your family, your closest friends, or your work colleagues about your inner and outer congruency, would they reply, "You walk your talk," or would they become nervous and change the subject?

One of the most interesting assignments in my classes concerns the assessment of personal values as determined by behavior. Each class participant does the following exercise over a two-week period. On the first day they list what they think their values are. Then, as they are consistently challenged each day regarding their behaviors and how those actions actually determine their values, they have to list their true values as reflected by their behaviors. They really struggle and choke on this one. But I push for absolute honesty.

One tall young man stood in front of the class and said, "I'm really afraid because last night my buddies all told me, 'If you don't tell the truth, she'll nail to you the wall in front of everybody!' So, I have to admit that my actual values really aren't anything at all like I thought they were and listed on the first day."

The students who have the valor to be excruciatingly honest are usually shocked when they begin to acknowledge their actual values, as expressed through their behavior—are far different from the values they believed they held. The following statements were made by various health professionals and clergy when honestly stating what their values were in reality, as defined by their actions:

- It is very important to me that I have a good reputation with my work colleagues and in my profession—I need this to build my self-esteem. It also is okay that I spend the majority of my time at work while ignoring my spouse and children. My family should understand this because I am bringing in the money we need."

- "My parents should give me everything I want now to make up for how much they neglected me when I was a child."

- "If anything goes wrong, it never is *my* fault—someone else did it, or sabotaged me."
- "My body is worthless and deserves to be assaulted by alcohol and cigarettes."
- "It is OK to lose my temper and rage at my wife and children, and still say I am a good Christian pastor."
- "If my spouse does not meet my needs physically or emotionally, it is completely acceptable for me to have sex with someone else. Having an adulterous affair is reasonable."
- "It is all right to give mixed messages to my children and to be incongruent; I can tell them not to smoke and drink, and then do those things myself."

These people looked respectable and genuinely thought they had high moral values—but after courageous work in this exercise, they came face to face with the blatant reality of their actual values. Most of them stated that this exercise was significant in helping them to genuinely evaluate their behavior. It challenged them to decide what they wanted their values to truly be, and to begin the crucial task of changing themselves to bring their behaviors in line with those values.

They also realized that in order to make this a permanent transformation, they alone had to determine their values—those moral directives could not come from me or anyone else. These values had to be what that individual felt and believed were correct for them. If that occurred, then the process of changing behavior would be a matter of breaking old habits and rejoicing in establishing healthy new ones that could become permanent as they aligned with heart-felt values. Please consider the following exercise with daring honesty.

(Exercise 16: Behaviors and Values)

In Summary

Your faith in your Higher Power will deepen and expand as you reflect upon the special gifts with which you were endowed at birth. It is helpful to contemplate the people and events which have been blessings in your life and which did not occur by chance but were placed there by God to validate the truth of your personal worth and value. If you accept this affirmation, it will provide you with an inner strength that will not fail as you proceed on this challenging portion of your healing journey.

We are created to innately seek balance in our lives, including having congruence between our values and our behaviors. Even though we might think we have a good value system, if our actions do not reflect that premise, then the incongruency will cause emotional and physical stress. In order to relieve that pressure, either your behaviors will change to get in line with your values or—your values will shift to support your destructive behaviors. A willingness to critically assess your values and behaviors, and to shift them in order to become congruent and healthy, are among the primary missions of a healing journey. If you genuinely love and respect God, yourself, and others, this mission can be accomplished.

CHAPTER 9

Wanted: A New Baseline for Normal

Each child is an adventure into a better life—an opportunity to change the old pattern and make it new.

—Hubert H. Humphrey (1911–1978)

The Sins of the Father...

Arizona State Prison, Florence, AZ; trustee yard; August 1986, 112 degrees.

A dust devil swirled about the old trailer sitting in a far-off corner of the yard as a rusty swamp cooler struggled to make the inside air more bearable. Earl fidgeted as he listened to the other men's stories. The heat exacerbated his growing irritation with what he was hearing. Abruptly, he stood up and headed for the door as he blurted out, "Man, I don't be-long here. My parents weren't anything like any of yours. They loved me." And he left.

I thought, "Well, you can't win them all," and continued lis-tening to incredible stories of abuse and neglect from the re-maining seven men. Nearly an hour later, the door flew open and Earl barreled in, banging the door so hard the entire trailer shook.

With his dark face drenched in sweat, he stormed, "That was abuse!" All eyebrows in the room went up in silence. His words tumbled into the air as he paced the room. "I've been walking around out there in this heat thinking about when I was little. And for the very first time I realized there was nothing I could have done as a two-year-old that was bad enough to deserve being disciplined with a baseball bat!"

Breaths were sucked in, a few gasped audibly, heads nodded—the other men understood. Earl's voice dropped as he lowered himself back into his vacant chair. "The sad part is I never knew that wasn't normal because every other kid in our neighborhood was disciplined the same way."

Two years later, at age thirty-five, Earl was being released after spending his total adult life in prison. He came to me and said, "I really would like to be married one day and hope to have several children. I want you to know if I hadn't been in this program, and especially in your group, I would have disciplined my kids exactly the same way I was. But I promise you, I will never, never treat my little ones like that—I will not be abusive to them, ever."

Common = Normal = Healthy, Or Does It Really?

In most cultures, the most common behaviors set the standard for what is considered normal. That supposition is then extended to the point that most people tend to believe that what is normal is also healthy. People travel the familiar paths of their ancestors because those roads were considered common and normal. Today, however, we realize that quite frequently, common = normal = unhealthy. Not only can standard "normal" behaviors be unhealthy, they can also be dysfunctional and sometimes quite abusive.

From the beginning of time until the last century, our world was in what I term, a colonization mode. People went out to conquer the savage land, the savage beast, and what they assumed was the savage man. As such, they were constantly in a state of survival. Because the average life expectancy in 1900 was age forty-seven (or less in some countries), most women died in their childbearing years. People rarely lived long enough to go beyond simply surviving. The majority of people lived in an agrarian society where children were often viewed as commodities; the more of them you had to work the farm, the better off you were.

Almost every family lost one or more children. A friend who researched our ancestors who lived in Russian villages, where loss of life in families was commonplace, told me that they had a saying: "Don't become too attached to people or things, because you will always lose them." No wonder many of them did not allow themselves to become close to their spouses or children. Inwardly, they believed: "I cannot allow myself to love you because, it will hurt too much when I lose you."

While we can acknowledge that this type of reasoning was emotionally unhealthy and prohibited intimacy, it did enable such cultures to survive—and for those people, survival was the number one priority. No one role-modeled to them how to be feeling people who could still survive without becoming swamped by emotions and being rendered incapable of working or fighting to protect themselves in times of death and loss. "Life must go on," was the motto. They repressed emotions as a way of life, something necessary and expedient.

How was the "baseline for normal" established in your family and culture? In many families that practice the old paradigm, children are seen as extensions of their parents, (the beliefs and actions of these parents are similar to some of the beliefs and actions of a narcissistic parent.) As such, parents have the right to do anything they want with a child—they can treat them lovingly, poorly, or both. The child is there to meet the needs of the parents and the family. The family is more important than the individual. What a person does directly reflects upon the parents and the family; therefore, if a child misbehaves it casts a shadow on the parents. Likewise when a child does well, the parents take the credit. Because the child is not viewed as an individuated, separate being, independent thinking is harshly criticized. One simply obeys parental commands.

Most parents genuinely love their children, but they parent the way they were parented. In short, they do the best they can. For those who desire to change and become healthy mothers and fathers, it can be difficult if they still interact daily with extended families, churches, and cultures that are ruled by traditions handed down through the centuries, traditions based upon survival.

Today nearly every inch of the earth has been mapped and charted. We are no longer in a colonization mode, yet most of the world's inhabitants continue to live as though they are still in a state of survival. Unfortunately, many people still do live in states of poverty, chaos, or war, and for those people, survival truly is the priority. With global awareness, however, even some of those who are nearly destitute are beginning to understand they can move beyond just surviving. But what about the fortunate people who do not live in those circumstances? Why is it they also live as if in a survival mode? The answer: because that mode is what has been common and normal for generations—it feels familiar. In the twenty-first century, we have the opportunity and privilege of moving beyond surviving to thriving. But where does one begin?

Our Most Fundamental Needs

(Illustration 3: The Survival Foundation)

As I listened to clients over many years, I realized there are essential survival requirements for every human being and created the "Survival Foundation" to illustrate this concept. These are the elements of that foundation:

- **Safety:** a physical assurance that you will not be harmed, that you are safe from abuse and trauma. You can live a lifetime without love, you can live days without food and water, but, you cannot survive if you are not safe.

- **Security:** an emotional assurance that you are valued and loved—by parents and others— which creates self-worth for a child. You also need the security of knowing that you are competent and skilled in your abilities as you grow and mature into an adult.
- **Stability:** a material reality that ensures you will have enough food, clothing, and shelter to survive.
- **Consistency:** actions which are consistent help a child to feel safe, secure, and stable. Children become confused and insecure when a mother and father are not parenting "out of the same book" and when the parents are not congruent with their own actions and teachings. The atmosphere of consistency is often violated in alcoholic homes where the addict's behavior is sometimes good and other times destructive (which is very disorienting for a child).
- **A Sense of Control Over One's Environment:** the fight for control over one's environment begins at birth with parents, continues through school, jobs, marriage, child rearing, and so on, up until the final moment of death. It is important to understand that every other person on this planet has as great a need for control as you do, and so, is technically your competitor in the fight for control of the space in which you reside. Ultimately, however, we must realize we live in a world in which we will never be in control—the only one who is truly in control, is God. The way in which we cope with this need for a sense of control over our environment greatly determines our health—physically, emotionally, spiritually and intellectually.

These fundamental needs represent our primal requisites, and dictate all of our decisions and actions. They form the foundation upon which everything else is built.

I have found that *every* conflict (in marriages, families, relationships, governments, and so on) begins with a violation of one of these basic needs. Most people do not move beyond their efforts to satisfy these needs; they become stuck and spend their entire lives trying to maintain their personal safety and security, often through other people, or through work, money, success, power, or addictions. As a result, they never develop and mature beyond the survivalist mentality. This is a tragedy as it denies them the potential for growth, maturity, and real intimacy.

(Exercise 17: Our Essential Foundation)

Survival History

During the 1980s I developed a psychological, mathematical equation to determine human behavior which I taught to my Ottawa University graduate students. As part of their final exam, the students who participated in the Treatment of Trauma, Abuse and Deprivation program were required to present research on three generations of their families—and to show how the survival traits (the fundamental needs of safety, security, stability, consistency, and a sense of control over their environment) had affected those families. They also traced the origins of addictions and various family styles regarding the processing of emotions, especially sadness and anger.

Each participant contacted relatives and frequently uncovered information kept secret for generations. They also gained numerous insights into understanding their own process as they learned more of their family history. They often developed pride in their ancestors' ability to survive—acknowledging the courage demanded of them—and gained admiration for their relatives' strength and perseverance. Stories of hardship and abuse suffered by parents and grandparents, for whom they previously felt only anger and hurt (or apathy and indifference), fostered an attitude of compassion and respect.

Students look at their families in a more balanced manner; those who had only seen their families in a negative light begin to accept their imperfections and recognize that their families also contain positive aspects, and those who saw their families as "perfect" acknowledge the human shortcomings and flaws of their loved ones. The entire process becomes incredibly healing as the students determine to forge new paths beyond just surviving.

While their personal insights and growth were most profound, the students also gained professional awareness and understanding into the backgrounds of their clients (present and future), particularly as they observed and listened to the presentations of the rest of the class. From that time forward, when presented with difficult cases, they knew to look far beyond the people sitting in front in them in their therapy offices. They could then help their clients discover the roots of their dysfunctions and claim freedom from those insidious entanglements of past generations.

My Russian students in our advanced classes now are also presenting their "Equations" with incredible results. In their families, discussing years of trauma under the Soviet System, surviving WWII, enduring torture in a Gulag, starvation, and multitudes of other horrific events has never been an option before. Much to everyone's surprise however, the majority of the students found that elderly family members were finally willing to open up and discuss these extremely painful years. Everyone who has participated in this class stated it had a profound effect upon them and gave them deeper respect for the courage and stamina of their loved ones in their struggle for survival.

I encourage you to look at your own family and claim your inheritance, which can be one of strength and emerging wisdom. I invite you to learn from the paths taken by your forebears—both from their successes, and their failures.

(Exercise 18: Roots)

Systems

To have one foot in your old survival-only paradigm and the other foot in a new, healthier paradigm may feel scary and uncertain.

How can you determine what will be healthy or unhealthy on that new, unfamiliar path? How can you be sure you won't repeat unhealthy patterns in the future? It is important to evaluate the numerous systems in which you live, or have lived, in order to establish a clear path upon which to travel in the future that will engender personal health and relationships, not hinder them.

As you assess the following systems, remember we all live in many systems: family, culture, religious group, ethnicity, race, school, business, government, and so on. Please keep these various systems in mind as some may be healthy while others are unhealthy, and many will have combinations of both negative and positive traits.

Unhealthy Systems

Justice without strength is helpless,
Strength without justice is tyrannical . . .
Unable to make what is just strong,
We have made what is strong just.
—Blaise Pascal (1623–1662)

There are two main types of unhealthy systems, which have the following foundational maxims:

1. Unquestioned Obedience to Authority
2. No Rules, No Boundaries

1. Unquestioned Obedience to Authority

In this system, there is one rule: *implicit submission to an immutable authority.* The good of the people is not considered; the only thing that matters is what benefits the person in authority. The walls surrounding the system are thick and high, made up of strict laws and rules set by the person in command. Allegiance goes to the authority figure, rather than to the law, because that person in authority can change the law at will. Strength and dominance prevail; power and control form the foundation. The bottom line issue always is one of control.

The walls in this system become a collective boundary, which encases everyone therein. The people within have permeable boundaries that can be invaded at will by the person in charge. Individuals have no right to say "No." They are not allowed to think for themselves, and have no personal worth. Their only value is to serve the system and especially the one in authority. This is a closed, tight system with inflexible parameters. Outside influences are rejected and dismissed as erroneous or threatening. This type of system can operate in an abusive or alcoholic household, an inflexible workplace, an authoritarian religious system, or a dictatorial state.

(Illustration 4: Unhealthy System - Unquestioned Obedience to Authority)

I often have my clients and students list the rules that are the "bricks" that make up the walls of their Unhealthy Systems (and have discovered that more than a few can also be found in my own). Such bricks can be overt or covertly implied messages. A few unhealthy messages do not necessarily render a system unhealthy. A system becomes unhealthy when the messages are pervasive and unquestioned obedience to authority is the mandate. Do any of these sound familiar to you?

- "Children should be seen and not heard."
- "Stop crying or I'll give you something to cry about."
- "What will other people think?"
- "Do as I say, not as I do."
- "Never air your trash/dirty laundry in public."
- "Never cry, to cry is to be weak."
- "The end always justifies the means."
- "Don't take risks."
- "Peace at any price."
- "Anything that goes wrong is always your fault – you are to blame."
- "We're right, anyone outside our system is wrong."

- "Never discuss sex; it's dirty."
- "Behave, obey without question."
- "It's not okay to be angry." (Except for the person in authority.)
- "Do not feel."
- "Just do as you are told and do not try and think for yourself."
- "Never, never ask questions of the authority."
- "Leave the past in the past."

(Exercise 19: What about your "Bricks"?)

An unhealthy system has a distinct gender, racial, religious, and cultural bias. Roles are clearly defined. Rigid black-and-white thinking prevails. Mistakes are not tolerated and are often punished harshly. Any slight is taken personally, and grudges may be held for years, even throughout generations.

Keeping a perfect front for the rest of the world is imperative. Maintaining a faultless image of strength and superiority is mandatory because to allow the perception of weakness or inferiority would invite invasion and destruction from outside sources. Secrets abound; but when problems occur within the system, they are never spoken of, even within the system. If a weakness or mistake does become exposed to the outside world however, someone from that "foreign" world is always blamed as the saboteur. The authority never takes responsibility for any internal errors.

This endogenous, closed system can be a setup for abuse—verbal, emotional, physical, and sexual. Tragically, abuse and domestic violence are most common and severe in this type of home and system, even though religiosity may characterize these homes as well.

Children in these families are encouraged to go only to system-schools and teens and young people are also told to date only others within their system. Adults limit social and business contacts to people within the closed community; outside socialization is restricted.

Issues such as alcoholism or problems with drugs, sex, and abuse are recognized, but, they supposedly exist only outside the protective boundaries of the system. The prevalence of these grievous problems is adamantly denied in order to maintain the image of perfection. These people refuse to see the enormous elephant of addictions and abuse in their living room, lumbering about chaotically and destroying their own families. There is great denial regarding any perceived weakness within the system's walls. The answer to any outside threat is simply to build the walls thicker and higher.

People inside the system grow more and more alienated from outside society—they become prisoners of their own fears and insecurities. Being taught that they are the elite, they may become condescending toward (and suspicious of) outsiders, who are seen as inferior and untrustworthy.

Because people within the system's walls have no options other than unquestioned obedience to authority, they may develop irrational thinking. Under duress, their distorted thoughts may propagate appalling tragedies. Depression, mental breakdowns, and suicides are not uncommon. Mothers, without the choice of birth control, become so overwhelmed by the pressures of having one child after another that they may kill or abandon their children, and/or have abortion after abortion.

Men and women sometimes murder their spouses because divorce or marriage counseling are not viable choices. When these people are prosecuted, lawyers and the media pontificate endlessly on the cause of these homicides, blaming mental illness, emotional stress, and postpartum depression. In actuality, it should be the authority figure who set the rules for the system— the spouse, the parent, the culture, the government, the church— who should stand trial.

These heartbreaking tragedies could be avoided if the participants knew they had another alternative: the right to say, "No, I will not live this way." But saying "No" is not an option for people in a system of unquestioned obedience to authority. For those who try to say "No," there may be devastating, even catastrophic, consequences. Yet, some do begin to question. One of my students in Moscow stated, "I remember as a young teen beginning to doubt the Soviet system and thought, 'If we are the best country in the world, why are we so poor?' "

Keeping traditions and rules is more important in these systems than respecting feelings and lives. People may be disowned, families may be torn apart, employees may be fired, parishioners may be excommunicated, battered wives may be killed, and people (especially children) may die because medical care is denied them or because they are continually placed in unsafe situations to accommodate the one in authority. The inhabitants of this unhealthy system can be repressed, sent to prisons, Gulags and executed for the slightest sign of disobedience.

These unhealthy systems not only are large entities such as a government or culture, they also include our families.

It is Always about Control

The father and three brothers of one of my clients were prominent religious leaders. The men were accustomed to being regarded as special, and the mother waited on them hand and foot. When my client married, he expected his household would be the same. He saw his place in the family as an entitlement. He stated, "I just naturally assumed it was my role and privilege to be in control," adding, "I don't know what it's like to be 'less than.'" His attitude of superiority created havoc with his wife and children as he expected that they always would obey him, no matter what he demanded. It never occurred to him to put himself in their places and feel what they felt. This type of relationship or system is never about equals relating to equals, it is a narcissistic dictatorship.

Male authority figures in such systems can be physically, emotionally and sexually abusive and consider it their right to do so. Violence and abuse are always exacerbated by alcohol or drugs. Women, girls and boys can be beaten, and emotionally or sexually abused. They have no right to say "no" and suffer a life-time of catastrophic consequences as a result of this cruelty and exploitation.

Offenders, however, are not always male, a significant numbers of females play the abusive authority role as well. They just use different weapons.

About Unhealthy Systems—Why Do People Stay?

Patience. A minor form of despair disguised as a virtue.
—Ambrose Bierce (1842-1914)

Obviously, unhealthy systems are not all bad or some people would not stay in them. For scores of people, they provide security, stability, closeness, and a strong sense of belonging—all significant and essential elements for an individual's well-being. In addition, some people prefer to have someone else tell them what to do rather than exert the effort to determine their values for themselves. "You just tell me the rules, and I'll follow them," they say.

I have often heard my Russian students state, "We were taught that to be patient, to endure, to not complain, to merely accept things as they were and never seek to change them, were qualities of the highest value. As such, we became accustomed to not having enough food, adequate clothing, etc., and simply accepted that was the way our lives were meant to be."

Others also admitted, "But, we also have to concede that it takes hard work and commitment to bring about change, and many of us did not want to make that effort. It was easier to let someone else take care of us and to make our decisions for us. Then, when something went wrong, we could always blame them. It was not our fault that things were so bad."

I am not intimating that patience itself is wrong, but it can be destructive when people allow themselves to continue to be victimized and it is used as an excuse for not confronting an unhealthy system or relationship; or when the concept of "patience" is cited as justification for irresponsibility and apathy.

Perpetuating Unhealthy Systems

Accepting a destructive system and not challenging it, enables this impairment to continue over the years. Children raised in an unhealthy system of unquestioned obedience to authority are not prepared to deal with a life outside the system when they become adults. They are vulnerable and defenseless, waiting for someone else to come along and invade them. Or they may have been trained to be an entitled invader. When "a vulnerable" and "an invader" connect, they start their own unhealthy system, and perpetrate it generation upon generation.

Unfortunately, unhealthy systems can also become the breeding ground for extremists. Wars, riots, terrorist activities, and radical cults are born in the womb of despotic systems, nurtured by deplorable arrogance, blind bigotry, and fanatical prejudice. "We're right, you're wrong" is the virulent bacterium that spreads the plague of ignorance and hatred throughout the world. Intoxicated by this brutal infection, souls become barren and unable to feel compassion or guilt. People become merciless, ruthless robots who can destroy a school filled with laughing children, parents and teachers; or fly a bomb made of steel, gasoline, and blood into two towers of concrete, glass, and human spirits, without remorse.

Catholics and Protestants fight in Ireland; Palestinians and Jews battle in Israel; Blacks, Whites, Hispanics, and Asians riot in cities across America; and endless battles continue throughout the former USSR. Autocratic, charismatic leaders become depraved when lost in a sense of their own power—Adolph Hitler, Josef Stalin, and Osama Bin Laden ignited history and destroyed multitudes of innocents in their self-righteous infernos. For centuries people have fought against such tyranny, but it still exists. Some fight with weapons, some with words.

2. No Rules, No Boundaries

Rebellion comes in various forms. In America in the 1960s and 1970s, young people rebelled against what they perceived as rigid unhealthy systems, saying, "Screw the rules!" They wanted the freedom to do whatever they desired, with no boundaries at all. It was "Sex, drugs, and rock and roll," "Make love, not war," and "Whatever feels good, do it."

But a system with no boundaries at all also becomes destructive. Some of those young people grew into irresponsible parents, allowing their children to run free with no restrictions to guide them. While the children may have enjoyed this at first, it lacked the security and stability they needed for inner survival. They ended up not feeling valued, as if their parents didn't care about them, because their mothers and fathers had not set protective boundaries around their behavior.

(Illustration 5: Unhealthy System – No Rules, No Boundaries)

This type of system is common in homes with chemical addictions where the parents are so absorbed with alcohol or drugs that they do not have time for their children or for their own health and welfare. Children are left to take care of themselves and often end up "parenting" their parents in order to survive. Because there are no boundaries, the children are at risk for physical and sexual abuse which leave the child confused, damaged and also susceptible to developing their own addictions to numb their pain and loneliness.

I have numerous clients who are products of this era. Some of their most frequent comments are:

- "I don't know how to 'do life!' "
- "My parents were so busy partying, they didn't want to bother with me."
- "Dad and Mom said they didn't want to restrict me with rules like their parents did to them, but to tell you the truth, they just didn't want to be bothered with learning how to be good parents because that would take effort and time—neither of which they were willing to give. They simply were lazy and selfish."

- "Our house was always full of their friends; they'd drink and do drugs all night. I couldn't sleep because of the noise, and I had to go to school the next day. In the morning, I'd have to step over bodies of wasted druggies in order to get out the door. I really hated it."

In many other families, the mothers and fathers are so committed to their professions that they become workaholics, ignoring their sons and daughters by leaving them alone or passing them off to others when available. They become narcissistic and resent taking any of their valuable time for their children's needs. The children live in a vacuum. Children from this type of Unhealthy System grow up feeling unloved, rejected, abandoned and worthless.

A Healthy System

If you plant forgiveness, generosity, kindness, and respect for all persons, you will reap contentment.
—Dr. Marie Chapian, Discovering Joy

Mutual Love and Respect

In contrast to the unhealthy systems that have overly rigid boundaries or have no boundaries at all, there is a better way. In a healthy system, both the external boundary and internal personal boundaries are based on the guiding principle of mutual love and respect.

(Illustration 6: Healthy System – Mutual Love and Respect)

In a healthy system, the external boundary is penetrable but firm. Because it is based upon the law of mutual love and respect, it is reflected in the Golden Rule: "Do unto others as you would have them unto you." The external boundary is not as rigid or monolithic as the rules imposed in an unhealthy system.

The internal personal boundaries are flexible and solid. When a person inside that boundary feels safe with another, his or her arms open in welcome; if not, their personal boundary can close protectively. Leaders and parents role-model the external boundary, assuring that each person is considered worthy of respect and of equal value in God's eyes. A healthy system provides safety and security by promoting freedom rather than captivity.

Unlike the closed system, a system of mutual love and respect is open to new ideas and cultures. A Muslim teen from Iran is welcomed as a foreign exchange student; a boy or girl from the healthy system is encouraged to visit a family in Japan. Children develop strong personal principles by living in a mutually respectful system, yet they are allowed to question their parents' values and beliefs. They are free to think for themselves, while they are nevertheless held responsible for their own behaviors, and they learn to accept whatever consequences may ensue as a result of their choices.

I have developed a list of descriptors that help to determine whether a system is healthy or unhealthy. I have my clients and student review the following list and, to place a number by each word which describe their own systems (for example: 1. Childhood family and culture; 2. Their personal behavior; 3. Present family; 4. Place of employment; 5. Church or other organization; and any other current systems that affect them).

A Healthy System is:	An Unhealthy System is:
Loving and Respectful of God, Self, and Others	Based on Unquestioned Obedience to Authority
Mutually respectful	Ruled by fear and intimidation
Open	Closed, territorial
Healthy, with appropriate boundaries	Unhealthy, with rigid or no boundaries
Supportive of independent thinking	Restrictive, only I/we know the truth
Positive	Negative
Friendly	Aloof, cold

A Healthy System is:	An Unhealthy System is:
Cooperative	Antagonistic, belligerent
Accepting	Critical, judgmental
Appreciative	Thankless, rude
Humble	Superior in nature
Gracious	Easily offended
Considerate	Selfish
Patient	Impatient
Loyal	Unfaithful
Straightforward	Devious
Kind	Harsh, hostile
Compassionate, empathetic	Uncaring
Respectful	Inconsiderate, invasive
Responsible	Irresponsible
Groundbreaking	Traditionalist only
Supportive of the value of all people	Close minded, We're okay, you're not
Optimistic, looks for the good in people	Pessimistic, looks for the bad in people
Curious, seeking truth and knowledge	Creed bound, I/we tell you the truth as it is
Honest	Deceitful
Trustworthy, reliable	Undependable
Appropriate	Tactless
Creative	Unchangeable, fixed
Balanced	Narrowly focused
Congruent	Discordant, does not "walk the talk"
Clear and consistent	Unclear, sending mixed messages
Flexible	Rigid
Vulnerable	Defensive
Encouraging, Building up others	Oppositional, Intimidating
Assertive	Very aggressive, passive-aggressive
Inclusive	Restrictive
Dedicated to individual and group health	Dedicated to the one and only authority figure

A Healthy System is:	An Unhealthy System is:
Cooperative	Conflict-ridden
Joyful, peaceful	Restless, antagonistic
Successful when the feelings of individuals and the group as a whole are successful	Successful only when the feeling of the leader (or leaders) is successful

(Exercise 20: How Healthy are Your Systems)

This exercise will help you determine what your "baseline for normal" was, and is, in all your systems. It can also be used to decide what you would like your new baseline for normal to be.

Ruling with Fear, or Respect?

You may be thinking, "But there are times when unquestioned obedience to authority is imperative." I agree. When a fire fighter orders onlookers to step back from a burning building, those orders should be obeyed. During wartime soldiers depend upon the knowledge that everyone is obeying their commander's orders; otherwise, there could be tragedy and chaos. Yet history has shown that great military leaders can lead respectfully rather than autocratically. Athletic coaches who treat their team members with mutual respect have had more successful track records and are highly regarded by those under them—far more than those who rule with fear and intimidation.

How do you rank as a parent, spouse, employer, teacher, or leader? Do you role-model mutual respect or do you rule with fear and intimidation? Are you still demanding respect from others rather than earning it? What do others say about your leadership style?

I see change and healing happening daily in many lives and families as they seek to become part of a healthy system. There are times, however, when I become so enthusiastic about the results that I have to remember to use some restraint. Revolutionizing old systems does not guarantee positive results.

The Soviet System initially was formed in rebellion to an autocratic, aloof Russian Tsarist regime that was often brutal, and was insensitive and unresponsive to the desperate needs of the people. For many of the original Bolsheviks, the objective was to create a structure where people were treated with mutual respect. Tragically, this ideology was overtaken by hard-line Soviet dictators who turned it into a vicious system even worse than the one it replaced.

In America, labor unions were formed to defeat the abuses of oppressive, self-serving employers who demanded that their employees work excessive hours for low pay under substandard working conditions. Unfortunately, some of those unions also became deeply flawed and many became as destructive as the systems they sought to correct.

Communism and some labor unions had imperfect leaders who were unwilling to address their own character defects and unhealthy belief systems. Even though some of their ideologies originally were founded upon mutual respect, the leaders assumed they were entitled to rule, and they discarded the foundational precepts of healthy systems.

In Summary

We live and work in systems, many of which are also within other systems, like a nest of stacking matroishka dolls. We have nuclear families, within extended families, within ethnic groups and cultures, within countries. In addition we also interact with other systems such as schools, jobs, churches, organizations, governments, and so forth. All these many systems have an affect on our daily lives. Identifying how these systems influence your behavior, and determining what beliefs and actions you wish to retain and nourish, and also defining those which you desire to eliminate, represent some of the most important mountains you will climb on this healing journey.

The people I know who have scaled those peaks successfully now live and thrive in healthy systems. These people, young and old, are creating fresh pathways that are beautiful, safe, and inviting for multitudes of others—their journeys, however, have often been difficult. But to take such a journey is one of the most courageous, rewarding undertakings in human existence—to live a life of faith based upon mutual love and respect of God, self, and others.

CHAPTER 10

Who's on First?

He that obtains wisdom loves his own soul;
he that keeps understanding shall find good.
—Proverbs 19:8

When I entered into therapy in 1980, there were very few books available regarding addictions or abuse issues and almost none regarding codependency or boundaries. Those terms were not commonly used—I thought a boundary was a fence. But, my therapist, Dr. Danylchuk, realized that part of my physical illness was caused by the extreme stress I felt from the pressure of my lifestyle, a lifestyle of my own making. He began insisting that I take care of myself and encouraged me to read a new book on healthy assertiveness so I could learn to say "No," a word that wasn't even in my vocabulary.

A New Healthy System

In the middle of the journey of my life, I came to myself within a dark wood where the straight way was lost.
—A. Dante (1265–1321)

The day I finally realized, at a deep level, that part of the path I had traveled for forty-four years was actually destructive and unhealthy, I wept for hours. I had always tried to do everything correctly, but now I saw that no matter how sincere I had been in traveling upon it, my pathway was wrong. For a perfectionist, such knowledge was devastating.

I have numerous clients who come from backgrounds like mine. Good people who genuinely believe they are on the correct path, but whose lives and relationships are coming apart. My friend and colleague, Ken Wells, a former pastor and now a therapist, said it so well, "Publicly I was driven to excellence; privately I felt, 'The wheels to this wagon are falling off!'"

My parents were not harshly demanding of me; *I* was demanding of me. Once I finally realized the course I'd set for my life was detrimental to me and to my family, I actively began to seek the path that I felt God had originally intended for me to walk.

To exit my unhealthy system and commit to a healthy one, I had to be willing to leave the homeland philosophically. The farther I traveled away from my old trail and system, the better I began to feel—physically, intellectually, emotionally, and spiritually. I found that I needed to make the task of keeping myself healthy in these four areas my number one responsibility—no one else could do that but me. Even God couldn't help me if I didn't cooperate.

Our Internal Dictators

We have discussed the "bricks" that make up the thick, high walls of an unhealthy system. I found that those "bricks" became like internal tapes that played unendingly in my mind. Some were recorded in my conscious mind and I was very mindful of their messages; but some were only heard in my unconscious, and I was not even aware of their existence. But they were very forceful and played a role in determining my values—and my actions every day—even though I was not alert to their power over me.

Who plays the tapes in your head? Do they originate in homes where parents were loving, but living in an unhealthy system? Or did your parents rule with an iron fist or a baseball bat? Whether old tapes and pressure come from parents, family, culture, government, school, peers, employers, church, or self, these powerful messages create an injurious climate, emitting noxious waves that threaten to smother generations to come. One student used several eloquent metaphors to describe the tapes that played for her:

"My grandmother's constant phrases about the unhappiness of life plowed my mind."

"Her words were like nails into my head."

"Those tapes became an impenetrable fence that surrounded my life."

Some tapes play in our heads all the time; others only on specific occasions. Some tapes may tell a lie, some tell the truth, and others tell a misapplied truth. Certain tapes have two messages playing on top of each other—they are the mixed messages we have all experienced ("Do your very best!" "Don't be proud.")

It is helpful to look at your Trauma Egg and see how many of those events and long-term stressors created a new destructive tape, or reinforced an old one. The more a tape is reinforced by events in your life, the louder it plays in your conscious, and unconscious mind. One example comes from my own past: As a child I loved to read and often walked around with a book in front of my face. My mother would say, "Put that book down and watch where you are going because if you don't, something bad might happen to you—you might step onto the street in front of a car." When I was eight I had been reading on the bus and missed my stop on the way to choir practice. As a result I became lost and my sexual assault occurred. Even though the assault was not my fault, I interpreted the tape I inherited from my mother to mean this: "If you make a mistake, something bad will happen to you." That message became dramatically reinforced by that very traumatic event. From that moment forward, my unconscious drove me to become a radical perfectionist who was terrified to make a mistake because it literally felt as though nearly everything I did was of "life or death" significance.

A New Message

It is time to discard the old ways of thinking; today be lifted up above the sorrows of yesterday; today, receive new vision, new hope, and new strength.

—Dr. Marie Chapian, His Thoughts Toward Me

My students often state that the following exercise on "Tapes" is as powerful and important to them as their Trauma Egg, I also found that to be true for me. In this exercise you make three columns: in the first one, list all the Tapes you hear playing in your conscious and unconscious mind; in the second column, list where the Tape originated and whether it was overt or covert; the third column is ultimately the most important—in it you list how God and you, as healthy parents, would respond to a child who came to you playing this Tape. Most of us have helpful answers for someone else if they come to us for counsel or comfort, however, we very often do not apply that same wisdom to ourselves.

When I started working in Russia and we first discussed the Tapes exercise, it was obvious that the majority of the students had no concept of a healthy response that would counteract the overwhelming, destructive tapes that played non-stop in their heads. As a result I decided I would use two devotional books that are a special blessing in my own life: *His Thoughts Toward Me*, and *Discovering Joy* by Dr. Marie Chapian, (in which verses from Old and New Testament scriptures are paraphrased and combined by subject matter) to bring new light and understanding to their spirits.

Starting with my first Level II class in Moscow in January 2003, I have begun every Russian class (even when I am teaching in a State University) with verses from what my students call the "God says..." books. They sit listening intently, often with tears in their eyes, and many on the edge of their seats. They begged me for the books in Russian—and thanks to generous American donors—they were translated and printed as one book in 2006. The majority of my Russian students now use these devotionals regularly (and buy them as gifts for family and friends). They also find these verses to be exceedingly helpful when filling in their third column. Many put their third columns on their walls where they can read them daily in order to drown out the incessant, vicious mantras of their old tapes.

As you complete this homework, be aware of the various types of internal messages you listen to and where these tapes originated. I usually ask my clients and students to complete the first two columns and to work on this exercise over a period of several days. Then, when they are finished, I have them gently (and prayerfully) address the third column. Completing this final column may take a rather a long time, and that's all right.

Please do this exercise and be especially sensitive to what God and you are imparting regarding your own wellbeing as you complete the third column. This is essential as it does no good to destroy a harmful message tape without replacing it with a healthy one.

(Exercise 21 & Illustration 7: Tapes)

The Circles of Intimacy, Responsibility, and Impact

In order to shut down those tapes for ourselves and the future generations in our families, we need to learn about boundaries and priorities in our lives. In attempting to understand this process, I created what I term The Circles of Intimacy, Responsibility, and Impact. These circles reflect the levels of intimacy we have with various people, the responsibility we have for ourselves and others, and the impact people and events have on our lives.

(Illustration 8: The Circles of Intimacy, Responsibility, and Impact)

In order to maintain healthy balance in your life, your priorities should be as follows:

Circle Number 1—God (your Higher Power) and you:

- If you truly want to discover your soul, then it is imperative that you develop a healthy Circle #1.
- If only you are in your Circle #1 and God is absent, you will be narcissistic and selfish.
- If only God is in your Circle #1 and you are absent, you are apt to be a martyr and suffer from religiosity, which will adversely affect your physical and emotional health.
- If you have anyone or anything else (other than God and you) in Circle #1, it will cause dysfunction— physically, intellectually, emotionally, and spiritually—and in your relationships.
- You can be intimate with someone else (even God) only to the degree that you are intimate with, and know and understand, yourself.
- One of the primary purposes of a healthy Circle #1 is to enable you to serve and give to others out of health, not through exhaustion or illness.

Circle Number 2—Intimate relationships

- Occupants of Circle 2a and Circle 2b:
  - When you are a child:
    2a—parents
    2b—siblings
  - parents and siblings should be moving out to Circle #3 in order to leave an empty, clean space so that when the person becomes an adult, there is room for:
    2a—spouse or significant other
    2b—minor children living at home; children should always be moving out toward Circle #3 so they learn to "fly" on their own
- May be empty
- There will be emotional pain if:
  - *a.* anyone leaves your Circle #2;
  - *b.* you have someone in your Circle #2 but they do not have

you in theirs, or vice versa (for example, you are in love with someone who is not in love with you);

c. once you become an adult, you have more than one adult in your Circle #2a (for example, you cannot have your spouse *and* a lover, or a parent, or an adult child); #2a is for your beloved one only and is not to be shared with others.

Circle Number 3—Other Intimate Relationships

- Occupants of Circle 3: Older children, minor children not living at home, grand-children; close family and friends with whom you share intimately
- Many people have plenty of friends and acquaintances but do not feel free to share confidences and feelings with them thus these persons belong in Circles #4 or #5, not in #3.
- Men often do not have any friends in their Circle #3. They may have buddies with whom they hunt and fish, attend sporting events, work, etc. but none with whom they can share intimately. These men usually expect their spouses and/or children to fill both their Circle #2 and Circle #3.

Circle Number 4, 5—More Casual Relationships

- Occupants of Circle 4,5...Family, friends, work colleagues, etc.
- These circles can go on ad infinitum depending on the quantity of your various relationships.

When a Circle #2 becomes empty as a result of the end of a relationship, many adults immediately try to fill it with someone or something else. Leaving it vacant for a period of time, however, is essential to cleanse the circle from any left-over unaddressed "garbage" before bringing a new resident into that intimate space. Allowing one's #2 circle to stay empty can also be a motivating factor that compels one to concentrate on strengthening both Circle #1 and #3 instead of becoming totally captivated by acquiring a new inhabitant for Circle #2. Many people live their entire adult lives with an empty Circle #2 and are still happy and fulfilled as they give their attention to Circles #1 and #3.

Your responsibility to and for others directly relates to their position in your circles. Your circles may fluctuate often, especially if you move or travel frequently.

In addition to people, your circles also contain other aspects which affect your life, such as your job, sports, exercise, school, computers, TV, video games, music, church, organizations, hobbies, other activities, and pets. Of course, addictions wield the heaviest influence on a person's life—often occupying circles #1 – 3 (or more).

To determine the rank for a person or activity in your circles, consider how great their impact is upon you. The level of their ability to cause you joy or pain determines their nearness to the center of your circles. The frequency of contact also determines the rank of the person or thing in the circles.

Confusion and Clinging

Please pay particular attention to the above explanation of the circles where it states: "There will be emotional pain if, once you become an adult, you have more than one adult in your Circle #2a." That means there will always be problems if you, or your spouse, is having an affair. No amount of justification or excuses can make this acceptable. It will always cause pain and destroy relationships.

In addition, you cannot have your parents in your Circle # 2 once you become an adult. Nor should your adult children occupy space in that circle.

It is not uncommon for parents and adult children to become enmeshed and continue to remain in each other's #2 circles—clinging to each other and thinking they are being extraordinarily loving. I challenge this type of distorted thinking with the image of a mother bird and her babies in a nest. If she holds onto them and does not allow them to fly when the appropriate time arrives to do so, then their wings atrophy and they never become capable of flying. They eventually die without becoming who God intended them to be—wonderful creatures who are able to soar and be free. Yet, even knowing this, some adults selfishly would trap those babies in the nest to help keep themselves as parents comfortable and warm, even at the expense of their children's lives. There are, however, those baby birds whose parents are urging them to fly, but the babies refuse and adamantly cling to the side of the nest even as the parents try to pry their little claws off the edge so they will be forced to learn to fly. Either way it is a most unhealthy situation.

Whose Garbage is This?!

There always are three entities in any relationship: 1. You, 2. The other person, and, 3. The relationship itself. As a consequence if there are any unresolved issues in that relationship, even if the other person dies, or the people move out of your circles (as a result of a divorce or break-up), those unsettled problems in the relationship still remain. If you do not actively work on cleansing your circles (especially Circles # 2 and #3) of those unprocessed painful issues, the next person to be brought into that intimate space immediately steps in the "old relationship garbage" and so the new relationship becomes instantly tainted. Of course, you are probably stepping into their old garbage also. No wonder relationships become so complicated.

The following are comments from students regarding the challenges they face with Circles #1 and #2 in their lives:

- "My youngest son married and left me. I am devastated by this abandonment. I cannot understand how he could love and care for this strange girl more than for me— his mother who has loved and cared for him since birth. I had such a hard life and sacrificed so much for him and now, he deserted me. It breaks my heart."
- "My wife's parents live with us and it creates lots of problems. My father-in-law is alcoholic and sits around the house

drinking and being extremely abusive verbally and emotionally to everyone. My mother-in-law keeps interfering when my wife and I try to discipline our teen-age son. She spoils him and tells him not to listen to us. I have told my wife many times that her parent's behavior is very disruptive and destructive to our relationship and our immediate family, but she refuses to do anything about it. She says her mother and father are her first priority and that I should just adapt to that. I am seriously thinking about leaving but I do love her and am worried about our son."

Recently when I taught the concept of the Circles of Intimacy, Responsibility and Impact, a young woman looked shocked as she asked, "You mean I am supposed to place my husband before my parents?!" She was stunned by the concept of having her own life and being committed to developing a healthy family with her husband and potential children.

Whenever I hear comments from clients or students regarding the people they feel they must place in their Circle #1, I usually ask this question, "What would they do if you did not exist?" One startled mother whose thirty year-old son refused to work and sat at home drinking, watching TV or surfing the Internet, replied, "Why, he'd have to go out and get a job!" So—if you have recognized yourself in this discussion and are having a difficult time setting boundaries and continue to be a co-dependent caretaker, please ask yourself, "What would they do if I did not exist?" The answer is: they would survive. They would not die; the world would continue to revolve—and perhaps, they just might learn to be responsible for their own welfare.

Conversely, if you are the person who expects someone else to take care of and be responsible for you—answer this question, "What would I do if they did not exist?" A young Russian woman, age thirty-two recently told me that she and her twenty-eight year-old sister still live with their parents in a very small apartment. Their father was an alcoholic and she really did not like living there. I asked her what she was doing about changing her situation. She replied, "Well, I have prayed and asked God to give me an apartment of my own." I said, "And what else have you done?" The answer was "Nothing, I guess I expect God to take care of it." When I asked her, "What would you do if your parents and their apartment did not exist?" She was stunned and sat silently. I asked if she had ever considered checking into the price of renting a one-room apartment or sharing an apartment with a friend. She sheepishly admitted she had never, ever thought of that. She was just expecting someone to take care of her—either her parents, or God. (The next time I saw her, she was excited to tell me that she had moved out and proudly stated that she was now taking responsibility for herself.)

I often have counseled families in conflict whose children were over age twenty and still living at home. These young people wanted all the privileges of remaining in their parent's #2 circle (e.g. free rent, food, and laundry service, Mother's great cooking, and a nice place to live) but wanted the freedom of a #3 circle to come and go as they pleased. I always stated that they could not have both. If they lived at home, they lived by their parent's rules and values; if not, they needed to move out and take the responsibilities that come with the privilege of freedom. Unfortunately, the parents were often exceedingly co-dependent and enabled these young adults to remain children by continuing to maintain the distortion of their circles. Until the parents were willing to set boundaries, with consequences, the conflict would continue with everyone being the loser.

Parents and Adult Children as Friends

Too many people feel that if they move their parents and/or their adult children into the appropriate Circle #3 it will mean they do not love them and are abandoning them. This action does not mean that you will ignore and reject your parents or adult children, not at all. It only means that you will be setting boundaries regarding your priorities. It also means creating a new atmosphere in your relationships: you will now become adult friends—not caretakers and dependents. As a result, you may be amazed to find that it has not destroyed your relationships. Instead, making this move can actually enhance them as you release unattainable expectations and obligations, and become free to love and be loved for who you are as people, not for what you do, or do not do.

The following was related in a class by a female psychologist and university professor: "My mother is a widow but she is only sixty-two. She refuses to have any social life and expects me to take her everywhere with me. She wants me to fill all of her Circles #1, #2, and #3. She calls me constantly and cries and yells at me if I do not visit her daily. Of course she also calls the other family members and tells them how selfish I am if I do not do what she demands. But, I have a husband and two daughters who are suffering greatly from my lack of attention to my own family so I am angry and resentful about all of it. I dread going to see my mother and only want to yell back at her. It is an awful situation, not only is my family affected but it also affects my own health. I am having terrible headaches and other physical problems from all the stress,"

Several months later, after going through the seminars and doing all the exercises and home work, she made some major changes in her life and relationships. Her firm commitment to changing her circles and boundaries enabled her to resolve the situation in a healthy manner. She reported the following to one of our classes:

"I finally realized I could not change my mother; I could only change myself. My life was a mess and I had allowed it. I went to see my mother and quietly sat and told her that I loved her, valued her and wanted to spend time with her. I went on to tell her how much she meant to me and mentioned many things that I remembered from over the years that truly were special to me. Then, I gently, but firmly said, 'Mother, I have to take care of my own health and I also now have a family of my own. It is my primary responsibility to become healthy and to be there for my husband and daughters. So, I am going to change how I relate to you and the time I spend with you.

"I will call you once a day (do not call me unless you are dying), and I will come to see you once a week. During that time I will give you my full attention and enjoy being with you. I will also see that you come to our home at regular intervals to see your grand-daughters and of course for special occasions. This does not mean that I do not love you. On the contrary, it means that I really value our relationship and want it to change and improve, because I am very resentful of it the way it has been in the past.'

"Of course, she began to cry and raged that I was abandoning her, did not love her, etc., but I just sat quietly and listened, and was not swayed by her hysterics. In the following days, I made certain to call her daily, but only talked for a few minutes and remained cheerful. When I went to see her I took along some flowers, or a special sweet that I knew she loved. I found myself thinking in advance about what she would like and actually began to look forward to my time with her. She gradually settled down because she found that I was consistent in my love and care for her—and had not abandoned her. Now our times together have become a truly enjoyable time for both of us. Occasionally, she will try to hook me in with some of her old complaints but I do not allow myself to pick up the bait and simply change the subject.

"She has now even started to cultivate some new friends in her neighborhood and has called up a few of her old ones. She is actually getting a social life of her own. I am amazed and so pleased with the results of having set healthy boundaries with her. My health also has improved drastically and needless to say, my relationship with my husband and daughters is much better now."

It would be wonderful if all cases turned out this well, but they do not always do so. Some people will continue to rage and be extremely angry when you start to set boundaries and adjust your circles. Be prepared for this, but please do not be discouraged, and do not allow yourself to be sucked back into their old unhealthy systems.

I have found in my own life, and in the lives of many of my clients and students, that often, the people who are resistant and upset when you move them from your Circles #1 and #2, will later admit that it was the best thing that could have happened because they were forced to become responsible adults. Usually, they are glad it happened, even though it was painful at the time.

Then there are those who will continue to remain in a victim/child state, making you the "abandoning scoundrel" and will demonize you to all your relatives. They will not change as long as they can find another co-dependent caretaker who they can manipulate and exploit. Remember you can only be victimized by someone like this if you allow it.

Even if you live in a small apartment or house crowded with many family members, you can still set "emotional boundaries" which will enable you to take care of your own Circle #1 and personal health, but still be attentive and caring of your loved ones as you move them to Circles #2 and #3 in your life. But this difficult task cannot be accomplished alone; it is not a solitary task. Having God as your partner will give you the wisdom and strength you need to achieve this complex undertaking in a manner that will bring healing to you, and to your family.

How Distorted Are Your Circles?

(Exercise 22: Circles of Intimacy, Responsibility, and Impact)

Please be scrupulously honest as you do this exercise. Fill in two sets of circles: the first one on how your circles actually look now; and the second on how you would like them to look. If you are in a relationship, please request your partner to do the same exercise. Each of you should also complete an additional circle, indicating the way you think your partner's circles are prioritized. Then compare the circles.

This last set of instructions always brings up many issues when I use this exercise with clients who come to me for marriage counseling. Many people will say, "My husband/wife is in my Circle #2," while their spouse sits there adamantly shaking his/her head "No." One partner often feels their spouse's addictions, job, children or an outside activity (such as sports or hobbies) is in their Circle #2, adding, "I feel like I am out somewhere about Circle #7 or #8. I'm not a priority in his/her life."

Intimacy dwells in Circles #1, #2, and #3. I give couples the following list to distinguish whether they are truly in each other's Circle #2a. Even though they may feel responsible to that other person and have an effect on that person's life, responsibility and impact do not necessarily create an intimate relationship. This list also applies to children in your Circle #2b and to close friends or family in your Circle #3.

Evaluating a Circle #2 or #3 Relationship
1. Is this a safe relationship?
2. Am I willing to be vulnerable with this person?
3. Do I trust this person?
4. Is this person honest with me?
5. Is this relationship mutually rewarding with mutual respect, sharing, and nurturing?
6. Do I enjoy being with this person?
7. Is this person glad to be with me and does he/she act pleased to see me?
8. Can I be all I am created to be with this person or do they find me threatening?
9. Does this person encourage and bring out my natural creativity?

10. Am I comfortable and relaxed with this person or am I uptight and anxious?

11. Do we find each other interesting?

12. What is my history with this person? Have we shared happy, sad, and interesting times together over a long period of time?

13. What are our shared interests?

14. Do we have shared values?

15. What is our frequency of contact?

I encourage you to go over the following list with your loved ones and appraise your relationships. After doing so, discuss what you can do to improve your level of intimacy where appropriate.

Intimacy and Health—Not Selfishness and Dysfunction

Most people, if they are honest, will admit that their circles are messed up. Many people have great difficulty placing themselves in their Circle #1 because it feels narcissistic to them. However, if God genuinely is there in Circle #1 with you, you will not be selfish. Your primary responsibility is to keep yourself healthy: physically, intellectually, emotionally, and spiritually—especially in your relationship with your Higher Power.

Some religious leaders become quite agitated when they hear the concept of putting oneself in Circle #1. They are immediately fearful that this implies a self-centered, self-serving attitude. What I propose is actually the reverse. The reason for placing yourself and God in your Circle #1 is not for you alone. In fact, being in a close relationship with God in your #1 circle and also taking responsibility for your own health, enables you to be loving and strong enough to extend yourself to others in an authentically altruistic manner, not in a codependent, destructive way.

Before I started my therapeutic healing journey in 1980, I felt like I was a Mercedes sports car that had never been serviced or maintained. It was as though the engine, (representing my capacity for emotions), had been taken out and replaced by an engine from VW. The exterior of the car was dirty and beat-up and the tires were bare threads. My little VW engine was stuck on full throttle and I was barreling down the road without the faintest idea of where I was headed. No wonder that when I reached the age of forty-four I was drained, exhausted, and contemplating taking my own life.

During the 1970s, with my friend Kay, I had helped to establish some of the first support groups for women in the United States. I retired from my work at the art gallery and devoted my full time to heading this organization—which was called *More Than Friends*—and to helping hundreds of women. But, I knew nothing about boundaries and so, in the process of this work, I became totally depleted.

I felt it was my obligation to be a loving, supportive friend to anyone and everyone who needed me, and did not feel that I had the right to take time to maintain my own health. I had God in my Circle #1, my spouse and children in Circle #2 and all the rest of the world in Circle #3. I was somewhere out in the hinterlands, not even on the chart. Years later, after I became a therapist, one of the reasons I developed the Circles of Intimacy, Responsibility and Impact was to try and understand my personal process and to reconstruct my own circles

Now I always try to keep these circles in the forefront of my mind. If I become weary or start to feel sick, I know it's because I've allowed my circles to become distorted and I have to stop and think, "Who's on first?" I usually recognize that I've taken God and me out of our healthy position in my Circle #1.

Today, when my circles are balanced appropriately I feel God uses me to influence and help thousands, not just hundreds, and I am not tired or ill. In fact, it's entirely different; I feel energized and love my work and my relationships. At age eighty, in many ways I am now in better condition than when I was in my twenties and thirties. Right now I'm planning my 105th birthday party (and you're invited!)

Other people may have a problem the opposite of mine. Because they put themselves and their wants and needs in their number Circle #1, but with God absent, they become narcissistic and unbalanced.

Then there are others who have allowed both God and themselves to be disenfranchised from their rightful places in their Circle #1 by jobs, addictions, spouses children, parents, friends, activities, sports, and so on. For example, numerous employers today assume their employees will work sixty to ninety hours per week, and people are afraid to set boundaries regarding their work hours for fear of losing their jobs. At the present time, addiction to activities (sports, shopping, gambling, computer games, Internet surfing, talking and texting on the phone, partying with friends) is almost as common as addictions to drugs, alcohol, sex, or food. Addictions, whatever the focus, always end up in a person's Circle #1 and often extend to Circles #2 and #3.

In addition, as stated earlier, feeling responsible for taking care of parents or extended family members at the cost of your own health or the health of your spouse and children is considered normal in cultures where blood relationships always come first.

Having a solid Circle #1 is the pinnacle from which everything else flows. If that circle is depleted and invaded by people, addictions and activities, you will be in a state of disequilibration, your personal balance destroyed. Your personal and relational health will suffer and be in chaos.

Ministry, not God in #1

Religious leaders are notorious for having radically confused circles. While they feel they have God in their Circle #1, if they are truthful, many have to admit that their ministry is in Circle #1, their denomination or mission board is in Circle #2, their congregations or constituents in Circle #3, and themselves, their spouse, and children are out about Circle #10. And because their actual relationship with God is greatly fractured, they feel spiritually bankrupt. They have very little time to spend in true intimacy— meditating, praying, and reading.

Even though they preach and teach God's love and grace to others, for them personally, God may seem an unreachable entity in some far off universe. Their head may have knowledge of grace, but their heart may lack an understanding of it. One of my clients worked for a pastor who actually said, "I do not know of anyone who is successful in ministry that lives a balanced life."

I well remember my dad's bitter words when talking about his minister father: "If he had paid his children one fraction of the attention that he gave to his congregation, it would have been an entirely different story. But, he left us with harsh, resentful memories instead of memories of love and caring."

I presented an all-day workshop several years ago for the pastoral staff of a large church in California. I had each pastor fill in their Circles of Intimacy, Responsibility and Impact, and then discuss them with the group. There were more than a few tears shed by the end of the day. Several participants said, "If we made our priorities like you've suggested, we'd all lose our jobs. The church board and the congregation expect us to be on call whenever they need us. They would feel we weren't being pastoral or appropriately spiritual if we set boundaries around our time and efforts." How tragic.

One Russian pastor related, "My church urges me to keep working and said, 'You may rest in heaven,' so I do not know how to begin to take care of my own health, or how to adequately care for my family."

During our Level II seminars I often take masking tape and lay out the Circles of Intimacy, Responsibility and Impact on the floor. Then we act out various scenarios from the lives of the participants. I remember one such time when I placed a pastor in the circles and surrounded him with many other students to represent the members of this congregation. His (actual) wife and other participants portraying his children were far outside the circles. Everyone was attached to him by ropes. I asked his wife what she wanted to do—and she frantically began to try and pry an opening between all the "parishioners" in a futile attempt to reach her entangled husband. But, he simply stood there and did nothing to help her, or himself. It was a very powerful moment and caused much discussion afterwards.

Several times in using this role-playing exercise, the "hero" literally becomes choked and finds it difficult to breathe because of the stress and pressure coming from the multitudes of people pleading and pulling on him or her for help. After a few moments of allowing this distress, I then have everyone step back and I take off all the ropes, and rearrange people in the circles the way they should be—if they were healthy. It is amazing how different everyone feels and looks, not just the greatly relieved protagonist.

The participants gain a compelling new insight into the validity of being committed to having their circles become healthy and to being the person that God created them to be.

While almost all clergy feel their work is a ministry and therefore must come first before their own health and their families, many health professionals also have similar beliefs and the same resulting difficulties. How about you, what do you put before your health and your loved ones?

In Summary

Consider what it would mean for you to change the configuration of your own Circles of Intimacy, Responsibility, and Impact. I realize it may feel frightening even to consider doing so. But if you literally take the high road, with faith, and commit to being balanced and healthy— physically, intellectually, emotionally, spiritually, and in your relationships—God always takes up the slack. It may be one of the most challenging things you have ever done— and whether it means setting boundaries with family members, friends or colleagues, quitting your job, or getting treatment for addictions—your ultimate well-being is worth the concerted effort and commitment.

Walking this new path may not be easy at first, but it's the path you were designed to walk. One day you will feel blessed. I know that to be true, not only from my own experience, but from the lives of countless others who have made that commitment. It does not mean you will never have problems again, but it does mean you will have the strength, energy, and wisdom to move through them in a manner that is healthy and rewarding for you and the loved ones in your life. You were created to live in balance and you have the right to claim that in your life. Have faith in yourself, in God, and in the process.

GUIDEPOST FOUR

ACTIONS, ATTITUDES, & ACCOUNTABILITY

Actions are outward indications of inward *attitudes.*
Accountability reflects a commitment to
transforming *actions and attitudes.*

The fourth guidepost rests upon the first three trail markers of this healing journey and features the critical elements of Actions, Attitudes, and Accountability.

Honestly addressing your personal attitudes and their affect on your actions may seem like an insurmountable mountain or a very deep valley on this healing journey. Looking at how you have been a victim in your life is a painful experience; but even more so, is evaluating how you have also been a victimizer. As you ask God to help you and are willing to become accountable for the manner in which you have contributed to the pain in your life and in the lives of others, you will overcome some of the greatest obstacles on this journey.

This segment of your passage will initiate a soul-searching quest regarding aggression, passive-aggression, and addictions. Generations of noxious attitudes will leave a legacy of destructive actions if not acknowledged and actively eliminated. This honest self examination can be accomplished only if you are willing to be accountable in this recovery process to God, yourself, and others.

CHAPTER 11

From Victim to Victimizer

Why, all delights are vain; but that most vain
Which, with pain purchased doth inherit pain.
—William Shakespeare (1564–1616)

It Takes Two to Tangle

Her rage scorched the ceiling of my office: "I had nothing to do with this! His affairs are the problem here, not me! Sure I get angry once in a while, who wouldn't. But, he's a man; he should be able to handle my anger. He's just a lousy son of a bitch who runs away and finds some other female to make him feel good. I can't trust him as far as I can throw him!"

She was a sharp businesswoman who owned an advertising agency and whose tongue could lacerate a steel wall. At her office she had total control of her staff and colleagues; at home, her mild-mannered husband could not stand up under her onslaught. So he had affairs.

They were both married to other people when they met at a business conference. What had started out as a professional relationship ended up in an affair. Divorcing their spouses, they had now been married five years. Their marriage was built upon a cracked foundation of betrayal; and the resulting lack of trust, tension and anger continued to erode that damaged base.

On another day, a polished, handsome man in his mid-forties with a cunning smile sat on the couch in my office as though he owned it. I asked, "Why are you here? Is it just because you were caught again with another woman, or do you genuinely want to give up your sexual addiction?" With a devious smile in place, he allowed, "Well, I suppose I have to admit that what I'm doing isn't okay. But each time I'm caught, I know that if I say I'm sorry, my wife will forgive me and take me back."

"And that's happened five times now?"

"Yes, but you see, my wife's church doesn't believe in divorce, so I know she'll never really throw me out. And besides, she likes having the elegant home and social position I provide for her plus being able to buy just about anything she wants at Neiman's. She really doesn't want to have to go to work and give up her tennis and golf games with her friends."

Later that week, a couple sat on opposite ends of my couch trying to stay as far away from each other as possible. His dark eyes glared at me as his silent rage filled the room, while her sad eyes seemed betrayed by the smile painted on her pale, round face.

They were there because of problems with her rebellious teenage son from a former marriage. They said the boy was belligerent, sullen, and refused to cooperate with them or his teachers. They wanted to know what could be done to "fix him." Because I don't believe in making the child the IP (identified patient), I first wanted to know what life was like at home for the boy. How did his parents handle conflict between themselves?

The woman with the plastic smile spoke: "Well, we almost never argue. When my husband is upset, I usually just go in my room and stay there reading or leave and go to the mall. It doesn't do any good to try and talk to him because he discounts everything I say and won't listen to any of my input anyway. So why try. But, at least he doesn't rage at me like my first husband did. He just leaves and goes and spends time with his friends."

The man's shoulders flexed and his foot kept moving as he responded: "She doesn't know anything anyway, so why should I put any value on what she says. Plus, she's gained so much weight she really turns me off. I much prefer the company of my buddies at the shop or at my lodge."

With a deep sigh she said, "I really do make an effort to make him happy. I keep things nice around the house and cook good meals, but it seems like no matter what I do for him, it's never, ever enough. He's critical of everything I do. And all I ever ask from him is for him to spend just a little time with my son. He really needs a dad, as his real father abandoned us when my son was a baby."

Her husband's agitation was visible as his eyes widened: "Look, I work really long, hard hours to provide a home for her and her boy, and I resent having to take any of my free time to spend with that kid. He's just a loser anyway."

These people, like the majority of my clients, are intelligent people. They usually have known some success in their varying professions and are not ignorant about many of the basics of life. Yet they have learned to rationalize and excuse behaviors that so obviously need to be corrected. They either blame someone else for their actions or justify why it's okay for them to continue with their injurious conduct.

Two Destructive Children

One of the primary goals of this healing journey is to enable the Original Child, the Controlling Child, and the Sobbing Child to integrate and mature into a Healthy Balanced Person. The three children, however, can also unite in unhealthy ways, creating injurious amalgamations that need to be eliminated.

A child whose fundamental needs for love, nurturing, touch, safety, and stability were not met, is left with holes in their psyche. As a result (unless there is intervening therapy), that person will continue to try to find other people, things or activities to fill those holes. It's as though their Sobbing Child is going around with outstretched hands, saying, "Please come here and fill this empty place in me."

But no matter how much the Controlling Child pours love, attention, money, alcohol, sex, food, power, or other people into those holes to try to fill them and comfort that child, it will never, ever be enough. Only you and God can fill those inner holes.

As the Sobbing Child continues to search for the ever-illusive means to fill the holes from some outside source, the Controlling Child may become weary from years of futile efforts at soothing and placating the needy Sobbing Child. Previously these two worked independently. Now, however, the exhausted Controlling Child says, "If you can't beat 'em— join 'em." And as the unhealthy Sobbing Child swings into action, so too does the unhealthy Controlling Child. When they connect, they are like two live electrical wires connecting—they explode and create the Angry Rebellious Child (whose initials just happens to spell ARC).

(Illustration 9: Angry Rebellious Child)

The Angry Rebellious Child

The Angry Rebellious Child:
- is overtly hostile
- is aggressive
- is demanding
- operates with a very short fuse
- is into power and control
- resembles two electrical live wires, arcing as they connect
  Common statements by an Angry Rebellious Child are:
- "Don't tell me what to do."

- "I'll do it my way."
- "It's my way or the highway."
- "I don't give a ---- what you think!"

The Angry Rebellious Child is born in early childhood when someone tells the child to eat or to do something he or she doesn't want to do. Rebellion at this stage is normal and is an expression of the child's need for independence and individuation. If this attitude is not modified, however, and it continues into adulthood, it becomes damaging to the person and others.

Everyone has had times of being an Angry Rebellious Child. It can vary from deciding to eat a second dessert, even though the doctor warned of a possible heart attack, to extreme violence, as anger escalates into out-of-control rage over something as simple as being asked to help get the kids ready for bed.

Unfortunately the Angry Rebellious Child is not our only inner tyrant. There are other times when the Sobbing Child's needs have not been met and the Controlling Child is weary of the pointless struggle to meet insatiable desires, and they join forces again—only this time they swing down and bring the Original Child into their destructive collusion, resulting in the emergence of the Stubborn Selfish Child.

(Illustration 10: Stubborn Selfish Child)

Stubborn Selfish Child

The Stubborn Selfish Child:

- is covert
- is passive-aggressive
- is manipulative
- is a game player
- is sarcastic
- is sneaky
- is revengeful
- is sometimes seductive and promiscuous; sexual addiction can start here

- has a sense of entitlement and grandiosity (fueled by the Original Child)
- Comments and attitudes by a Stubborn Selfish Child include:
- "I deserve this."
- "I want to do, what I want to do, when I want to do it."
- "If it feels good, do it!"

The Stubborn Selfish Child is also first seen in early childhood and, unless guided to share and care for others, will become a prime candidate for delinquency and addictions.

As with the Angry Rebellious Child, the Stubborn Selfish Child is no stranger to the majority of us. We all have times in our lives when we feel entitled to do something simply because we want to do it, and we don't consider the impact of the consequences. Or we withdraw, withhold, and refuse to talk. The Stubborn Selfish Child's motto is "I don't get mad, I get even."

While the Angry Rebellious Child is overt and in your face— the Stubborn Selfish Child is covert and much more subtle. In fact, the Stubborn Selfish Child often looks like the innocent one in many relationships because that child is usually quiet and looks good on the surface— unlike the Angry Rebellious Child who is so obviously out of line. While the Angry Rebellious Child is aggressive, the Stubborn Selfish Child is passive-aggressive, which can be more dangerous because you don't realize you've been stabbed in the back (by someone with a smile) until much later. At least the Angry Rebellious Child operates with a frontal attack so you know what's coming and can perhaps defend yourself.

Both the Angry Rebellious Child and the Stubborn Selfish Child:

- are unreasonable
- will rationalize to justify their behavior
- are unwilling to look at the consequences of their actions
- refuse to take responsibility for their behaviors
- consistently blame other people or events for their deeds

- will do whatever they want even though they know their actions will be destructive to themselves and/or to others (we often refer to this as "crawling out on a limb and sawing it off behind you.")
- see themselves as the victim, but become the victimizer, to themselves and to others

The Angry Rebellious Child and the Stubborn Selfish Child behave in harmful manners due to the unhealthy combination of the Sobbing Child, the Controlling Child and the Original Child, and they must be eliminated. Addictions are born here.

I have heard endless stories of viewing or being the recipient of aggression and passive-aggression:

- "I used to hide under the table when my father was beating my mother and sister so badly – I felt really helpless. I think it was harder having to watch him beat them than when he hit me. I was always terrified he would kill them. Today I have a very hard time standing up for my own needs."
- My mother was the 'ice queen' – she would not talk to me or my father for weeks at a time. She would leave and spend time at bars with her female friends from work. I had to do cooking and laundry for my father and me from the time I was very little."
- "I work at a children's colony where abused and abandoned children are sent. They have been so horribly mistreated it is as though cruelty is imprinted upon their souls."

Not by Chance

There is a fine line between victim and victimizer. We have all been victims and we all become victimizers, to ourselves and/or to other people.

While some people rationalize violence and abusive behavior by saying it is cultural and normal, others say, "A person is born bad and always will be that way; he or she cannot change." But I do not agree. Offenders don't "just happen," they are created.

I believe every child is created in the image of God. He or she is also given free will and therefore has the capacity to choose to do good or evil—however, these decisions are often formed early in life.

This precious child is like a little sponge—a receiver, a responder, a receptor. If darkness and pain are poured into that sponge, when it is squeezed, darkness and pain will pour out. Then often, someone stuffs that dirty little sponge into a box in which it does not fit. One day when it becomes an adolescent, it comes out of the box—all dark and misshapen—and parents, teachers, and other adults look at it and say, "Bad sponge!"

As with the other "children" exercises, I ask my clients and students to fill out a worksheet concerning their Angry Rebellious Child and Stubborn Selfish Child and then to draw these victimizers. After finishing, this sheet, they often arrive holding their homework at arms length in front of them, saying, "Oh, I really don't like looking at this. It was hard enough getting in touch with the way I have been victimized as a child and as an adult. But to see how I've victimized and hurt myself and others, especially those I love, is very difficult and painful." I ask you to have the courage to answer the same questions.

(Exercise 23: Victim to Victimizer)

When sharing their drawings of their Angry Rebellious Child and Stubborn Selfish Child with our classes, the following narratives have been given regarding their own victimizer behaviors :

- "I threw terrible temper tantrums as a child and my parents would give in to my demands because they became exhausted from my screaming. I still use rage as a way to control everyone around me—my family at home and my colleagues at work. People will let me have my way so they don't have to endure my wrath. "

- "I am more passive-aggressive and sneaky. I can provoke outbursts in others, and then I go and tell our friends how bad my "victim" behaved so they feel sorry for me."

- "I am an intense fire, inside a huge iceberg. My mother is the same."
- "Sarcastic humor is my great weapon. I can annihilate most people with it. If they act wounded, I simply ridicule them by saying they cannot take a joke and are childish. I feel powerful and in control. "
- "I pout and manipulate; it is very effective in getting my husband and my parents to do what I want."
- "I have fangs and a tongue like a sword. I enjoy carving people up with my words and spitting them out."
- "I scream at, swear at and threaten my terrified children, just like my mother did to me. And I promised myself I would never do that."
- "If someone offends me, I never forget. I am cold, calculating and wait for the moment to get revenge, even if it takes years."
- "This spider is also a provocative, beautiful woman who represents how I enjoy luring men into my web with sex, and then destroying them."
- "I have often hit my children, and sometimes even my wife, especially when I used to drink. I always blamed it upon the alcohol. Even though I don't abuse them physically anymore, I still am abusive verbally and emotionally."
- "This closed door is my passive-aggressiveness. When things don't go the way I would like, I simply leave—either physically or emotionally."
- "My mouth is zipped shut with a padlock. I can punish my family by not talking to them for weeks. But to our friends and other relatives I am gracious and loving so they never know how I act at home; and they won't believe it if my spouse tells them differently."

Fortunately, these people are courageously admitting to their very abusive, victimizing behaviors. Often they argue and try to rationalize their actions by saying that an "eye for an eye" is completely justified. But I relate one of my favorite quotes from Mahatma Gandhi, "An eye for an eye only leaves the whole world blind." They gradually begin to realize this is not the behavior they want to bequeath as a legacy to their children.

If you truly desire to become healthy and have a healthy family, then the destructive actions of your Angry Rebellious Child and your Stubborn Selfish Child must be eliminated. They are not your friends. They will destroy you and all your relationships if given permission to run rampant through your soul.

Predators and Prey

Moving from victim to victimizer is never acceptable, neither is staying forever a victim.
—*Marilyn Murray*

I am quite confrontive with all my clients regarding not only their victimizing behaviors, but also their victim stance. When you are a child being victimized, you have no choice. But if you are an adult, you have a choice.

When I worked at the prison, I once asked a group of rapists how they picked their victims, to which several replied: "I look for someone who has already been a victim." In the world of nature, a predator is basically lazy, looking for a wounded animal first before having to exert the effort to chase down a healthy one. In Arizona in years past, hunters who went after coyotes used a whistle named a "varmint caller." When blown, it emitted the sound of a wounded rabbit, to which coyotes responded eagerly.

Humans are no different. If you look, walk, talk, and act like a victim, you emit "the sound of a wounded rabbit," which assures your continued victimization. I also realize that many people who are victimized do not have a victim stance and were chosen at random or by accident. This kind of victimization cannot be avoided, no matter how healthy a person looks or acts. By eliminating a victim stance, however, you can at least protect yourself from those lazy coyotes that are looking for a wounded rabbit to abuse.

To stop abuse, it is necessary to address the issues affecting both victims and offenders, by:

1. Enabling victims to
   a. heal their victim wounds
   b. establish self-worth
   c. set boundaries with consequences
   d. release their victim stance
   e. acknowledge and change their own victimizing behavior.
2. Working with offenders to
   a. identify offender behavior and its origins
   b. provide treatment for offenders as a preventive measure to protect victims from further abuse
   c. heal their own victim wounds

Victims and Violence

Many people are in violently abusive situations where they are fearful for their lives and know that setting boundaries or trying to leave may get them killed. Those cases need to be handled in an entirely different manner from those relationships that do not include violence of this type. Specially-trained personnel at domestic violence shelters, abuse hotlines, support groups, friends, and extensive preparations are needed to make it safe for these victims to leave. Even then, many victims, especially women and children, are tragically killed whether they leave or stay.

She only came to my office one time. Her body visibly shook as she tearfully told me of her husband's violent temper and wild mood swings. They were both professionals, had moved to the United States from South America about six years ago, and were expecting their first child. But she was terrified as her husband had a long history of manic-depression and was refusing to take his medication. He was coming home soon from an extended trip, and she begged me to please pray with her for the safety of the whole family. I can still feel the intensity of her hands as they clung to mine while we prayed. She wept profusely.

She called me several times over the next few weeks, saying she had not made another appointment to see me because her husband was back and things seemed to be going better. They had already named the baby, a boy, and his delightful bedroom was ready and waiting for his expected arrival in about a month.

The next time I saw her was in church, only a few weeks later. It was a triple funeral: for her, her husband, and their unborn son—just days away from birth, now joining his parents in death.

Her husband had been driving. As they started to climb up a long hill, the nose of a mammoth eighteen-wheeler truck emerged over the top of the incline.

The giant semi barreled toward them down the oncoming lane of the freeway. Suddenly, her husband smashed his foot to the floor, and their small car lurched forward as its engine raced and the speedometer hit maximum. Deliberately turning the steering wheel, the man who should have been their protector instead propelled himself, his wife, and his unborn son across the median with deadly velocity, and drove head-on into the giant executioner. The little car and its three occupants were instantly annihilated.

The truck driver was not seriously injured physically, but his spirit never will recover from that memory. That young family's loved ones will never forget either. I, too, will remember.

Abuse Respects No One

Domestic violence is far more common than is generally imagined. While violence is commonly equated with alcoholism, drugs, mental illness, and poverty, it also takes place in the homes of the average family and affects people in all social and educational strata. And it is not gender specific.

All victims are not female, and all victimizers are not male. I consistently fight this bias, and I assure you, after twenty years of specializing in trauma and abuse, there are almost as many female victimizers as there are male—especially toward children. In the past, violent female offenders have not been as prevalent as male offenders. Today, however, teenage girls comprise one of the fastest growing populations of violent offenders. [1]

The constant onslaught of violence being unleashed through modern media and video games is brainwashing millions of individuals, especially young people, male and female, to see abuse as "normal." Lt. Col. Dave Grossman (a former Army Ranger and paratrooper, who taught psychology at West Point and is currently the Professor of Military Science at Arkansas State University) addressed this issue in his exceptional book, *On Killing: The Psychological Cost of Learning to Kill in War and Society*. In this book, Lt. Col Grossman explains that in times of war, young soldiers are prepared for battle through operant conditioning by practicing military maneuvers over and over again until the act of shooting to kill becomes second nature and the soldiers become numb to the reality of taking a life. He states that long-term exposure to violence and harsh aggression in the media and in video and computer games produces the same kind of conditioning. The observers and participants become conditioned to accept violence, abuse, and killing as acceptable behavior.

The Frog and the Pot

While we need to pay serious attention to physical and sexual violence—verbal and emotional abuse, neglect, and rejection

---

1 *Violence by Teenage Girls: Trends and Context*; U.S. Dept. of Justice, May, 2008; Girls Study Group, Understanding and Responding to Girl's Delinquency

are equally damaging. Though physical aggression that results in black eyes and broken bones may not occur, verbal and emotional aggression and passive-aggression may abound in a relationship. Too often, victims of nonviolent abuse rationalize that they don't have it so bad and so they put up with horrible situations—all the while thinking that these abusive relationships are better than nothing.

Most of the time a relationship starts out fairly well; the couple loves one another and treats each other fairly respectfully. But for some couples, as the years go by, unresolved anger starts to build and leaks out in passive-aggressive ways. Because it is not confronted and stopped immediately, the offenders continue with this behavior, which becomes a long-term habit.

What starts out as ninety percent good and ten percent bad gradually shifts until the bad increases as the good declines. There are many couples who have been married thirty or forty years who can rarely speak a decent word to each other. Their relationship is now ninety percent bad and ten percent good. They have slowly become accustomed to the dysfunction, and say, "Oh you know Dad, he really doesn't mean it when he says those things. That's just the way he is." Or, "Please be patient with your mom, you know how agitated she gets if things don't go her way. We just have to fit in and keep her happy." I often hear, "Well, even if he constantly puts me down and says horrible things to me, at least he doesn't beat me," or "My wife and I haven't had sex in five years, but she takes good care of our kids." The abusive behavior is never confronted and worse yet, the victims make excuses for the victimizers.

I am reminded of an old fable, to which I have added a few phrases of my own, about the frog who was dropped into a pot of boiling water and immediately jumped out, highly offended that anyone would do such a thing to him. He warned his children, all his family, and his froggy friends to avoid that hot pot at all costs. Then one day, someone picked him up and set him in a pot of nice cool water. Since it felt very good, he relaxed and went to sleep.

His body hardly noticed as the water slowly, gradually became warmer, just a degree or two at a time. He awoke and still felt comfortable; having a nice warm bath was okay. He even thanked the one who put him in the pot and called out to his children, family, and friends telling them that this pot was safe if they wanted to join him. Point by point the temperature increased, and the frog paid no heed to the fact that his body kept adjusting to each increase. But the adjustment took a toll: each rise in the water temperature meant the frog had to shut down part of his body and his spirit to maintain the balance between him and the intensifying heat. Finally the moment came when he realized the water was getting too hot and that maybe he ought to try to get out. But he couldn't—it was too late. As the remaining life drained from his body and spirit, he whispered, "But the cool water was so nice and pleasant, I'm sure it will return again if I just wait long enough.

Many people never confront their abusive relationships because addressing them means facing unpleasant consequences. They'd have to wake up and pay attention to the fact that the pot was getting too damn hot! Plus, they'd have to tackle the issue of facing the person who put them in the pot, and that might get rather heated too. So rather than deal with the consequences, they allow their bodies and spirits to become more and more adjusted to the rising level of the abuse. Until one day, they find their whole life has gone, and not only have their spirits died, but they have role-modeled that their children should only fear a fiercely boiling pot, not a slowly warming one. They have become a victimizer, to themselves and to their loved ones.

Payoffs: The Victims' Compensation

A boundary without a consequence isn't a boundary; it's just a fence with a hole in it.
—Marilyn Murray

Many people stay in abusive relationships and are afraid to leave because of the great fear instilled in them by what they have received—for example, battering and broken bones, or threats of being killed if they try to escape. In other types of abusive relationships, however, the victim stays, not only because of what they have received, but also because of what they will lose.

Some people put up with all types of abuse because they hope that maybe, just maybe, their partner will be a little nicer to them—perhaps one day out of ten. They don't make waves, so the nine bad days won't be quite so severe. And they fantasize and dream about the times past when the good days outnumbered the bad and their partner actually said pleasant things at the dinner table. They feel that the few, fleeting good days now are better than living alone and having no one.

Or, there are those people who know that following a really bad episode of abuse, whether verbal or physical, their partner will feel guilty, apologize and do something special to make up—bring gifts or plan an evening out and even act loving, romantic, and caring—just like a perfect mate. And besides, the sex is really great then.

However, predictably, the stretches of abusive behavior continue to lengthen over the years, while the days of loving actions shrink to hours and minutes. But the victim continues to maintain the status quo of abuse in order to gain the little snippets of (perceived) love that are waved about like bits of bread before a starving child.

Very few relationships are all bad or no one would stay in them. Even in really bad relationships, there is always some kind of goodie that keeps a person from leaving. Each of us has to weigh the costs, and ask ourselves, "What am I willing to give up in order to become truly healthy?" You have to make the effort to be responsible for your own feelings and work at the changes necessary in your own life.

One of the biggest hindrances to obtaining healing in abusive relationships is getting the "identified victims" to recognize how they, too, can become victimizers. Few of those on the receiving end of abuse are willing to recognize how their silence, coldness, sarcasm, addictions, and verbal put-downs are passive-aggressive actions instigated by their Stubborn Selfish Child—and, as such, are no more tolerable than the overt abuses of their partner's Angry Rebellious Child and Stubborn Selfish Child. Both these children are victimizers who must be eliminated.

Sometimes an "identified victim" just wants someone else to listen and sympathize with their grievances; they really don't want to have to change themselves. I have had many clients, female and male, complain about a dysfunctional relationship in which they are being verbally and emotionally abused, and yet they stay. We discuss how to set appropriate boundaries. But invariably they come back and report that even though they spoke up and told the other person how upset they were about the abusive behaviors, the abuse continued and sometimes even grew worse. They state that their attempts to bring their abusive spouse to couple's counseling sessions, were also rebuffed.

I then ask, "When you set the boundaries, what type of consequence did you give if the abuse did not stop?" Silence almost always greets that question, because, to set a boundary, the victim has to be willing to give up good things as well as bad. I then confront the clients and ask, "Why do you continue to stay? What type of payoff are you receiving by staying in the relationship? Is it financial security, social standing, having a home, time to do things you want, not having to live alone, having someone to help raise your children, having the approval of family, friends, or your church? Or do you gain sympathy and support from others who see you as a long-suffering martyr?" The clients who are unwilling to answer these questions honestly most often remain stuck in their destructive relationships. How about you, what is your excuse?

Can you answer the (preceding) questions I posed to my clients, as well as these: "Do you genuinely love your partner and want to work things out? Are there enough good things to outweigh the bad? Is your partner willing to some concentrated individual and couple counseling? Do you believe that God can help change your relationship?"

Unfortunately, belief in God alone does not guarantee a healthy relationship. It can be, however, one of the strongest aids to healing a broken bond if other factors of emotional health are also considered.

Only you can decide how you wish to address the unhealthy relationships and systems in which you are involved. Are you willing to give up the payoffs you receive, in order to become healthy? If not, and you feel you are duty bound to remain, are you willing to ask God to help you eliminate your resentful attitude, stop complaining, and then go about making the best of the rest of your life?

(Exercise 24: What Are the Payoffs?)

Boundaries: Complaints, Change, and Compliments

He had beautiful gray hair and walked with the aura of a Southern gentleman. His speech was soft and slow. He seemed the perfect, courteous, respectful husband. But he had Attention Deficit Disorder, was very passive-aggressive, and drove his perfectionist wife absolutely crazy. Her mind, her tongue, and her temper were bright and quick. She would rage, and he would usually leave. On occasion, he too would rage, and at times they both would become physical, with her being the major offender.

They had been married twenty years and genuinely loved each other. When they weren't fighting, they enjoyed many things and had a grand time together. They were like that old nursery rhyme, "When they were good, they were very, very good, but when they were bad they were horrid." When they began communicating through their "children," they found they could interject humor and greatly diffuse much of their fighting.

*One day, she was really in his face, her anger rapidly esca-
lating out of control. But instead of leaving, he looked at her
and said in his soothing southern drawl, "Darlin,' I just love
your Original Child; she's the one I fell in love with years ago.
But right now, would you mind steppin' back just a bit please
as your ARC is singeing mah eyebrows."*

Their commitment to healing their childhood wounds and
taking responsibility for the adult wounds they have caused each
other has been a long, intense journey for them. Although it still
isn't over, I continue to be encouraged and amazed as I hear of
their progress. They have become active in a place of worship near
their home, and their faith in God has been enormously empow-
ering for them individually and as a couple.

Not all clients are as committed to doing their own work as the
couple I've just described. I refuse to listen to people who complain in session after session about the same issues regarding
what someone else is doing or not doing to them. Unless clients
are willing to genuinely work on changing themselves, I suggest
they find another therapist. Many clients are upset when forced to
address their own participation in a destructive relationship. They
want to make the other person the identified problem; it's always
so much easier to blame someone else. But until a person takes
a hard look inside at their own Angry Rebellious Child and their
Stubborn Selfish Child, the relationship will continue to decline.

Please do not think I am an advocate for divorce. In the relationship counseling that I do, reconciliation and restoration are always
my goals, but not at the cost of a life—physically or emotionally.

Unfortunately, some victimizers, even when faced with the loss
of a relationship, will give up the relationship rather than their detrimental behavior. In that case, the victim has to choose whether
to leave or to stay in a relationship that will probably never improve, and may indeed become worse. Of the numerous people
with whom I have worked over the years, however, the couples

who have stayed together and are happy and healthy today are the ones in which one person had the courage to set a boundary with a firm consequence. Boundaries are necessary in all relationships, especially those that require fairly consistent contact.

As I mentioned previously, I spent more time in therapy learning about boundaries than in working on the issue of my sexual abuse. It seemed to take forever for me to fully grasp this concept. About six years after I started my own therapeutic journey, I realized I had made great progress in boundary setting when something happened that I never will forget:

I had been working part-time on a pro bono basis in the Sex Offender Treatment Program (SOTP) at Arizona State Prison Florence for about two years when the program psychologist told me about a new inmate in the program. "This guy is one tough, hardened con. He's a rapist and probably one of the most extremely violent men down here. He's been in and out of prisons all of his adult life. I hope you can work your magic and 'Marilynize' him; he really needs it."

Group is almost ready to start when the intimidating inmate swaggers in. He is huge, so tall he has to duck to come in the door. The intensity of his presence seems to occupy the entire room in the old trailer. He looks a lot like "Mr. Clean"—with his shaven head (unique in the mid-1980s) and his muscles exaggerated by the rolled sleeves of his tight white T-shirt—but without the smile. He glares at me as he layers himself into the frayed armchair, challenging me, no daring me, to try and engage him in emotional combat.

The day is long and painful. I follow my normal pattern of starting the marathon day by sharing my own story of sexual abuse (even after all these years, it never gets any easier). An audio-tape of one of my therapy sessions, where I re-experienced being gang raped as an eight-year-old, is played while the rapists and child molesters are compelled to view slides of me in childhood and look at me standing before them. Fear and pain laser through the darkened room; no one escapes the hysteria of the screaming, terrorized child.

At last the tape goes silent and the lights return. Gradually, the men begin sharing, many for the first time, talking about their own battered childhoods. Tears escape from their life-long captivity and etch the faces—white, black, and brown.

But my challenger sits sullen and brooding. As I look past him and through the dusty trailer window, the sun is descending across the razor-wire fence that surrounds the prison yard. We are running out of time, and he is the only one left who has not opened his own Pool of Pain. As I begin asking questions, his answers are short and strictly "from the neck up." He sits ramrod straight, absolutely refusing to speak about his past.

"Jim, I would rather talk to the logical adult part of you later. Would you please consider giving that little boy in you permission to speak to me here in this safe place?"

He refuses to speak, rapidly shaking his head back and forth, signaling, "No, no." He clutches the wooden arms of his chair so tightly it seems as though they will disintegrate in his vast palms; his knuckles are as white as his heaving T-shirt.

I edge my chair a trifle closer as I speak softly to that hurting child inside him. His body begins to shake and sweat pours from his face. His jaw muscles twitch and flex and he clenches his teeth so tightly you can almost hear his jawbone crack. The veins in his arms and neck pulsate, then leap to the surface, appearing as though something inside him is fighting fiercely to burst through his every vein, pore, muscle and bone.

Suddenly an immense shudder starts at the top of his glistening head and stampedes all the way to his toes. His chin drops to his massive chest as an enormous sob bursts from the depths of his being, from a child buried so deep he has not seen daylight since age two—a child who has been chained in solitary confinement with walls far thicker and higher and more restrictive than any prison that ever held his physical body. At long last that terrorized little boy is allowed to cry, to sob and speak of horrific deeds done by a mom and dad who should have given him love, not torture.

A little over a year later, at a follow-up group, I look at Jim and find it difficult to remember the hardened, violent man who looked like Mr. Clean. Now he has an easy, kind manner and is one of the first to encourage and support new group members. They all understand about boundaries and know that as long as they are honest, open and respectful, we will get along fine. No bullshitting is allowed.

It is the end of the day and, although group is over, everyone is sitting around. When there is a lull in the conversation, Jim turns toward me with a slight smile that speaks of gentle strength and says, "Marilyn, we all know that the scared little boy part of us, the part you call the Sobbing Child, is always safe with you, that you never will hurt us, but..." He stops and shifts his powerful body, leans forward, and connects directly with my eyes. A slightly crooked grin creases his face and his eyes twinkle as he continues, "We also know that there is always part of you that says, 'Don't f--- with me!'"

The rest of the group roars and nods in agreement. For someone who has had severe boundary problems all her life, it is the nicest compliment I have ever received. Everyone is capable of change—even me and even those who have manifested an extremely violent Angry Rebellious Child practically their entire lives, such as Jim.

It is never tolerable to abuse a child, whether an actual child or the child who resides within you. It is never tolerable to abuse anyone, whether a four-year-old or a forty-year-old. Abuse—physical, sexual, verbal, emotional—is never justified. As long as abuse is tolerated—in families, in communities, in schools, in churches, in businesses, in government, in any unhealthy system—abuse will continue to breed and give birth to its incestuous progeny: cruelty, violence, exploitation, neglect, and contemptuous disrespect.

As long as victims remain victims and avoid recognizing when they have transitioned from victim to victimizer—and that, instead of being mere followers, they now lead those who come behind them, their children and loved ones, to a path of victimization—abuse will continue.

In Summary

I believe we have all been victims, and have also been victimizers—both to ourselves, and to other people. Aggression and passive-aggression are a way of life to many people world-wide. Unfortunately, the attitude towards, and acceptance of, these behaviors, especially passive-aggressiveness, is so common that it is often difficult to sort out these destructive actions from healthy ones. Unless we are willing to challenge ourselves and ask God to help us eliminate the Angry Rebellious Child and the Stubborn Selfish Child from our daily repertoire of conduct, we will continue being both victim and victimizer. We will also role-model that destructive stance to our loved ones, and pass on a bitter legacy of abuse. If you permit this to occur in your life, you will create a dead-end detour that will bring your healing journey to a crashing halt. However, if you are genuinely sincere about breaking the chain of dysfunction in your family, God is waiting by the side of the road to enable you to continue your healing journey with His encouragement, love, help, and support.

CHAPTER 12

Facing the Enemy: Addictions

Lord grant me the serenity to accept the things I cannot change, the courage to change the things I can, and the wisdom to know the difference.
—Reinhold Niebuhr (1892–1971), "The Serenity Prayer"

When Love and Caring Is Not Enough.

She was fourteen, blond, and vivacious with a delightful smile. Her parents brought her to see me while I was speaking at a conference in Texas in 1982. They had adopted her when she was only a few weeks old and loved her dearly. But despite all their efforts to let her know she was loved and valued, she fought deep-seated feelings of rejection and abandonment. Depression and rebellion marked her young life. Her exhausted parents were willing to try anything to help her. I encouraged them to continue to love her and provide as much supportive therapy as possible. Two years later, her father was transferred to the San Francisco area, and they relocated a short distance from my therapy office at Restoration Therapy Center, the treatment facility I had co-founded with Dr. Peter Danylchuk and his wife.

Shortly after they arrived, she did an Intensive with Dr. Danylchuk and myself and worked hard on her issues. Despite the therapy, her need to be seen as someone special who would not be rejected was a powerful force in her life at sixteen. At her new school, she became involved with a crowd of well-to-do teens who were actively involved in drugs, and her new boyfriend was a dealer. It was not long before she became addicted.

Her parents put her in an inpatient treatment center for teens where she did quite well. She wrote me a letter while there, telling me that she genuinely wanted to start therapy again and was committed to sobriety and staying healthy. Only a few days later I received a frantic call from her parents saying that her boyfriend had come to the treatment center and somehow had managed to sneak her out. They had no idea where she was. Months went by without a word from her.

Late one night the call came; she had been found in convulsions and was at a hospital. When I arrived she was in a coma, her beautiful hair filled with vomit. She had evidently ingested a bad batch of designer drugs, and her condition was critical. I took turns with her parents and two younger brothers, sitting by her side day after day. Her young body continued to convulse, which was hideous to watch. How I wished I could have videotaped this to show to every person who thought that overdosing on drugs is a quick, easy way to go.

Her parents, brothers, Dr. Danylchuk, and I held her hands while she died, twenty-one days later. I still think of her.

Addictions—The Number One Adversary of Health, Freedom, and Relationships

Working with chemically addicted people has not been my specialty over the years. But I have become thoroughly acquainted with the devastation of those demon addictions because I have had multitudes of clients who have been the victims of parents, spouses, or children with these tormentors. Alcohol and drugs always exacerbate violence and abuse of every kind; they are fuel poured over smoldering coals that can burst into brutal eruptions and unleash tormenting flames that consume all within their path. However, alcohol and drugs are not the only destroyers of individuals and families, addictions of any kind are always destructive.

I am often asked, "What is an addiction anyway?" My thesaurus supplies several related words: habit, compulsion, dependency, need, obsession, craving, and infatuation. My basic definition is: *An addiction consists of anything that controls your life rather than you being in charge of your life.* Addictions are really bad habits. Because habits are formed, they can also be broken. However, this is not done easily.

We have discussed how each of us has a Pool of Pain that forms our Sobbing Child, and how our defense mechanism, our Controlling Child, uses various substances and diversionary tactics to anesthetize our pain (such as, alcohol, drugs, nicotine, caffeine, food, sex, work, power, money, sports, gambling, or religion). But these substitutes only create temporary relief—they never totally obliterate the pain. Our Controlling Child, then, has to keep upping the ante, adding more and more of our anesthetic of choice. But it is never, ever enough.

Eventually the anesthetic of choice increases to the point that it literally has a mind of its own, one that has forgotten the reason for its initial use. Then, you have a full-blown addiction, a long-term habit and a physiological compulsion to use the anesthetic, no matter what it costs you: money, time, reputation, loss of family and loved ones, in short, everything. Now you are not acting out of your Controlling Child, but from a roaring, out-of-control Angry Rebellious Child and a truly Stubborn Selfish Child. The addiction arena is the playground where they most often reside.

I have found that to effectively treat addictions, the addict must be willing to:

- **stop the active use of the addictive agent** by seeking help (and possibly medical care) at an inpatient or outpatient treatment center for detoxification and therapeutic healing; and to focus on changing their behavior to maintain long-term sobriety by using a Twelve-Step program or similar groups for support and accountability (an essential step for this portion of the treatment);

- *address root cause issues*—ideally by working with a competent professional in individual and group counseling sessions; or through using the methods outlined in this book and sharing the results with another person/s for support and accountability,

Sexual Addiction—The Ultimate Entrapment

Because I began working with sexual victims and victimizers in the early 1980s, I became very aware of the reality of sex addiction. At the time, this addiction was just being acknowledged as a reality and I was fortunate to work with several of the pioneers in this field. Dr. Patrick Carnes, a long-time friend and colleague, wrote one of the first books about sexual addiction in 1983, titled *Out of the Shadows: Understanding Sexual Addiction.* My associates, Dr. Ralph Earle and Dr. Greg Crow co-authored another major book in this field, *Lonely All the Time: Understanding and Overcoming Sex Addictions.*

While working with Dr. Earle at Psychological Counseling Center in Scottsdale, AZ, we specialized in the treatment of sexual addiction. That work gave me the opportunity of seeing the enormity of the consequences of this malicious addiction. Since then, we have come to realize that sexual addiction is one of the fastest growing addictions in the world.

The root causations of sexual addiction are multi-layered. We have found that many sexual addicts come from lonely, isolated childhoods and have often been exposed to sexuality (via pornography or sexual activity or abuse) very early in their lives. They learned that the high they received from sexual orgasm brought both an ecstatic feeling, plus a way to numb their emotional pain.

I found this particular addiction to be one of the most difficult to treat. Often, sex addicts did not respond as quickly to treatment as those with other addictions because, although we are not created with an innate need for alcohol, drugs, or nicotine, we are created with a natural desire for sex (and also for food). As such, sex and food addictions are some of the most difficult to overcome, not only because they are innate drives, but also because you have to learn to modify your use of sex and food. With alcohol, drugs, or nicotine, there is a distinct line over which you do not cross. If you want to remain sober you simply do not pick up that glass, pill, or cigarette. But modifying a natural desire is an extremely difficult challenge.

When clients come for treatment of sexual addiction, I explain the levels of this addiction to help them understand that the actions they are engaging in are extremely destructive for themselves and for other people; and that sexual addiction can create long-term injurious consequences that go beyond the norm for many other types of addictions.

Levels of Sexual Addiction

- **Level One:** With yourself—masturbation, usually with pornography
- **Level Two:** With someone else, a willing partner—affairs, promiscuity, prostitution, massage parlors, group sex, phone sex, computer sex, strip bars
- **Level Three:** With someone else, an unwilling partner, and without touch—obscene phone calls, voyeurism, exhibitionism
- **Level Four:** With someone else, an unwilling partner, with touch—rape, molestation, harassment

Sexual addiction, like any other addiction, is always progressive; the addict continuously looks for a higher high, the same as with people addicted to drugs. Not everyone starts at Level One, and not everyone progresses through the levels in the same order. A person usually stays at one level until a satiation point is reached, then progresses to another level.

The Pornography Prison

Pornography is the annihilator of intimacy. It creates a fantasy world in which reality cannot compete.

—Marilyn Murray

Because of the Internet and the "Three As: Availability, Anonymity, and Affordability" (discussed by sex addiction treatment professional, Robert Weiss), pornography has captured the minds and souls of countless millions. Some people deliberately seek out sexually explicit material on the web. Others accidentally stumble onto pornographic web sites, often via innocent looking e-mail, and then, out of curiosity, begin to view the seductive images and find they are unable to stop. Unfortunately, a computer and an Internet connection can be like having a heroin or cocaine dealer in your child's bedroom or in your office. Today, in addition to the predictable sex addict, we are seeing a new, different generation of addict, including children under the age of twelve, housewives, even pastors and missionaries. The adults are often people who never would venture out to buy pornography or rent X-rated videos, whose moral values are opposed to such activities.

When people hear that I treat clients with sexual addiction, they often make comments like: "A person never can have too much sex," or "Don't you think you're being too old-fashioned? Sexual freedom happened years ago." To which I answer, "This is not sexual love, this is sex addiction. I wish you could listen when my clients tell of being caught in the insidious web of this addiction, of what it has cost them—their spouses, children, extended family, friends, jobs, dignity, self-respect, and untold amounts of money. I hear heartbreaking stories of betrayal, never being able to have sex again with their loved one without seeing the image of some porn star, loss of trust, and sexually transmitted diseases."

More and more families are being affected by this infectious disease—good families, normal families, families in your neighborhood, maybe even your family. If you doubt the seriousness of this plague, I encourage you to discuss this with your spouse, children, loved ones, friends and acquaintances. I assure you that you will find that this horrific disease has already begun to affect people you know and love.

If a virulent plague of such gigantic proportions that affected the physical body began infecting the world, the United Nations and every government worldwide would immediately rally together their largest and finest resources to stop the catastrophic sickness and create a vaccine to bring it to a halt. Time, energy, and money would be no object. The severity of the problem would be the primary topic of the media in every language until the pestilence was brought under control. However, a deadly, infectious plague that decimates personal integrity and freedom, devastates families, destroys health, and ravages the spirit, today is left to rage about the world unchecked.

A Devastating, Abusive Education

Researchers at the University of Pennsylvania found that in 2001, an estimated 325,000 girls and boys, age seventeen or younger, are prostitutes, performers in pornographic videos, or have otherwise fallen victim to "commercial sexual exploitation." [1] Unfortunately, the use of children and teens in pornography will continue as long as the demand exists.

Because I view every person as containing an Original Child, pornography featuring people of any age violates a child. In working with sex addicts, I often lead them in a visualization where they see the young child in themselves. Then I have them envision taking that vulnerable child with them as they go to a sleazy strip bar, or to pickup a prostitute, or to a dangerous drug

---

1   (reported in *USA Today*, September 10, 2001).

house; or they picture involving that child in pornography. The client has a very difficult time with this painful process as they begin to realize that each and every time they participate in those activities as an adult, they also are taking along that child. They now have become the abusive, victimizing parent to that vulnerable child within themselves. For most clients, realizing that they have picked up where their childhood offenders left off is one of the most sobering aspects of their therapeutic journey.

After a therapy session in which an addict re-experienced visiting bath houses for anonymous sex, he tearfully stated how his inner little boy felt, "Those acts were terrible—my body wasn't my own—it was passed around like a cheap snack. I hated it and was so afraid." Then the adult addict added, "I lost my dignity over and over."

The Seductive Slide

In years past, it was not uncommon for an addict to remain at Level One of sexual addiction, especially if the person was prominent in the community or religiously opposed to sexual promiscuity. The addict would not take a chance on being seen with a prostitute or at a local strip bar. Their pornography stash might not be extremely hard-core because they also would not risk being observed going into an adult bookstore. They would purchase such items when they were out of town. Even then, because of their position or beliefs, their collection of porn might be somewhat limited. They could spend a lifetime at Level One and not necessarily become satiated; they were still able to obtain a "higher high" within Level One.

Today, however, anyone having access to a computer can view perpetual pornography on the Internet, including extremely obscene images and perverted live activities. This means that a satiation point can be reached in a matter of weeks, rather than a lifetime. This explicit pornography bombards the senses with force so great that an addict can become quickly immune to its onslaught and no longer receive a high from it. The addict then needs more intense stimulation from a live contact, not from a still photo or a video and they move on to Level Two, or perhaps even Three, or Four.

As a consequence of pornography and other sexually related sites on the Internet, we are seeing more people rapidly progressing through the levels of sexual addiction than ever before. This is a major consideration because it presents an increasingly large population at higher risk of becoming sex offenders.

Because the perversion seen on most Internet pornography sites is so vile and extreme, the addict may become conditioned to the violence and demoralizing actions of the participants so that sadism and perversion become mundane. Soon the visitor begins to desire more than just watching the computer screen and wants to be actively involved. Moving to Level Two, the addict may participate in group sex, bestiality, sadomasochism, or potentially lethal activities such as autoerotic asphyxiation.

I always stress the importance of recognizing the severity of this deadly trap to all my clients with sexual addiction issues. When I tell clients who are at Level One or Level Two that they are facing a ruthlessly debilitating addiction—almost certain to lead to sexually transmitted diseases (including the possibility of AIDS) and even the potential of a prison sentence—they are usually appalled, responding, "Oh, I would never do any of those things described at Level Three or Level Four." I reply, "Ten years ago, would you have ever thought you would be participating in your present activities at Level One and Level Two?" Abashed, they whisper, "No," often with tears reflecting a deeply troubled spirit.

Pornography web sites almost always have many links that can immediately access sex chat rooms and video hookups with live sex and sexual addicts often take the opportunity to enter them. As a consequence, the addict immediately moves from Level One to Level Two where he or she becomes involved with another live person in sexual activity.

Viewing pornography is a type of voyeurism. But when a person is participating in a live video hookup, they have become an authentic voyeur. If this person's spouse becomes aware of this activity and has the computer removed (or for some other reason the Internet is not readily available), then the addict may start to peruse the neighborhood to see whose blinds have been left up in their bedrooms or bathrooms. It becomes an easy, predictable slide from Level Two to Level Three.

In the past, women have made up a smaller portion of the sexual addiction population. They were more likely to be sex and love addicts who were seeking relationships and intimacy— and the sexual activity was simply part of the relationship, not the primary focus. Females, however, are increasingly becoming genuine sex addicts as they view pornographic Internet sites. In fact, in recent years some of my most severely addicted clients were twenty-one-year-old girls. Also, women who previously spent a great deal of time watching soap operas on television or reading romance novels are now becoming addicted to sexual chat rooms, frequently emailing the people they meet. They spend increasingly longer hours on the Net to the exclusion of almost everything else. When they can no longer receive their higher high from written words, they may decide to meet their new "lovers" in person. This happens often, many times with tragic results.

Sexual addiction has existed since the beginning of time, and having lovers while married is commonly accepted in many modern cultures. In the United States, many individuals in positions of power and leadership, or prominence in the fields of sports and entertainment, have had extramarital affairs. I have found that the stronger the personality, the greater the capacity for weakness. Some persons with great professional strengths also have great personal weaknesses, especially when it comes to sex. Unfortunately, rather than admit to a sexual addiction and seek treatment, such issues are often skirted (literally) and healing never occurs. Fortunately, today, numerous well-known persons have broken this resistance and have sought treatment for sexual addiction. Hopefully they will make a genuine commitment to the path of recovery and will demonstrate that change is possible in a life formerly consumed by addictions.

Affairs of the Heart—Addicted to Love

Many affairs are emotional, never reaching the physical or sexual stage. I don't think anyone, if they are genuinely honest, will admit to never having had an emotional affair with someone who is married or otherwise unavailable. We develop crushes, which are usually one-sided, on another person from the time we are very young (school teachers, coaches, parents of friends); that's normal. When those fascinations with another person escalate, however, and especially if the other person responds, an emotional or a physical affair can develop.

Emotional affairs happen by the thousands every day in the workplace between people who are in constant contact on a regular basis. People see more of their colleagues than they do their spouses. They learn to respect their coworker's expertise and intelligence and some begin sharing more and more intimate details of their lives.

Many people think that if you are not having sex with someone, then it is not an affair. Some think that if it is only oral sex and not full intercourse, it doesn't count, or if "she's doing it to me and I'm not doing it to her, it doesn't count" either.

Among the greatest needs of every adult, is the desire for physical, intellectual, emotional, and spiritual intimacy. Those needs should be filled by partners in a committed relationship. Of course, no one person can fill all those needs—however, unless the couple has some connection in all four areas, they will seek to fill their intimacy needs with someone else—in an affair—or with their children, or with other family members or friends.

My definition of an affair is: any occasion in which an individual's efforts to provide and receive physical, intellectual, emotional, and spiritual intimacy are displaced upon another, who is not that individual's partner, even if it does not include sexual activity. When this occurs, the individual's partner is denied the full commitment to intimacy to which he or she is entitled.

In my private practice I saw numerous clients who were involved in emotional affairs, who became just as addicted to that relationship as people who are addicted to sexual relationships. While they do not face sexually transmitted diseases or prison sentences, their difficulties in maintaining sobriety are as complex and, in fact, may even be more perilous than the sex addict's. Because the emotional affair of the heart is not as tangible as a sexual affair, these addicts have more difficulty accepting culpability.

Offenders

It is important to note that not every sex addict becomes a sex offender. And, not every sex offender is a sex addict. I found however, when working in the Arizona State Prison Sexual Offender Treatment Program, that a high percentage of the men (both addicts and non-addicts) that become sex offenders have themselves been sexually abused as children or teens with both men and/or women as offenders. There is an alarmingly high rate of sexual abuse by females in the backgrounds of rapists, sex offenders and sexually aggressive men—59% (Petrovich and Templer, 1984), 66% (Groth, 1979) and 80% (Briere and Smiljanich, 1993).[2]

Facing the reality that women can also be offenders is an extremely sensitive area that numerous people, especially other women, do not want to acknowledge. In many years of working with male rapists, I found they were not born that way—that the basis for a male's rage at females almost always was his own

---

2   *Female Sex Offenders - Female Sexual Predators*; Canadian Children's Rights Council; http://www.canadiancrc.com/Female_Sex_Offenders-Female_Sexual_Predators_awareness.aspx

physical, verbal, emotional and/or sexual abuse as a child or teen by a female—usually his mother, sister, grandmother or aunt and he was unable to defend himself at the time. As he became older and stronger, he extracted his violent revenge onto some unsuspecting female who became the innocent victim of his brutal reprisal.

Most male victims of sexual abuse do not become sex offenders—however, their long-lasting damage is the same as for female victims of sexual abuse—a reservoir of pain, guilt, shame, confusion and anger—and often, also a seditious legacy of sexual addiction. Many men find it difficult to admit sexual abuse by females, calling it "a relationship," an "affair," "an early introduction to sex (wasn't I lucky?!)" Young boys and teens who were seduced by an older female, especially their mother, find their sexual distortion to be tragically deforming when they attempt having any type of sexual relationship in a marriage.

In order to reduce the number of males who do become violent offenders—either sexually and/or physically, it is critical that mothers and other female family members treat the boys in their families with love and respect, not with violence and abuse. Also for the men in the family to role-model to their sons that women are to be treated with love and respect. If adults—both female and male—became committed to changing their behavior toward their children and each other, then the level of future physical and sexual abuse could be dramatically reduced.

Addictions Know No Nationality, Race, or Status

I believe every individual has a propensity to become addicted to something, be it a person, a substance, an activity, or a belief system. I know I could easily become addicted to the computer. It activates both the right and left sides of our brains, both the creative and logical parts, making it a highly addictive resource. I deliberately limit my time on it. Because I also struggle with trying to be a recovering perfectionist, the computer is deadly for me (you can continue to correct and polish a manuscript perpetually). I also love to learn, and I can get on the Internet to research a subject only to find that five or six hours have passed and I have not moved.

As a therapist, I saw the amount of time boys and men spent on video and computer games escalate dramatically. They are becoming addicted and commonly spend many hours on the enticing games while their parents or spouses and children complain bitterly. When I confronted these addicts about their behavior and suggested that they set boundaries around their gaming time, I often met with great resistance. Some would give up alcohol and drugs quicker than those games. For adult men, this activity taps into the competitive nature they previously satiated by participating in sports as teens.

Preventive Maintenance

In the Alcoholic Anonymous program, they have an acronym known as "HALT" which stands for "Hungry, Angry, Lonely, and Tired." The program teaches that each of these words indicate a state under which a person may be most tempted to drink. After working with addicts of many types I added two more indicators which I also found were quite prevalent and created susceptibility for most addicts. One of my clients who is in recovery for sex addiction came up with the following acronym which I think is very appropriate:

When Am I the Most Vulnerable to My Bad HABITS?
1. Hungry
2. Angry
3. Bored
4. Isolated
5. Tired
6. Stressed

Adding "bored" and "stressed" to the "HALT" list, plus changing "lonely" to "isolated" has been exceptionally effective with the clients and students to whom I have given this therapeutic tool. I have them place this list in their home, office, and car, and when they are tempted to give in to their addiction, they review the HABITS list and determine which words best indicate their present condition.

I have found most addicts to be quite very vulnerable when they are tired and stressed (which is the state in which the majority of adults reside); and sex addicts to be especially at risk when they are bored.

My Russian students consistently report that they go to bed very late and rarely get enough sleep. I confront them strongly about this behavior because lack of sleep exposes you o a high risk of being open to your addictions. Further, the DeHavilland News Information Service reports that previous research from the University of Pennsylvania determined that those who sleep for six hours a night make eleven times more errors than they would had they gotten eight hours of sleep (and most of my students get less than six); and that you have a difficult time remembering and making good decisions. Plus, lack of sleep damages your ability to recreate healthy new brain neurons. As you can see, neglecting this portion of your health can impact you in many areas, especially your susceptibility to addictions.

If you truly are seeking to overcome your addiction/s, it will be helpful for you to be aware of the states in which you are most apt to act-out (Hungry, Angry, Bored, Isolated, Tired, and Stressed); and to eliminate or reduce those dangerous situations in advance—such as getting enough sleep. Your ability to stay sober will greatly increase as you decrease your exposure to risk.

Friend or Foe?

Many addicts, especially sex addicts, feel their addiction is their friend, and perhaps even their lover. It gives them solace when they are lonely, helps to numb their pain when they are hurting, and delivers a high when they are bored. It becomes the most important issue in their lives but, before they realize what has happened, their addiction will hungrily devour every other activity and person in the addict's Circles #1, #2, and #3 (from the Circles of Intimacy, Responsibility and Impact exercise), thus eliminating any outside competition.

Eventually, your addiction will no longer bring you a high, or numb your pain, or give you solace. Instead it will abandon you, leaving you a used-up junkie or alcoholic, a sexaholic entrapped by disease or the law, or a workaholic who lost love and family somewhere along the path to "success." Until you face the reality of these truths, you will continue to justify, rationalize, and make life-long excuses for your destructive addictions. I often confront my clients by saying, "Your addiction is not your friend, it really doesn't give a sh-- about you! It will eat you up and spit you out, then move on to romance your loved ones, your children, your grandchildren. Do you want to leave that kind of legacy? Is that what you really want? "

Codependency—the Major Enabler of Addictions

As you read the above information and acknowledge that addictions and other dysfunctions exist in your family, what are the excuses that allow them to exist? Why do you continue to be codependent and *enable* alcoholism and other destructive behavior in your loved ones? Why are you not setting boundaries, and moving family members, who do not belong there, out of your #1 and/or #2 circle?

You may be saying, "But our family tradition demands that I do this—I cannot do anything else." When my clients or students respond in this manner, I usually ask, "If you did set those boundaries, what would be the worst thing that could happen?" They almost always answer , "Well, my family would say I was selfish and unloving, an awful, uncaring person."

And...? "Then they would talk about me to the rest of my family and they would all agreed how bad I was!"

And...? "They would reject and abandon me!"

Are you also fearful of being rejected and criticized if you set boundaries regarding destructive behaviors? Or, do you gain positive strokes from being seen as a self sacrificing martyr who continues to put up with an abusive, alcoholic spouse? Or, does being needed by the addict in your life help to fill the "cracks and holes" inside of your spirit and make you feel worthwhile? Or, are you so fearful of what would happen to your loved ones if you stopped caring for them, that you continue to support them even though they are active addicts?

Being in recovery from codependency does not mean you stop caring about or loving others, it is about being balanced—you still express your love and at the same time, you do not neglect your own health or hinder God from working in the lives of others.

If codependency if your issue, I encourage you to challenge any belief systems that continue to keep you bound in an extremely unhealthy situation. Today, there are many resources available to help you become sober from codependency including the Twelve-Step programs of CoDa and AlAnon. However, if you choose to stay stuck and remain a codependent that enables addictions and dysfunction, you must accept responsibility for facilitating these destructive behaviors. *As long as there are codependents, there will be addicts.*

If addictions and/or codependency are an issue with you or in your family, I encourage you to address it immediately by using the tools and resources suggested in this chapter and throughout the book. Hope for healing is greater today than at in any time in history.

**(Exercise 26: Honestly Facing Your
Addiction and/or your Codependency)**

In Summary

Our Controlling Child uses various defense mechanisms, including anesthetics and diversionary tactics (such as taking responsibility for others), to protect us from our Pool of Pain. These devices are meant to be temporary, but when we lose ourselves in them, they become addictions and codependency. These bad habits and compulsions are far more dangerous than most people realize and can destroy lives, families, and reputations. Every person is vulnerable to addictions of some kind—be it work, ministry, food, alcohol, drugs, caffeine, nicotine, sex, and gambling; or the destructive behavior of codependent enabling. Whether we realize it or not, when we participate in these activities and/or abuse substances, our Angry Rebellious Child and a Stubborn Selfish Child take control. Addictions and codependency must be eliminated as they are the arch enemy of health. If they are a problem for you, I strongly encourage you to seek professional help or a Twelve-Step program. It takes courage and is a sign of strength to admit you need help. We can all use the assistance of others at some time in our lives. You are not alone.

Just as everyone is a potential candidate for addiction, and this malady does not distinguish among groups of people, everyone is also a candidate for accountability and recovery.

I hope you seriously contemplate this major segment of your healing journey for, as you and God dismantle your addictions and codependency, you will then be able to help others in their healing journey as well. Nothing, absolutely nothing, can produce a "high" equivalent to a changed life.

CHAPTER 13

Balance, Balance, Balance

If you were to think of yourself as I think of you,
how glad, how healthy, how satisfied you would be.
Peace I give to you my dear one...
peace to be yourself, and to enjoy being yourself,
To become all I created you to be.
—**Dr. Marie Chapian,** *His Thoughts Toward Me*

You have been created to go forth into life,
with great openness of heart.
You were born to love and live...
to discover joy.
 —**Dr. Marie Chapian,** *Discovering Joy*

Shining from Within

The eyes of the beautiful woman sitting in my office glistened
with tears as she spoke, "How can I possibly celebrate the tal-
ents God has given me and genuinely enjoy my present life-
style when so many others are in such great need and are not
as fortunate as I am in natural abilities? It seems terribly self-
ish and prideful." She had a Ph.D. in psychology, and was a
highly intelligent, gifted public speaker and talented writer
who had been a child prodigy on the piano. Married to a suc-
cessful executive, she had wonderful children and grandchil-
dren; she lived and looked like the perfect wife, mother, pro-
fessional, and church leader. She had spent years in ministry,
giving of herself unselfishly to help many hurting people.

Amazingly, this woman's father was in prison when she was born and her childhood was shattered by abuse, neglect and alcoholism. Fear of abandonment and violence had taken its toll on her psyche. Despite the knowledge that she was a valuable child of God, at a deep unconscious level, she felt she did not deserve good things in her life and was defective and unworthy. As a consequence, she continued giving and giving of herself until she was completely exhausted and depleted.

During and after her therapy, she focused the majority of her efforts on establishing a relationship with God as a loving parent in her life—someone who would always be there, validating and loving her unconditionally in a way that her earthly father never had.

She also worked to accept that her Original Child was a very special creation who needed to be nurtured and affirmed. It was essential for this woman to understand that she could take healthy pride in growing into the person she was created to be and that she need not worry about intimidating others with her skills and talents. Her painful past made her caring and compassionate, but the ongoing issue she had to address was the need for boundaries.

Today, this lovely woman sets firm limits around her lifestyle and is well-known internationally as an author and teacher. I am delighted each time I see her, as she appears younger and more vibrant now than when we first met. She is a mentor and role model for many, demonstrating what it means to be a Healthy Balanced Person.

Transformation does not come easily; it takes courage and a commitment to a healthy, balanced life, often in the face of criticism and fears—both your own and those of others. While narcissism and selfish pride are very real issues for many individuals, I have found that it is far more common for people to under-value their self worth than to over-value themselves.

You may agree with me on this issue while nevertheless wondering: "What about those of us who are not so fortunate, who do not have exceptional talents or who are lacking in personal achievements, relationships, or material possessions?" Every person is given special abilities and has a unique role to play in this lifetime that no other person can fill. That unique role is to become the Healthy Balanced Person that only you can be. I know individuals in prison and many people in oppressive countries who have almost no resources available, and yet, they are actively becoming fully functioning Healthy Balanced People. It's not what we have, but rather what we do with what we have, that counts.

The Ultimate Balancing Act

My clients and students sometimes tease me about having a "B" for balance engraved on my head since I emphasize this quality so much in our lives. I find most people tend to be rather polarized, not balanced; I certainly was before my own therapeutic journey. In the process of learning about balance, I developed several schematics to illustrate how I perceived a Healthy Balanced Person would evolve.

I believe the majority of people act and react mostly from the viewpoint of their Controlling Child and their Sobbing Child; these inner children are in charge of their lives rather than their adult. Their Original Child is small and generally ignored. I sometimes imagine people with their Controlling Child and Sobbing Child attached by two ropes to the wrists of their Original Child, and the two "outlaw" children are flying across the desert, with their Original Child helplessly in tow, being dragged over cactus and rocks, covered in spines and bitten by rattlesnakes. Not a very inviting scene.

Other people have a strong Sobbing Child and a small, neglected Original Child, while their Controlling Child is weak, or nearly nonexistent. These people often act as though they had a "V" for victim stamped on their foreheads as they are perpetually being victimized by others. They also constantly seek to find someone else to take care of them. They take very little, if any, responsibility for their own lives.

In addition, there are other people who behave as I used to with a very strong Controlling Child, and a weak Sobbing Child whose existence is not acknowledged, along with a devalued Original Child. For this group of people, the issues of control, doing things correctly, maintaining appearances, and work are of primary importance.

Then, there is the person who has a large, active Original Child with an underdeveloped Sobbing Child and Controlling Child. While this person can be creative, exciting, and a delightful friend, they often may appear to be a perpetual child, rather like Peter Pan who never wanted to grow up. The people in this group, while enjoyable at times, can also be immature, irresponsible, hedonistic, and they often live in a fantasy world as graphically illustrated in the movie, *Arthur.* As a party friend, they can be fun, but over the long-term they are unreliable and self-centered unless they decide it's time for them to grow up and become a healthy adult.

In order for your Healthy Balanced Person to develop, your three inner children need to be in manageable proportions. Your children need to learn to work together as a unit rather than pulling against each other as individual components.

The Team

Sitting on my little patio in California, I was intrigued by the story of my new friend. He had an infectious laugh, clear blue eyes, and the look of an "all-American boy." He had been the quarterback and captain of his football team, president of the student body, and an honor student. His grandfather, father, and brother all were physicians; the town hospital was named for his father.

He longed for a connection with his dad, but the doctor was always too busy—his patients came first. When my friend was twenty-one, his father finally started to take time for himself

and his family, but it was too late; the esteemed physician suc-
cumbed to a heart attack at age fifty-one.

Instead of following the family practice of medicine, this young man chose to attend the London School of Economics, a highly prestigious school, and became a CPA in the San Francisco Bay Area, where we eventually became friends. One day he said, "You talk about this Sobbing Child—what does that mean?" After I described my concept of the children, he laughed rather sardonically, saying, "Oh, I think I know all of them pretty well. When I drive to work in the city on Monday morning, it's as if I pull on one of those old-fashioned, tight swimming caps, which is my Controlling Child. I arrive at my accounting office and it's filled with other Controlling Children, all diligently working away on their calculators and computers.

"I stay that way all week until Friday night when I rip off that restrictive cap—I am so glad my work week is finished and my Original Child takes over. My friends and I hit a single's hangout or I have a date. Then Saturday I play golf or basketball with friends and maybe attend a sports event that night. But, when Sunday arrives, my Sobbing Child comes out and says, 'You need to call and check on your mother.' Then Monday morning rolls around, and I pull on that imprisoning Controlling Child cap again.

"And that's the way it goes, week after week. It seems as of each of those children sits in a different corner of the room, waiting for a break in the action just so they can jump in and take control of my body—and they all have completely different agendas. I wonder what I would be like if they worked together as a team?"

I explained the following diagram of a Healthy Balanced Person to him, and over the next four years we spent many hours discussing these concepts. He incorporated them into his lifestyle and also actively worked on his personal issues with a therapist. Today, he continues to grow, becoming a mature, balanced person. What would it be like for you if your inner parts responded as a team?

(Illustration 11: Healthy Balanced Person)

As this title implies, a Healthy Balanced Person is a balanced, healthy combination of all the attributes of the Original Child linked with the positive strengths of the Sobbing Child and the Controlling Child. This combination creates wisdom and maturity, and is a lifelong process.

I once thought I needed to eliminate my Controlling Child and Sobbing Child, but I realized that they had very important roles to play in my becoming a Healthy Balanced Person. When I was a child during World War II, there was a popular song called *"Accentuate the Positive, Eliminate the Negative."* I found I needed to apply that maxim to each of my inner "children", and had to focus on and encourage the positive traits of each child and to let go of their negative influences. Being a Healthy Balanced Person does not happen just because we desire it. I encourage you to begin to look both at the positives and negatives of those portions of yourself represented by each child as you contemplate becoming a fully Healthy Balanced Person.

Sobbing Child

You may be a deeply feeling person but perhaps it has never been safe for you to allow those emotions to surface. Or maybe you are more inclined to be a thinking person, rather than a feeling one. In either case, you need to pay a great deal of attention to your Sobbing Child, and learn to listen to the feeling parts of yourself. As you do so, give yourself permission to allow the feelings to flow, but within healthy boundaries.

Every person should cleanse their own Pool of Pain until it feels to be at a manageable level, with its negative influence minimized. I do not think any of us ever empties their Pool of Pain entirely. Furthermore, it is not necessary to do so—just reduce its level until it no longer overwhelms you.

Learning new communication and relationship skills are valuable tools to help keep your Pool of Pain cleansed. It is futile to work on emptying your Pool of Pain only to then turn around and put more pain back into it. If you are able to deal with current issues and process them appropriately, they will disappear. However, if you do not process them at all, or you deal with them but do it inappropriately, they are dumped into your Pool of Pain and create new pain.

Remember, your Sobbing Child also provides empathy and compassion, graciousness, and caring. I know I could not have acted as a therapist for many years with incarcerated rapists and child molesters if I had not first worked on my Sobbing Child. I would have made them the inappropriate recipients of all my anger and rage toward my own offenders, or I would have been very fearful and unable to be effective with them.

By dealing with my Sobbing Child first, I was able to work with this prison population as victim to victim, rather than as victim to victimizer, or as almighty therapist to lowly scum. Because of my prior therapy and my willingness to share my own story of sexual abuse with them, they could open up and share their own Sobbing Child stories with me. For most of them, it was the first time they ever told anyone about their own childhood abuse.

Controlling Child

If you are person who is more feeling and tends to be reactive, strengthening your Controlling Child will be an important aspect of your healing journey. Let your mind to be your "feeling's manager." Allow your feelings to come up through your mind and be processed with the aid of your Controlling Child. When you do so, you create an effective synthesis of head and gut and therefore, you will act responsibly instead of simply reacting, and possibly regretting your actions later.

As I have mentioned before, your Controlling Child provides a defense mechanism that is essential in times of pain and crisis; you do not want to lose this value attribute. It is necessary to evaluate your childhood and adult defense mechanisms, so you can choose which ones are positive and should be kept, and which ones are negative and need to be eliminated. If addictions have been one of your defenses, then you should consider professional help, as well as a Twelve-Step program or an appropriate support group, to help you overcome them.

Your Controlling Child also keeps you responsible, with financial, occupational, family, and social obligations. Additionally, your Controlling Child sets boundaries, a very important role, which takes time and work to develop. A boundary exists for two reasons: so you don't victimize me, and so I don't victimize you. Too often, people think a boundary is set in place only to protect themselves from others; they do not realize it also is necessary to protect others from them.

Original Child

Your Original Child is literally the captain of your team. This child is of ultimate importance because it is who you were created to be and contains your innate abilities. It is where your soul abides and enables you to connect with God. If left to develop on its own however, without the compassion of the Sobbing Child or boundaries and responsibility of the Controlling Child, the Original Child can become narcissistic and childish. But, if you spend the greater portion of your time developing your Original Child, while still valuing the positive attributes attained through your Sobbing Child and Controlling Child, you will create the ideal setting for a Healthy Balanced Person to develop.

Understanding this concept has been profound for me as I grow older. It gives me permission to make my Original Child a priority in my life: to devote time for my own health and especially my relationship with God; to enjoy my family and friends; to relax in the park with a good book—and not feel guilty because there still is so much work left for me to do. I have experienced many painful times in the past thirty years including the death of family members and close friends, plus undergoing numerous surgeries and other major difficulties, yet, if my Healthy Balanced Person is solidly supported by a strong Original Child, I am able to walk through the pain of these events without falling. It has been extremely rewarding for me to realize this truth.

The Road Map

A master views the parts with compassion,
because he understands the whole.

—From the Tao te Ching, Translation by Stephen Mitchell

I use the following exercises to enable individuals to prepare a Personal Road Map for their own healing journey using the diagram of the Healthy Balanced Person (Illustration 11). It is unique to each person, containing only what that individual feels is correct and attainable. Because the whole process can seem a bit overwhelming, I have broken it into small achievable pieces that support the old saying, "You eat an elephant one bite at a time." I hope you will join us in this part of the journey by answering these questions and filling out the worksheet.

(Exercise 27: Controlling Child)

(Exercise 28: Sobbing Child)

(Exercise 29: Original Child)

(Exercise 30: Healthy Balanced Person Worksheet)

After you finish these exercises write what you would like to address first on the Healthy Balanced Persons diagram (see example on Illustration 12) under the circle of each child, indicate which things on the diagram are negative that you want to eliminate and which are positive that you wish to keep and accentuate. Over time, as you accomplish each goal, choose another from the above exercises.

(Exercise 31 & Illustration 12: Your Personal Roadmap)

Becoming a Healthy Balanced Person is one of the most valuable gifts you can give yourself. We discussed that a healthy Circle #1 consists of God and you, which can happen only if you are a Healthy Balanced Person. I hope you will dedicate the time and energy needed to enable yourself to enjoy who you were created to be. Toward this end, I challenge you to do the following:

- Make a commitment to begin working on your Healthy Balanced Person
- Ask God, your Higher Power, to help you

Keep your Healthy Balanced Person Worksheet and your roadmap posted where you can see them daily. Always balance your goals regarding your physical, emotional, intellectual and spiritual aspects, do not become over invested in just one or two. Do not stress yourself or become overwhelmed; your goals need to be attainable and desirable or you will procrastinate and accomplish nothing.

Preparing the Team for the Journey

If any of the three children is allowed to completely overshadow the others, an unhealthy imbalance will develop:

- If your Controlling Child is allowed to be the dictator, you will be into power and control, focus on image, and be a workaholic.
- If your Sobbing Child dominates, you will remain an eternal victim, always needing others to care for you and rarely taking responsibility for your actions; or you will become so empathetic and compassionate (without any boundaries) that you die a martyr at an early age.
- If your Original Child is on the throne and does not acknowledge the other two, you will be hedonistic, self-centered, and childish (as opposed to childlike); or you can become "so heavenly-minded that you are no earthly good."

Likewise, if any one of the three children is unable to contribute positively, the whole will become imbalanced:

- Your Controlling Child brings stability and safety. Without this influence, the other two would be irresponsible, with the Sobbing Child always seeking care from others and the Original Child always playing and partying.
- Your Sobbing Child brings graciousness and empathy. Without this quality, the other two would be selfish, with the Controlling Child into power and control and the Original Child being totally self-centered.
- Your Original Child brings not only the essential, important spiritual component, but also life and vitality, keeping the other two from being boring. Without this attribute, the Controlling Child would work all the time and the Sobbing Child would cry all the time and neither could genuinely connect with God in a significant manner.

Maintaining balance sometimes feels like walking a tightrope. One of my clients, an intense young man, desperately wanted to be who God designed him to be. We talked about allowing his Original Child, who housed his soul, to enjoy time with God. He got excited and said, "I know; I need to really, really seek God!" Then he stopped and said rather sheepishly, "That sounds just like my Controlling Child trying to make my Original Child really work at finding God, instead of just taking pleasure in time with Him."

A Healthy Parent

Your Healthy Balanced Person is a healthy, mature parent. With God helping you, you can learn how to care for your "children" in the ways you always desired from a parent. You can:

- be attentive and genuinely listen
- be loving and kind
- be fair to all three
- keep them safe and secure
- be responsible and trustworthy
- be willing to admit when you are wrong

- be supportive and willing to risk
- encourage creativity and talent and
- laugh and have a joyous time

If you have a family, use the basic common sense parenting skills you already know, and when in question, stop and consider how you would resolve the problem with three actual children.

A popular exercise is to keep a journal, listening to and recording feelings from your inner children; my clients call it Journaling the Parts. One of the reasons group therapy works so well is because people learn to listen to others, and in doing so, they become less judgmental and more accepting. After a while the group starts to function more as a whole, while keeping each individual's identity intact. This is the same phenomenon that happens when keeping a journal which gives a voice to each of your inner children.

You may be quite surprised when you discover how different each one of them reacts to the same event—I certainly was. It will also help you better understand why you feel so conflicted about certain relationships and situations.

I encourage you to make this a daily practice and to especially use it when you are confronted with difficult decisions; it will help you make choices that are much healthier and will cause fewer regrets later.

(Exercise 31: Journaling the Parts)

I personally have used this tool for Journaling the Parts for many years. After a while, all my children start to work more as a team and are not so set on their own agendas. They still know what is important to them, but they are also willing to listen to the others. My clients have found this to be true for them also. One client, a prominent businessman, used to send me his copies of this type of journal. At first, his Controlling Child was always the dominant soloist, but over time that child melded with the others, and eventually they all sang in harmony, each part unique but now blended as a whole.

I have used this exercise for so many years that now I quickly do it in my mind rather than writing it out. However, if I have a major decision to make, I still write down all the nuances that emerge about that specific matter. When I decided to move back to Scottsdale, Arizona, after thirteen years in California, I definitely used this process in written form to evaluate several issues. I was especially interested in my answers to the question, "What type of home should I buy in Arizona?" My responses were:

- My Sobbing Child wanted a place that was safe
- My Original Child wanted something pretty, with space for my flower garden and roses
- My Controlling Child wanted to know how much everything cost: the price of the house, taxes, the mortgage interest rate, utilities (electricity for summer air-conditioning), and future appreciation

I considered almost forty houses before I found one upon which all three children agreed. It would have been easy to just give in and settle on a majority vote of two out of three. But I knew if I did that, I would never be fully satisfied; something always would feel wrong for some facet of me.

When I finally found the right house and stepped inside for the first time, all the inner parts of me exclaimed, "Yes!" The house was in my price range, it was beautiful, and it was located in a small, safe neighborhood. For many years, each evening as I returned from the office and drove into my garage, I felt a huge inner sigh of contentment and peace—I loved it.

Today I am deeply grateful that my Healthy Balanced Person persisted. In the past I would have listened to the part of me with the loudest voice (my Controlling Child, of course) and have given in after I found a good bargain.

How about you, how often do you listen to only a portion of yourself? Do you make choices you later regret? Most of us, at some time (or times) in our lives, have followed our hearts by listening only to our Original Child and have discounted the caution of our Controlling Child and Sobbing Child, and as a result we have ended up spending too much or buying something we really didn't need, or found ourselves in relationships that were painful or destructive. Or perhaps you have listened only to your Sobbing Child who was afraid to risk, and lost out on what could have been a wonderful opportunity or relationship.

Part of being a Healthy Balanced Person is learning about healthy choices, and those choices come from listening to the combined wisdom of all of your parts and their past experiences. Maturity develops as the outward expression of this inward state.

The Roof

(Illustrations 13. and 13a: The Roof)

As I searched for my new home, I visualized a new symbol for understanding the Healthy Balanced Person: a *Roof.*

Imagine a bar-graph with three bars—the center is the largest and tallest representing the Original Child; the side bars are smaller and shorter representing the other two "children." Over them is placed a roof which portrays the Healthy Balanced Person. As long as the Original Child continues growing and is vigorous, the roof stays in place.

There also is open space between the Sobbing Child and Controlling Child and the "Roof" which enables flexibility in dealing with present-day crisis events. Because painful incidents continue to happen, this space is needed for the Sobbing Child to expand temporarily and the Controlling Child to be able to grow and provide protection during those difficult times. You will note in the "Roof" illustration that as long as the Original Child remains larger, the Sobbing Child and the Controlling Child can expand and retract when necessary, without disturbing the "Roof" of the Healthy Balanced Person.

If, however, when new pain erupts, the Original Child is neglected and small, then the "Roof" automatically caves in (see Illustration 13a.). It is impossible to stay a Healthy Balanced Person if there is no active nourishment of the Original Child.

This reality was brought home to me suddenly when I was writing my first book, *Prisoner of Another War*. During this process, I concentrated almost exclusively on my Sobbing Child and her story—and had completely stopped all the things I had been doing to support my Original Child (except for prayer.) I was so absorbed in listening to my Sobbing Child's voice, I became completely unaware that my neglected Original Child was beginning to shrivel and shrink. I was startled when my "Roof" came crashing down within just a few weeks. Fortunately, I quickly realized why my Healthy Balanced Person's "Roof" collapsed and actively began to rebuild some major trusses to support it once again by becoming attentive to my Original Child: I started taking breaks and going for walks in the sunshine, I spoke with family in Arizona on the phone and took time to have dinner with local friends, I started attending church again, I exercised, I rented funny movies and laughed!

How is your "Roof"—is it also on the verge of collapse?

What's in a Name?

By this time you may be sick to death of all the "children." Maybe you have heard about this inner child stuff before and discounted it. You may even have had some difficulty in the past when someone suggested you listen to your inner child and that child told you to leave your spouse and children and run off to some sea-side retreat. I used to receive quite a number of clients who had read or heard something like that, who didn't know they needed to listen to several inner children, not just one.

If the names bother you, you may be wondering whether you really have to call part of yourself a Sobbing Child. It doesn't matter to me what you call these parts of yourself; they can be "Jeff, Mike, and David" or "Sara, Kate, and Allison" or any other name you wish. The only real issue is to acknowledge that every one of us (including you):

- contains the person we were created to be (our Original Child)
- possesses a Pool of Pain, be it large or small (birthing our Sobbing Child)
- uses defense mechanisms (compliments of our Controlling Child)

How those three parts interact determines how we live our lives.

Feel free to use any name or designation you wish for your inner aspects, but please do not deny yourself the privilege of growing and thriving throughout the remainder of your life.

In Summary

While the goal in our healing journey is to become a Healthy Balanced Person—the unique person we were designed to be— we are always in a process of "becoming." We never become fully perfect; only God has this status. So, be gentle with yourself, understand that you will make mistakes, but be encouraged by the progress you have made thus far. As you learn to set boundaries around your own behavior and that of others, and are becoming healthy—emotionally, spiritually, physically and intellectually— you are well on your way in this healing journey. In addition, listen attentively to the combined wisdom of your valuable inner children; they will help you make healthy choices as a Healthy Balanced Person.

Perhaps you regard all this talk of "health, wisdom and maturity" as tiresome, and feel that a Healthy Balanced Person would be terribly dreary and tedious. I have found the reality to be exactly the opposite. People who are healthy and balanced are among the most creative, interesting and exciting people on this planet because at last, they have the freedom to become who they were designed to be. I invite you to find out for yourself.

GUIDEPOST FIVE

WISDOM AND MATURITY

Knowledge + Experience + Understanding = *Wisdom*
Wisdom + Application = *Maturity*

The guidepost for Wisdom and Maturity is placed upon the foundation of the previous four and is the culmination of our journey.

The fifth guidepost begins with the definition of wisdom: Knowledge plus Experience plus Understanding equals Wisdom. Many people have only one or more parts of this equation, but each part plays a fundamental and crucial role in the development of wisdom. No piece of the equation can be disregarded. For everything to add up in our lives, it is important to listen to the wisdom we have gained from our Original Child, Controlling Child, and Sobbing Child, as they each make a unique contribution to the personal wisdom that we seek on this final portion of our journey.

In addition to the concept of wisdom, the theme of maturity is a significant component of this guidepost. Maturity is not something that simply happens when you get older. Rather, it develops when you apply the wisdom you have acquired. Maturity encompasses your observable traits—your attitudes, actions and reactions. It determines your belief systems, your actions in rectifying past mistakes and your ability to react in healthy ways to new situations. To progress on your healing journey, it is important to respond from a new, mature strength and to let go of defensive, childish behaviors that are no longer beneficial, but which have instead become hindrances to health. Maturity enables you to experience peace and joy as a Healthy Balanced Person.

CHAPTER 14

The Healing Journey

Wisdom outweighs any wealth.
There is no happiness where there is no wisdom.
—Sophocles (495-406 B.C.)

Wisdom

Previously, I defined a segment of this final guidepost with this equation: Knowledge + Experience + Understanding = Wisdom. Many people have a great deal of knowledge, but they are not necessarily wise; nor could the people who only have experience be considered to be wise, and neither could those who have both knowledge and experience. Until you add understanding—especially at a deep level—to your knowledge and experience, wisdom is not possible. It is those "ah-has" and profound insights that come with understanding that engender the remarkable phenomenon know as wisdom.

So far, this book has focused on providing you with knowledge, asking you to add your own personal experiences to that knowledge with the hope that you will gain not only awareness, but understanding. You should already be feeling a little wiser if you and God are working together, and if you are:

- making your Controlling Child more responsible and setting boundaries so as to be neither a victim nor a victimizer;

- allowing your Sobbing Child to show concern and compassion for others while being protected by healthy boundaries;
- encouraging your Original Child to reclaim your soul, and to honor the gifts God gave you by allowing them to grow and thrive;
- actively working on being healthy and balanced physically, intellectually, emotionally, and spiritually.

In doing this work, you will also learn that, while each one of your children has bits and pieces of knowledge, experience, and understanding, they need the input from the other two to obtain wisdom, otherwise their individual efforts will be incomplete and imbalanced. The input from all three children brings wisdom to the Healthy Balanced Person.

(Exercise 32: Wisdom)

Take your time in filling out the chart for Exercise 32. As you complete this chart, you may be surprised at the extent of the wisdom you have gained from your past knowledge, experience and understanding. Do not undervalue the validity of that wisdom. Claim it, it's yours, you've earned it. I have my clients and students repeat the following phrase over and over: *"I know that I know what I know."* I ask you to do the same. Write this statement on sticky notes and place them in your home, your car, your office— any place where you can read them every day until that truth becomes a reality and is imbedded deep inside your unconscious where no one can ever take it away.

Maturity

People are like stained glass windows: they sparkle and shine when the sun is out, but when the darkness sets in, their true beauty is revealed only if there is a light within.
—*Elizabeth Kubler-Ross (1926-2004)*

Now that you are gaining wisdom about what contributed to who and what you are today, what about correcting past errors and ensuring a healthier new path for your journey in the future? How will you take this new wisdom and apply it to your relationships on this journey, personally and professionally? This is where the attribute of maturity is vital.

I define maturity as the outward expression of the inward state of a Healthy Balanced Person who acts upon wisdom (gained from knowledge, experience, and understanding,) and upon a value system of love and respect for God, self, and others.

Maturity is not about age; it is about applying wisdom. I know some children who are wise and mature beyond their years and many adults who are unwise, immature, and childish. A Healthy Balanced Person rejoices in maintaining a childlike (not childish) openness to life and love and always desires to continue learning and growing.

And, achieving maturity is not about perfection. We all still slip-up occasionally—because we're human. I always remind my clients and students, "Remember, maturity doesn't mean you'll never make a mistake, what matters is how quickly you course-correct when you do."

We never become fully mature—only God is in that state of perfection.

The Qualities of Maturity

Many of my clients come from families and systems where love and respect were not modeled. They say, "I would like to be mature and loving and respectful, but I haven't the least idea where to start. Please give me some specifics—describe a healthy, mature person to me." As a consequence, I developed a list of attributes that greatly impact our lives and the way we relate to ourselves and to others.

If developing maturity is your goal, then contemplate the following qualities and consider whether or not they describe you. Mark the traits you feel you already manifest, and, using a different color pen, mark the traits you wish to enhance.

Maturity is:

- being responsible for your own health—physical, intellectual, emotional, and spiritual
- having a healthy relationship with God in your life
- turning over to God the things that only God can handle
- realizing you are not God
- having healthy self-worth, balanced with humility
- being a feeling and thinking person
- being loving
- being passionate about what you love
- exhibiting gracious strength
- providing safety, security and stability in your life
- being congruent, "walking your talk"
- risking vulnerability by being open and transparent
- being honest and trustworthy
- being kind, caring and considerate
- being assertive, not aggressive or passive-aggressive
- being patient, especially with those who irritate you
- having an accepting, nonjudgmental attitude
- being compassionate and merciful but with boundaries
- being respectful of all people, regardless of gender, race, color, religious creed, political beliefs, or sexual orientation
- enjoying giving more than receiving
- being responsible and dependable
- having an attitude of gratitude
- seeing the good in others and sharing genuine compliments with them
- being able to delay gratification, to plan and save
- seeing cooperation as valuable, at home and in the workplace
- giving up childish immaturity and selfishness
- persevering in spite of opposition and setbacks
- being a good listener and really hearing others
- making decisions and following through

- knowing how to balance a positive attitude with the reality of pain when it occurs
- giving yourself permission to cry and to share your pain with others
- acknowledging all your feelings and learning how to express them appropriately
- being courageous
- being adventurous
- allowing your creative abilities to thrive and grow
- accepting leadership as an opportunity, not to control, but to inspire and enlighten
- being able to state your own needs and wants in a clear, respectful manner
- being forgiving and allowing past issues to stay in the past
- restoring broken relationships
- being willing to accept the responsibilities that come with your role as a child, parent, spouse, employer, employee, friend, or citizen
- laughing and enjoying life, deeply and often
- being gentle with others, especially family and loved ones
- being aware when your voice, tone, or manner is disrespectful and correcting it
- being courteous in a genuine manner, not just per learned etiquette
- not taking things personally
- letting your "Yes" be "Yes" and your "No" be "No"
- being flexible, adapting to change
- being fair and just
- being a good sport
- not assuming what someone else is thinking or feeling
- accepting criticism graciously by acknowledging what is accurate and needs to be corrected, and not taking on that which is not yours
- acting, not reacting

- separating the person from the deed, for yourself and for others
- not being a victim or a victimizer
- being able to process anger constructively
- giving yourself permission to risk and to make mistakes
- giving up perfectionism
- not berating yourself when mistakes happen, but learning from them and course correcting as soon as possible
- encouraging, supporting, and inspiring others
- actively reducing your stress level as a priority
- dreaming great dreams and going after them
- dealing in reality, not fantasy
- doing what you love
- relating to others in a mutually rewarding manner

While this may seem like a rather awesome, even daunting list, if you have started practicing being a Healthy Balanced Person, many of the above traits may have already started falling into place. You might also share the list with someone who knows you well and with whom you feel safe, asking them to identify those traits they feel you presently embody and those which they feel you need to strengthen. This takes courage, but we know others can see attributes in us—good and bad—that we are unable to recognize in ourselves.

Please be gentle with yourself. You do not need to undertake all your issues immediately; this is a lifelong journey, and God wants you to genuinely enjoy yourself along the way. No one is perfect; know that you most certainly will stumble and fall. You may also run into some pretty rough road blocks, and take a few lengthy detours along the way, and that's okay. I have, and still do. True growth and maturity are measured by how rapidly we acknowledge our mistakes and recognize what factors caused us to make those errors, and how promptly we get back on our true path.

The Guideposts

We have looked at the five foundational guideposts which have been provided for your healing journey. Guidepost One is Purpose and Preparation and consists of accepting the need for a personal healing journey in your life; trusting in the process of that healing, whereever it may lead you; and being willing to risk and actively participate with your actions.

Guidepost One: *Purpose and Preparation*

Accepting the need for a personal healing journey in your life;
Trusting in the process of that healing,
where ever it may lead you, and being
Willing to risk and actively participate with your *Actions*

The second guidepost, placed upon the first, is Balance and Health and declares the significance of being balanced and healthy—physically, intellectually, emotionally, and spiritually, and of integrating your Original Child, Sobbing Child, and Controlling Child. As you reclaim your soul from the core of your Original Child, you connect with your innate desire to have an intimate re-lationship with God as the primary relationship in your life.

Guidepost Two: *Balance & Health*

features:
You: becoming *Balanced* and *Healthy*—
Physically, Emotionally, Intellectually and Spiritually with
an Integrated Original Child, Sobbing Child, and Controlling
Child; and with *God* as Your Primary Relationship

Guidepost Three, resting upon the first two, represents Faith and Values: your love and respect of God, self, and others.

Guidepost Three: *Faith and Values*

Love and respect of God, self, and others

The fourth guidepost, positioned upon the previous ones signifies "Actions, Attitudes and Accountability." Actions are outward indications of inward attitudes; accountability reflects a commitment to transforming actions and attitudes.

Guidepost Four: *Actions, Attitudes, and Accountability*
Actions are outward indications of inward *attitudes*
***Accountability* reflects a commitment to**
transforming *actions and attitudes*

The final guidepost, placed at the pinnacle, symbolizes Wisdom and Maturity. Wisdom evolves out of the knowledge, experience and understanding gained while on your life's journey; maturity emerges from the application of that wisdom.

Guidepost Five: Wisdom and Maturity
Knowledge + Experience + Understanding = *Wisdom*
Wisdom + Application = *Maturity*

As these five guideposts are placed solidly one upon the other, they evolve into the final, and probably the most important aspect of your life—your Character—the legacy you leave behind. This overarching, powerful influence, if healthy, will bequeath gifts to those who follow you—of inspiration and love. This legacy will bless their paths; or if that legacy is corrupt, it will create a destructive chaos born of discouragement and dysfunction.

(Illustration 14: Character)

CHARACTER: Your Final Gift

Character cannot be developed in ease and quiet.
Only through experience of trial and suffering
can the soul be strengthened, vision cleared,
ambition inspired, and success achieved.
—Helen Keller (1880-1968)

Watch your thoughts; they become words.
Watch your words; they become actions.
Watch your actions; they become habits.
Watch your habits; they become character.
Watch your character; it becomes your destiny.
—Anonymous

In researching this quality I found character defined as:

1. a pattern of behavior
2. moral strength
3. reputation
4. the representation of who you are
5. a statement about the qualities of a person
6. an ethical point of view
7. a reflection of your values
8. a possession of a quality that distinguishes you from others
9. a person with the characteristics of integrity, honest, honor, courage, strength, fortitude, goodness, and sincerity

You alone decide the legacy you leave to your loved ones and to the world. Will it be the result of having lived a worthwhile life in which you genuinely sought to be loving and respectful of God, self, and others? Or will you allow yourself to become apathetic, narcissistic, into addictions, or so busy with your work that you ignored a healthy healing journey. One of the saddest epitaphs I can imagine would be to die and have someone say, "He or she was not a person of character." How will people remember you?

Fortunately, you now have an opportunity to determine what your legacy will be. There is no character defect of the past that cannot be changed if you allow God to help you turn it into a blessing for yourself, and for others.

Do you want your children, grandchildren, and future generations to remember you with love, respect, and admiration, instead of anger, resentment, or indifference? It is my hope that you take this opportunity to connect, or re-connect, with loved ones in a new, intimate way that will ensure that you leave a legacy of love.

(Exercise 33: Your Legacy)

In Summary

Our wisdom evolves when we combine knowledge plus experience plus understanding; maturity develops when we apply that wisdom. These maxims are the basis of our fifth guidepost, and they bring us to the final aspect of our healing journey. As we contemplate the guideposts and steppingstones which have been indicators of a healthy path, we realize they create that aspect of our lives known as character. It represents the legacy we leave.

What legacy will you leave? Is it a guidepost that directs others to a life of love, peace, and joy—or to one of isolation, despair, and destruction? You now have the opportunity to leave a wonderful legacy of health and balance—a pathway for others to follow.

Exercises

Exercise 1: Trauma Egg (see Illustration 1)

1. Use an easel pad or the plain side of a roll of wallpaper, and assorted felt-tip markers. You may find it easier to do this exercise while sitting on the floor.

2. Draw a large, empty egg to represent yourself, sitting on the "nest" into which you were born. Then, start at the bottom of the page, and, using the space under the egg, list the following:

    a. Your "mother" and "father" and any items about them that would affect their life at the time of your birth; for example: under Father - his father was a workaholic who was always absent; or under Mother – youngest of ten children; age six when her mother died

    b. if raised by someone other than your parents, also add their names and details about them

    c. if adopted, list items regarding both your adoptive parents and your biological parents (as much information as is available)

    d. date of your birth and any specifics about that era and time; for example: 1942 – WWII

    e. any prior siblings, abortions, miscarriages, or stillbirths

3. The items inside the egg represent specific events that happened to you that caused you to feel pain, fear, rejection, sadness, etc.; starting from the bottom of the egg and moving upward, list events chronologically from early childhood to present:

  a. indicate an event's intensity by the line's width

  b. name the event and your age at the time on top of the line

  c. also list events you may have been too young to remember but have been told occurred (premature birth, early illnesses and accidents)

  d. if you will be sharing your Trauma Egg with others and there is an incident which you wish to keep private, indicate the event by drawing the line and listing your age, but leave the nature of the event blank

  e. If deprivation rather than specific traumatic or abusive events have been experienced, the egg may remain nearly empty.

4. Around the outside of the egg, list long-term, chronic events and stressors, the things that created external pressure on you; for example: Mother always angry; Father violent alcoholic; also include long-term illnesses, family, cultural and/or government issues, and details of neglect and deprivation.

Exercise 2: Wounds and Shock

1. Have you ever been cut, burned, hurt, shot or been involved in an accident? If so, did you feel the pain immediately or did it take a while before you felt the pain?

2. Have you ever had a physical wound that became infected? What would have happened had it not been taken care of?

3. Using your Trauma Egg from Exercise I

  a. address each incident listed inside the egg and the long-term chronic stressors and, (using a different colored pen) list the feelings that your child or adult felt, or should have been able to feel, at the time of each event or stressor; (see list of feelings and words which describe emotional states below)

  b. put a check next to those painful events which you were able to process appropriately at the time, or which you were able to process at a later time *c.* put an X by the incidents that indicate emotional wounds that remain unhealed.

I am including a list of feelings that you may find helpful for this exercise:

ANGRY	Suffering	Deficient	Ignored
Resentful	Dejected	Incompetent	Left Out
Furious	Broken	Ineffective	Offended
Mad	Wounded	Defective	
Rage	Anguish	Imperfect	**HELPLESS**
Hostile	Grief		Hopeless
Wrath	Distress	**SHAME**	Overwhelmed
Infuriated	Miserable	Embarrassed	Burdened
Outraged	Despair	Bad	Out of Control
	Distraught	Ugly	Powerless
BETRAYED		Dirty	Dominated
Not Fair	**FEAR**	Guilty	Trapped
Injustice	Terror	Condemned	Vulnerable
Disappointed	Scared	Ridiculed	Impotent
Violated	Frightened	Humiliated	Disabled
Dishonored	Horror		Defenseless
	Panic	**HATE**	Unprotected
WORTHLESS		Despise	Exposed
Devalued	**DIFFERENT**	Shun	Unsafe
No Good	Don't Fit In	Detest	Crushed
Unworthy	Strange	Loathe	Pressure
Disregarded	Excluded		
Disrespected	Odd	**LONELY**	**ANXIOUS**
Damaged	Peculiar	Isolated	Frantic
		Lost	Confused
PAIN	**INADEQUATE**	Desolate	Frustrated
Hurt	Stupid	Forlorn	Nervous
Sad	Dumb		Agitated
Agony	Failure	**REJECTED**	Insecure
Grief	Wrong	Forsaken	Stressed
Sorrow	Defeated	Abandoned	Distressed
	Discouraged	Deserted	

Exercise 3: Narcissism, a Generational Affair

1. Be very honest and look at the narcissistic traits described in this chapter and list those which you possess.

2. Are you willing to actively work on eliminating them from your life—or do you feel a strong resistance to this suggestion? If you are resisting,

    a. list what you gain by keeping your narcissism (being able to do what you want, when you want)

    b. list what you lose by keeping your narcissism (loss of relationships, intimacy, loneliness)

    c. weigh the results of a. and b.—which is stronger for you?

3. Look at the narcissistic traits in this chapter

    a. list which ones are representative of each of your parents; each of your grandparents (if this information is available); and each of your siblings

    b. list which ones are representative of your own children and/or grandchildren (if you are a parent)

    c. list your feelings and thoughts regarding whether or not you want these traits to be an ongoing legacy in your family

4. If you genuinely desire to abolish your narcissism

    a. complete the exercises in this book

    b. prayerfully seek help from your Higher Power

    c. share with your loved ones your desire to change and become a loving, caring person

    d. commit to working with a professional who can help start you on your road to recovery

Exercise 4: The Five Stages of Recovery

1. Take your Trauma Egg and look at the untreated emotional wounds you noted with an X in Exercise 2 and make a list of the persons and/or events who were involved in creating or contributing to those wounds

2. Referring to the Five Stages of Recovery, determine in which stage you presently reside with each offender/event and make a list describing your condition at this stage.

3. Choose one or two persons from the list with whom you would like to complete working through the Five Stages of Recovery.

4. List the obstacles which have prevented you in the past from continuing through the stages with each of these people; allow yourself to be vulnerable and truthful as you look within— without blaming other people or circumstances for your inaction.

5. Has forgiveness been a problem for you? Why? Can you forgive others but not yourself?

6. Determine the specific steps needed to progress to the next stages with each person and list them. Share this list with someone you trust.

7. Consider seeking a therapist to assist you or joining a support group to encourage you and help hold you accountable.

Exercise 5: Cleansing the Pool — Listening to Your Sobbing Child

1. Start a journal and record your feelings in a variety of ways so they can flow freely.

2. Review your answers from Exercise 4 in this chapter regarding the Five Stages of Recovery. Look at the areas of Anger and Grief and allow yourself to openly acknowledge what your Sobbing Child actually feels in these areas. Give your Sobbing Child a voice by using your non-dominant hand to write with felt-tip pens on an easel pad or the plain side of a roll of wallpaper

   a. hold the pen in your fist like you would a dagger and write: "I hate it" and "Not fair;" continue allowing the words to flow without editing for spelling, grammar or punctuation; use as much paper as necessary (I have found that "children" do not like to write small or within the lines)

    b. write directly to the persons who have victimized you in the past; don't be polite or correct, just allow yourself to dump your feelings without restriction

    c. draw your feelings without restraint, especially anger, loneliness and pain

3. Using your dominant hand, compose "dump" letters, telling it all, but do not mail the letters

4. Share all of the above with someone you trust. Consider having this person accompany you as you create a ritual to dispose of the pages:

    a. tear them into small pieces or using other methods of shredding them

    b. burn the remnants in a safe receptacle

    c. use prayer or meditation to allow your Higher Power to receive the ashes

Exercise 6: Acknowledging the Wounds

1. Take out your Trauma Egg and look at the untreated emotional wounds you noted with an X in Exercise 2 of Chapter One. Choose one or two that you would be willing to address at this time.

2. Walk through each of the steps in the section on "Physical Wound Treatment" in Chapter Four which explains the proper care of a physical wound and prayerfully consider what you need to do to apply these same steps to the process of healing your emotional wounds.

Exercise 7: Releasing Your Sobbing Child

1. Use an easel pad or the plain side of a roll of wallpaper and assorted felt-tip markers. You may find it easier to do this exercise while sitting on the floor.

2. Draw your Sobbing Child, using your non-dominant hand if you wish.

3. Add the feelings of your Sobbing Child, using symbols and/or words.

4. Share your drawing with someone you trust.

Exercise 8: Controlling Child Past and Present

1. Using an easel pad or the plain side of a roll of wallpaper and some felt-tip pens, list what your Controlling Child did to suppress your Sobbing Child when you were a child.

2. Draw that Controlling Child.

3. List what your Controlling Child does to suppress your Sobbing Child as an *adult*.

4. Draw your Controlling Child as an adult.

Exercise 9: Affirming Your Actual Age

1. Using an indelible pen, write the current year and your current age in the palm of your hand.

2. Write the current year and your current age on small sticky notes, and place them in various places where you will see them often, at home, and at work.

3. Daily stand in front of a mirror and state the date and your current age.

Exercise 10: How to Say "Yes" and "No"

1. Do you often say, "yes" when you would like to say, "no"? Or, if you do say, "no," do you feel guilty?

2. Why do you have difficulty setting boundaries? Are you afraid you will make the other person mad, or sad?

3. Have you ever been in a situation like #5 where you responded with a "yes" to accommodate a temporary situation? Was it a crisis? How long did it last?

4. List the persons that are the most challenging for you regarding boundary setting.

5. Choose one person from the above list and commit to practicing the "Five Ways to Say 'Yes' or 'No' " with this person. Ask a friend you trust, a therapist or your support group to hold you accountable.

6. As your confidence increases, continue to choose additional persons from your list and commit to setting healthy boundaries with them.

Exercise 11: Creating Healthy Balance

Using the following chart as a pattern, fill in your own evaluations—make the chart as large as needed:

Aspect	How I Care for Myself Now	Additional Ways to Enable Health & Balance
Physical		
Intellectual		
Emotional		
Spiritual		

Exercise 12: Reclaiming Your Original Child

1. Using an easel pad or a roll of wallpaper and felt-tip pens, draw your Original Child as it would have been had you been raised in a healthy environment and encouraged to release all your natural talents and abilities

2. As a small child, what did you love to do? What made you really happy?

3. As an adult, what healthy activity brings you the greatest joy?

4. How often do you participate in this activity? If your answer is "seldom," what is the major obstruction? What are you willing to do to change that?

Exercise 13: Anger at God

1. As you look at your Trauma Egg and your drawing of your Sobbing Child, what do you feel?

2. Do you have many unanswered questions where God is concerned? What are they?

3. Are you angry with God? Are you willing to address this?

4. Write a letter to God and dump everything you feel, without editing yourself. Then give yourself permission to read the letter out loud.

5. Let God know whether or not you would like to have an intimate relationship with Him and prayerfully wait for an answer.

Exercise 14: Grace, Blessings and Prayer

1. Do you have trouble extending grace to yourself? If so, why?

2. Do you have trouble extending grace to others? If so, why?

3. What steps can you take to begin to extend grace to yourself, and to others?

4. Are you committed to being healthy spiritually? If so, list specific actions you can take (or are already taking) to fulfill this commitment.

5. As you look at your Trauma Egg, are you aware that God has taken any of those painful events and made something good come of them? If so, please list.

6. Start a "Blessings Journal" by buying a journal and each day listing at least one thing you feel is a blessing and for which you are grateful.

7. Review the above journal regularly and share it with a loved one.

8. Have you ever experienced the power of prayer in your life or in the lives of others? If so, please list several specific incidents.

9. Please consider praying daily—thanking God for past blessings and asking for help regarding your present situations. List the answers in your journal.

Exercise 15: Accidental or Purposeful? (Refer to your Blessings Journal from Exercise 14)

1. Write down all your Internal Positive Influences (IPIs) and the gifts your Original Child was given at birth. Don't be modest, list all your strengths and assets.

2. How have the above IPIs helped you to survive? (Be specific)

3. How does this make you feel? Are you gaining some new respect for how you and that Original Child within you survived?

4. List all your External Positive Influences (EPIs) from birth up to the present day (family, friends, teachers, coaches, bosses, schools, awards—any person or event that helped you to feel loved, appreciated, valued)

5. Put a check mark by the persons and events that you feel were

the most significant, and separately list why each one was so important in your life.

6. Consider writing a letter to these people and tell them what they mean to you and how they influenced your life.

7. Do you think your IPIs and EPIs all happened by accident?

8. Do you feel that your Original Child was designed for a specific purpose in life? How does this affect your relationship with your Higher Power? Do you feel loved and valued?

Exercise 16: Behaviors and Values

1. If someone asked you to state your personal values, what would you say? What are the foundational ethics upon which you base those values? Where do those ethics originate?

2. Look at your behaviors and realize that they determine what your values *actually* are. Now, rewrite what your true values are, based upon your behaviors. Be scrupulously honest with yourself in writing your answers.

3. Prayerfully evaluate what you would like your values to be and list them.

4. In regard to the concept of "Love and Respect of God, Self and Others," do you agree with this value system? Why, or why not?

5. Do you allow disrespectful actions to invade your psyche and cause you long-term distress? If so, what can you do to eliminate these actions and distress?

6. With whom do you have the most difficulty being respectful? Why? What do you specifically need to do to change?

7. Do you have faith in a power greater than yourself? If so, are you willing to ask your Higher Power to help you become congruent with your values and behaviors?

Exercise 17: Our Essential Foundation

1. Take each of the fundamental needs and list whether or not they were met, or violated, in your childhood and give examples:

   a. Safety
   b. Security
   c. Stability
   d. Consistency
   e. A Sense of Control Over My Environment

2. What have you done over the years to try and fill those holes in each one of the above areas? List those actions and state whether or not they have worked.

   a. Safety
   b. Security
   c. Stability
   d. Consistency
   e. A Sense of Control Over My Environment

3. What can God and you do now to fulfill those needs for yourself? List those actions and state when you will be ready to implement them.

   a. Safety
   b. Security
   c. Stability
   d. Consistency
   e. A Sense of Control Over My Environment

Exercise 18: Roots

1. Talk to parents, grandparents, and other older family members and encourage them to tell you about their years as children and as adults. Let them know you are genuinely interested in their pasts and how they have overcome the difficulties in their lives. Let them know you are not there to judge or

criticize them, but to learn and empathize.

2. What stories do they tell you that are new to you?

3. How are their stories similar or different from yours?

4. How do these stories help you understand your family and the way you were raised? Do these conversations change your feelings about your family? Are you gaining new empathy for them?

Exercise 19: What about your "Bricks"?

1. On pages 175-176, do any of the messages on the list of bricks/rules that help to make up an Unhealthy System sound familiar to you? Check those which influenced your own system.

2. Add any others which have affected you.

Exercise 20: How Healthy are Your Systems?

1. Working from the Healthy/Unhealthy Systems list, mark which characteristics describe the following (use the letters "a, b, c, d, e" to denote the systems):

    a. your family of origin
    b. your present family
    c. your culture
    d. your place of employment and any other systems that affect you (e.g., church, government)

2. What systems have most influenced you?

3. Which list describes your present attitudes and behaviors most often?

4. Are you the one in authority who sets the rules, or do you blindly obey them? You may find you are both, in different systems.

5. List the factors that represented "normal" for you as a child.

6. List the factors that represent "normal" for you today.

7. List the factors that you would like to represent your "new baseline for normal"

Exercise 21: Tapes

1. Using an easel pad or a roll of wallpaper and felt-tip pens, make three columns as noted in Illustration 7

2. In the first column, list the inner "tapes" that play (or have played) in your conscious and unconscious mind; (refer to your answers in Exercise 20 and add new ones).

3. In the second column, state the origins of those "tapes" (e.g. Mother, Father, Siblings, Grandparents, Other Family; School; Friends; Cul-ture; Media; Job; Church; Yourself, and any other areas that influenced you). Also indicate if the message was overt and/or covert (implied or role-modeled) by using the initials "O" and/or "C".

4. In the third column express what you and God, as healthy parents, would tell a child who came to you with one of these inner "tapes" playing. Some examples from the author's "tapes" include:

   a. **Tape:** "What will other people think?"

   Where from: My mother and my culture; it was overt and actively played in my conscious mind.

   God and I to child: "You were given the gift of an intelligent mind and are able to make healthy decisions with us guiding you. You are a person of worth and do not need to depend upon what others think of you to have value."

   b. **Tape:** "Girls are not supposed to be smart."

   Where from: My culture and also the era and time in which I lived; I was raised in the 1940s-1950s in America, in which girls were not always encouraged to go to college or seek professions; they often were encouraged just to support their husbands and not think for themselves; this was a covert message and played in my unconscious mind.

God and I to child: "You never have to apologize for who you were created to be! Use all your natural talents and abilities; enjoy them and also give them as gifts for others."

c. **Tape:** "Your priorities should be: Jesus first, then others, and you should always be last."

Where from: My mother and my church; it was a constant overt message

God and I to child:"Yes, you should love God and others, but you also need to love and take care of yourself; it is not selfish to pay attention to your own health—physically, emotionally, intellectually, and spiritually. If you do not do so, you will not have the energy and ability to give your love elsewhere"

Exercise 22: Circles of Intimacy, Responsibility, and Impact

1. Use a large easel pad or roll of wallpaper and felt-tip pens, and draw two sets of circles like those featured in Illustration 8.

2. List names and activities on one set of circles that illustrate the way your circles are now.

3. List names and activities on a second set of circles that illustrate the way you would like your circles to be if your life was balanced and healthy.

4. If you are married or have a significant other in your life, try having each of you fill out another set of circles illustrating the way you perceive the other's circles to be. Discuss these circles together.

Exercise 23: From Victim to Victimizer

1. When were you an Angry Rebellious Child as a child?

2. When are you an Angry Rebellious Child as an adult?

3. When were you a Stubborn Selfish Child as a child?

4. When are you a Stubborn Selfish Child as an adult?

5. Be specific. If you have a difficult time finding any answers, ask the members of your family (I'm certain they will be happy to oblige).

6. When finished, using your large pad or wallpaper, draw pictures of each of the children described above—you may find these to be very revealing.

Exercise 24: What Are the Payoffs?

1. List any unhealthy relationships or systems in which you are presently involved.

2. Honestly contemplate what payoff you receive by staying in those relationships or systems and list each reason next to the unhealthy relationship.

3. Take each of the above relationships or systems and determine whether or not you are willing to give up your present payoffs. If so, what are you willing to do to either end, or heal, that detrimental affiliation.

4. Do you set boundaries with consequences? If not, what keeps you from being firm about the consequences?

5. If you are not willing to set boundaries with consequences, or to leave your unhealthy relationships or systems, will you be content to accept them, as they are, and no longer grumble about the treatment you receive?

Exercise 25: Honestly Facing Your Addiction and/or your Codependency

1. Be excruciatingly truthful and list the activities and/or substances to which you feel you may be addicted.

2. Who in your family of origin, or your present family, also has similar addictive or codependent behaviors? Have they ever dealt with those issues and become sober?

3. Make a list of the "Cost of My Addiction/s" and address your losses regarding: health, family, friends, job, reputation, self-esteem, money.

4. What is the most frightening aspect when you consider the possibility of eliminating your addiction/s? Are you willing to address those issues?

5. What do you gain by staying an addict/victim/child?

6. Why do you stay codependent and unable to set boundaries with loved ones who are addicts? What are you most afraid will happen if you stop being a codependent/enabler?

7. What do you, as a codependent/enabler, gain by this behavior? What do you lose? What do the addicts that you enable gain? What do they lose?

8. List the steps you are willing to take, starting today, to eliminate your addiction and/or Codependency—such as a Twelve-Step program or other support group, or seeking professional therapeutic help. Then discuss this decision with a family member or friend. (You will find you have many people who love you and will support and encourage you regarding this brave step.)

Exercise 26: Controlling Child (refer to Exercise 8)

1. What did your Controlling Child do, as a child, to hold down the pain of your Sobbing Child?

2. What does your Controlling Child do, as an adult, to hold down the pain of your Sobbing Child?

3. Which of the above behaviors are healthy and should be kept?

4. Which of the above behaviors are unhealthy and should be eliminated, or have been eliminated? What can you do to actively work on eliminating those unhealthy behaviors which remain?

5. What do you need to do to learn how to set healthy boundaries (for example, take classes, join a codependency group)?

6. What boundaries does your Controlling Child need to set, and with whom? How can you activate those boundaries, and when will you do this?

Exercise 27: Sobbing Child (refer to Exercise 5)

1. What can you do to continue to drain your Sobbing Child's Pool of Pain (for example, individual therapy, support groups, self-help books, journaling, sharing with close friends and family)?

2. What can you do to keep your Pool of Pain cleansed and not become re-infected (for example, couple or family counseling, communication courses, books on healthy assertiveness)?

3. With whom do you need to show more compassion? From whom are you estranged? What active steps can you take toward expressing that compassion and possibly mending that relationship? When will you do this?

Exercise 28: Original Child (refer to Exercise 12)

1. If time and money were no object, what would you like to _be_ (a state of being: e.g. spontaneous, happy, sexy, more spiritual)?

2. If restrictions regarding money and the government did not exist what would you like to _do_ (e.g. learn to play the piano or

guitar, be an astronaut, start an orphanage, travel around the world)?

3. What are the biggest distractions and deterrents that keep your Original Child from being who he or she was created to be?

4. Are you genuinely committed to allowing that child to come out and fly? If so, what will be your first step?

Exercise 29: Healthy Balanced Person Worksheet

Use the worksheets from your above Controlling Child, Sobbing Child, and Original Child exercises to complete the following:

1. **Controlling Child**—choose and list <u>one</u> item from the following Controlling Child questions:

    a. Which of the above are unhealthy behaviors which should be eliminated, or have been eliminated? What can I do to actively work on eliminating unhealthy behaviors which remain?

    b. What do I need to do to learn how to set healthy boundaries?

    c. What boundaries does my Controlling Child need to set, and with whom? How can I activate those boundaries, and when will I do this?

2. **Sobbing Child**—choose and list <u>one</u> item from the following Sobbing Child questions:

    a. What can I do to continue to drain my Sobbing Child's Pool of Pain?

    b. What can I do to keep my Pool of Pain cleansed and not become re-infected?

    c. With whom do I need to show more compassion? From whom am I estranged? What are the active steps I can take toward expressing that compassion and possibly mending that relationship? When will I do this?

3. **Original Child**—choose and list <u>one</u> item from each Original Child question:

    a. If time and money were no object, what would I like to <u>be</u> and how would I go about accomplishing it?

    b. If time and money were no object, what would I like to <u>do</u> and how would I go about doing it?

4. Address your Balance chart from Exercise 11 and choose <u>one</u> item from each of the following:

    a. Additional ways I might care for my physical aspect

    b. Additional ways I might care for my intellectual aspect

    c. Additional ways I might care for my emotional aspect

    d. Additional ways I might care for my spiritual aspect

Exercise 30: Your Personal Roadmap

1. From your Healthy Balanced Person Worksheet in Exercise 29, set your current goals by choosing:

    a. One item from your Controlling Child section

    b. One from your Sobbing Child section

    c. One from each portion of your Original Child section

    d. One item from each aspect of your Balance chart

2. Write your goals on a sheet of paper that you can duplicate and then place in your home and at work.

3. Draw your own roadmap using the outline on Illustration 12 and list each goal underneath the appropriate child on your road map.

4. Continue working on your goals until you feel comfortable with them before you add a new one.

5. When ready, add additional goals.

6. Each time you complete a goal, list it in the open space of your road map leading up to your Healthy Balanced Person.

Exercise 31: Journaling the Parts

1. Use a journal or a piece of unlined paper.

2. At the top of the page, place the date and a brief description of the event about which you will be journaling.

3. List the names of the three children

4. Allow each child to express what they feel about the listed event. (You will find they often have very conflicting opinions and ideas.)

5. Allow each child to speak as often as they want; they will argue occasionally.

6. Fill as many pages as needed.

7. Try writing with your non-dominant hand, especially for your Sobbing Child.

8. Your Angry Rebellious Child and your Stubborn Selfish Child may also want to write. If so, explore the reason for their appearance; it is usually because your Sobbing Child has not been truly heard. Do not allow these two destructive aspects to dominate this exercise as you continue writing— they should gradually begin to disappear as you listen more carefully to the other three.

9. When the children are finished, have the healthy parent—the Healthy Balanced Person—give a summation and/or make a decision (if one is needed) based on listening to the needs of all the children.

10. If there is not enough information to make a wise decision, delay for a few days and actively seek the additional data you need to resolve the event.

Date:_____Event:_____

Sobbing Child:
(try using your non-dominant hand for this one)

Controlling Child:

Original Child:

Healthy Balanced Person:

Exercise 32: Wisdom

List the areas in which each of the following has contributed to your store of wisdom. When finished, evaluate the resulting wisdom from each child (note examples in parentheses).

Element of WISDOM	Sobbing Child	Controlling Child	Original Child
KNOWLEDGE of	(The prevalence of abuse)	(Being responsible for one's own actions)	(The gifts given by God, especially my soul which intimately connects with God; it is the core of who I am)
EXPERIENCE created the	(Awareness of the severity and consequences of abuse)	(Awareness of the definite need for boundaries)	(Need for freedom to be who I was created to be)

Element of WISDOM	Sobbing Child	Controlling Child	Original Child
UNDER-STANDING provided	(Compassion and empathy for others and their own pain)	(A desire to become balanced and a willingness to give up control)	(A feeling of deep joy from a genuine relationship with God and others)
Resulting WISDOM	(I realize now that my painful past experiences were not in vain as they give me compassion and empathy for others; I am a more loving person, spouse, parent and friend. I want to give to others out of love, but also to value my own health.)	(I now accept that I am not God. I am willing to allow God to be responsible to bring about growth in the lives of others; my responsibility is to change myself and also to set healthy boundaries so others do not victimize me, and I do not victimize them.)	(God gave me the gift of my soul which is my core from which flows many talents and other attributes; God expects me to use them and for us to enjoy a deep relationship with each other and with other people.)

Exercise 33: Your Legacy

1. Address the definitions of character and contemplate how someone else would describe your character, and the legacy you are leaving.

2. Review this book again and all the exercises, then determine which areas you wish to change. Are you willing to make the commitment for that transformation and growth?

3. Write a paragraph describing your character as it is today.

4. Write a paragraph regarding what *you desire your character to become and the legacy you wish to leave.* Post it in a place where you can view it daily.

ILLUSTRATIONS

Illustration 1: Trauma Egg

Trauma Egg examples featuring Specific Painful Events, Long-Term Chronic Events and Stressors, and details regarding the "Nest" into which child was born (see Exercise 1)

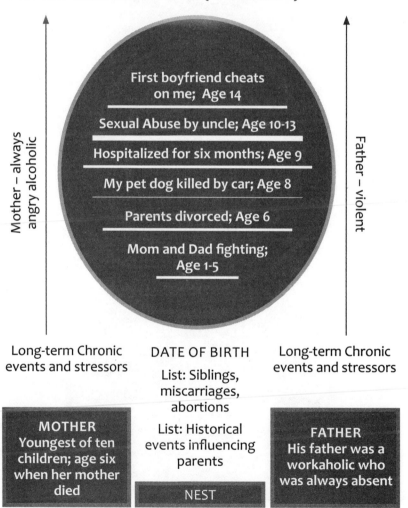

Illustration 2: The Circle of Love and Respect

GOD
Love
&
Respect
Others
Self

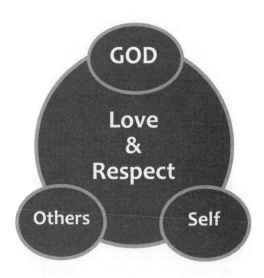

Illustration 3: The Survival Foundation

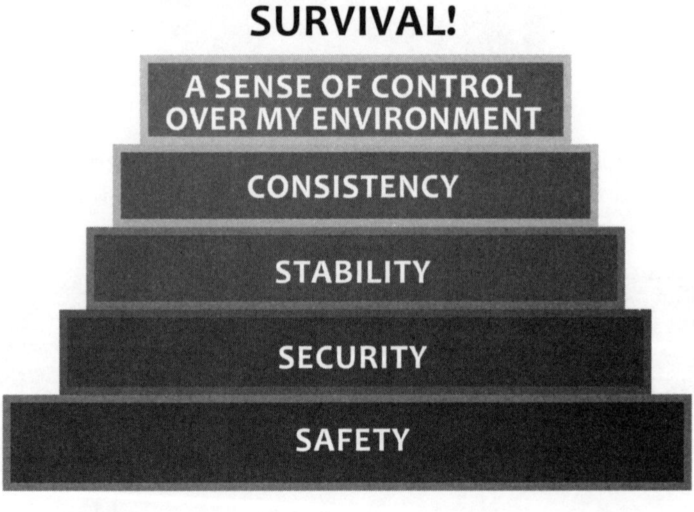

SURVIVAL!
A SENSE OF CONTROL OVER MY ENVIRONMENT
CONSISTENCY
STABILITY
SECURITY
SAFETY

Illustration 4: Unhealthy System
~ Unquestioned Obedience to Authority

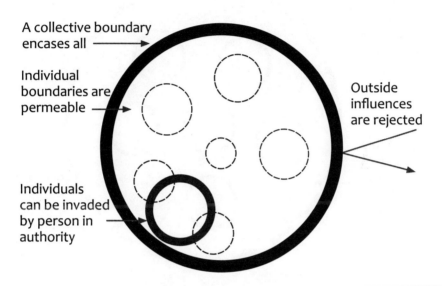

A collective boundary encases all →

Individual boundaries are permeable →

Outside influences are rejected

Individuals can be invaded by person in authority →

Illustration 5: Unhealthy System
~ No Rules, No Boundaries

Independent people with no external boundaries

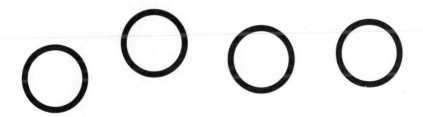

Illustration 6: Healthy System
~ Mutual Love and Respect

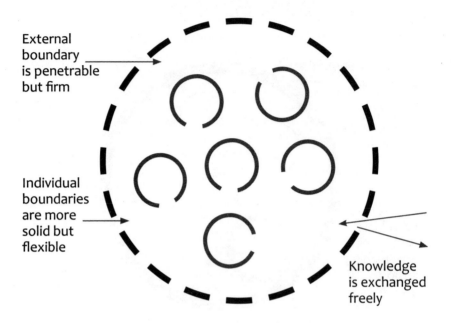

External boundary is penetrable but firm

Individual boundaries are more solid but flexible

Knowledge is exchanged freely

Illustration 7: Tapes

Tapes	Where from? Covert or Overt?	What would God and I as healthy parents say to a child who came to us playing this tape?

Illustration 8: The Circles of Intimacy, Responsibility, and Impact

(there are only five circles listed but you may include as many as needed)

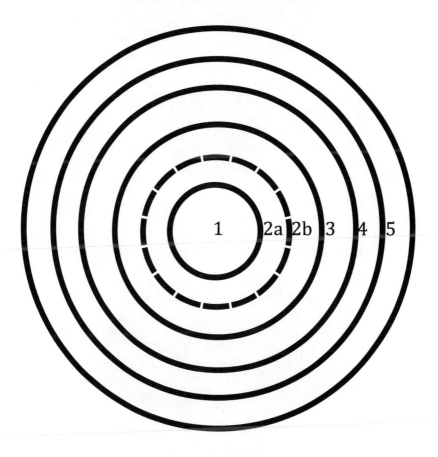

Illustration 9: Angry Rebellious Child

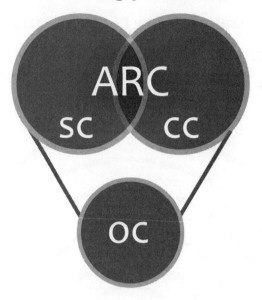

Illustration 10: Stubborn Selfish Child

Illustration 11: Healthy Balanced Person

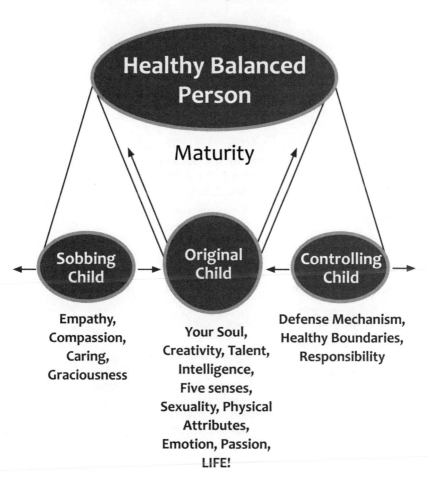

Illustration 12: Your Personal Road Map

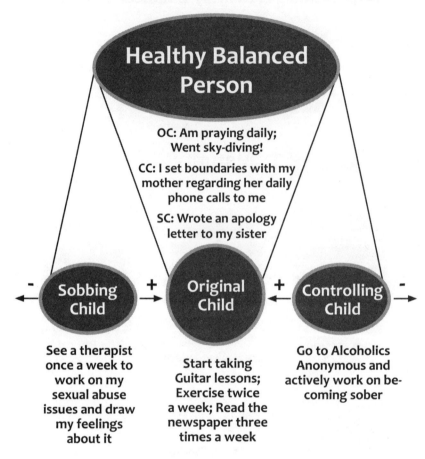

Illustration 13: The Roof

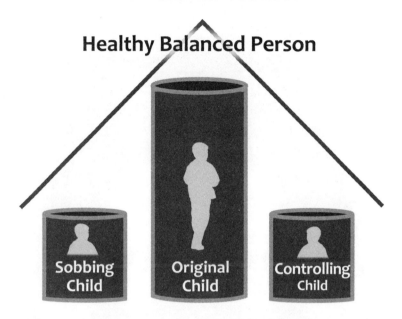

Illustration 13a: The Roof

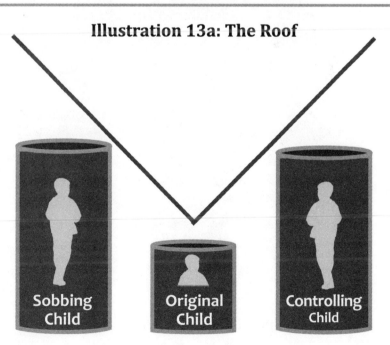

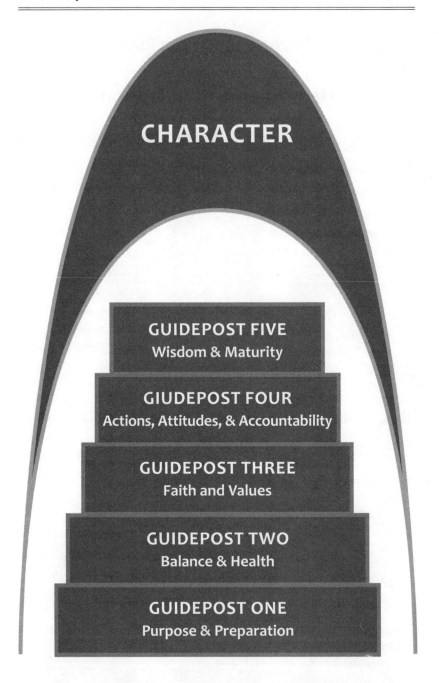

Illustration 14: Character

Professional Resources

(The following clinicians are recommended and have been trained in the Murray Method.)

Ralph Earle, MDiv, PhD, ABPP, LMFT, CSAT
Marcus Earle, PhD, LMFT, CSAT
Psychological Counseling Services (PCS)
7530 East Angus Drive
Scottsdale, AZ 85251
480-947-5739
email: **pcs@pcsearle.com**
website: **www.pcsearle.com**

Soozi Bolte, MC, LPC, LISAC
9260 East Raintree Drive, Suite 130
Scottsdale, AZ 85260
480-236-6682
email: **soozi@soozibolte.com**
website: **soozibolte.com**

Christopher J. Charleton, MA, LCSW, Fulbright Scholar
InterAct Counseling, President
2136 Penfield Road
Penfield, NY 14526
585-388-8010
email: **interact@frontiernet.net**
website: **www.interactcounseling.com**

Gayle Cordes, DBH, LPC, LISAC
11000 North Scottsdale Road, Suite 155
Scottsdale, AZ 85254
480-296-2050
Email: **gaylecordes@gmail.com**
Website: **gaylecordes.com**

Greg Crow, PhD
7510 East Angus Drive
Scottsdale, AZ 85251
480-947-1989
email: **worcgg@gmail.com**
website: **www.scottsdalecounseling.marriage-family.com**

Serine Graham, MC, LPC, LISAC
6735 E Greenway, Suite 2047
Scottsdale, AZ 85254
602-376-5002
Email: **serine@azics.net**

Lynn Husband, MA, EDS, NCC
6424 Johnson Chapel Road West
Brentwood, TN 37027
615-370-2885
Email: **lynn_husband@hotmail.com**

Sarah Matheson, MA, LPC
4202 North 32nd Street
Phoenix, AZ 85018
602-952-0680
Email: **sarah@matheson-counseling.com**
Website: **www.matheson-counseling.com**

Deborah Stelzleni, MAPC, LPC, CSAT
4300 North Miller Road, Suite 222
Scottsdale, AZ 85251
480-614-0900
Website: **epiphanycounseling.com**

Kathleen Thoren, MA
1420 East Whalers Way
Tempe, AZ 85283
602-315-5597
Email: **Kathleen.thoren@gmail.com**
Website: **thorengroup.com**

(Specifically for Clergy)

Dale Wolery, MRE
Clergy Recovery Network, Director
PO Box 52
Joplin, MT 59531
406-292-3322
website: **www.clergyrecovery.com**

Acknowledgements

To my editor and long-time friend, Roy Carlisle, my deepest gratitude for his never-ending encouragement, wisdom, expertise and professional recommendations. Without you, this book never would have been completed—you have endured with me for over twenty years as we worked through endless re-writes and new editing—THANK YOU! To *Mary Clare Blakeman*, the finish editor who polished this manuscript, my gratitude for your professional skills and your wise suggestions that contributed to a more complete text.

To my family: my children and grandchildren - *Jinger and Brad Richardson, Missy and Lyle Anderson, BJ and Ashley Richardson, Janell and John Grady, and Ashley Brammer*; and to my sister and brother-in-law - *Mary Sue and Wayne Watson* and my nephews and their families - *Tim and Joy, and TJ and Hannah, Randy, Zach and Dylan, and Josh and Sara Watson*—your unconditional love and constant support mean a great deal to me—I appreciate all of you so very much and I love you! Tim and Joy - your presence in Russia and participation on our Murray Method classes for eight years are some of the greatest personal joys I experienced there – thank you for all your efforts on my behalf and for your commitment to teaching the Method to so many others.

To *Dr. Ralph Earle*, my mentor, colleague and friend who first saw my Murray Method theory in 1982 and has never ceased to encourage the expansion of my work. I greatly appreciate your years of support and your confidence in the Method contained in this book. Having you and *Marcus* in my first Murray Method training was an unforgettable experience. A special thank you to you, and to Marcus and all the PCS staff for allowing me to continue to be a part of the PCS family.

To *Bill Swackhamer*, my deep gratitude to you for over thirty years of sharing your wisdom and expertise that has contributed greatly to numerous facets of this book and to the Murray Method—thank you for your constant encouragement and for helping me continue the work in Russia by your wonderful contributions of time and effort to Health Restoration International.

To *Greg Crow*, a good friend and colleague who attended my first Murray Method training session so many years ago—you have remained a source of professional encouragement, friendship and spiritual support which I greatly value. Thank you for all your interest in, and concern for Russia—I know it holds a special place in your heart, too.

To *Gayle Cordes*, dear friend, confidant and colleague—your loving help with Health Restoration International and wise counsel regarding this book has been extremely helpful—thank you. I am honored that you will continue to share this Method with others.

To *Kathleen Thoren*, a devoted friend who has believed in this Method and committed much of her life to sharing it with others— my special gratitude to you for your love and especially for your patience as you waited so many years for this book to be completed. I know God will continue to use you to be a blessing in many lives.

To *Arthur Flegel*, I greatly appreciate and thank you for all you and Cleo have done to support me and the work of HRI in Russia with your love, encouragement, and especially your prayers. Your long-term historical work regarding Russia has been a great motivator for me—you are truly inspiring as one who has lived a healthy, balanced life for over 90 years!

To *Jerry Bisgrove, Jim and Carol Hebets, Lyle and Missy Anderson, Ken and Randy Kendricks* – without you, the work in Russia never would have continued beyond the first years. I extend my love and deepest appreciation for your belief in this Method and the results it has attained in the former USSR thanks to your personal commitment of love, finances and prayers.

To *the Board of Directors of Health Restoration International, Ltd.* and to *everyone who has donated time, prayers and the financial resources* that have enabled our work in Russia to continue – your efforts have helped many hurting persons find hope and healing within their lives and their families – thank you.

To *Mike Tyson*, you have shown me that anyone can change—I am proud of the work you have done over the years even though you still struggle at times. Your brutal honesty is so refreshing and I know of your personal commitment to health—for yourself and in your relationships. Your love of Russia and your encouragement and support has been a special joy for me—thank you for being part of my family.

To my *clients and to my students at Ottawa University and the University of the Nations* who have applied the instruments and ideas of this Method and have excitedly shown me how their lives have been affected and changed—you are my teachers and my guides—I am certain I have learned more from you than you have from me. Thank you for your pledge to your own growth and health, and to your constant belief in who God created you to be—a valuable person worthy of love and respect.

To my *Russian students and friends* – there are no words sufficient to tell you of my deep admiration of your incredible talents and abilities, and for your courage and strength as you commit to healing the deep wounds you carry, not only from the present, but from generations past. I so appreciate your tender care for me, and your love and constant support. Thank you for the honor and great privilege of participating with you in your healing journeys. The amazing changes I have seen in your lives have been a great inspiration and a very special encouragement for me.

About the Author

Recognized internationally as a psychotherapist, theorist, author and educator, Marilyn Murray is a well-known presenter at psychological conferences, universities, churches, to the general public and in the media. As an authority regarding abuse and its consequences, she has specialized in intensive therapy in private practice and has given her Murray Method Theory and Training Seminars since 1983.

She created and taught a specialty program for Ottawa University graduate students in Phoenix, Arizona for seven years entitled, "The Treatment of Trauma, Abuse and Deprivation." She also has taught for an international university in Hawaii, Ukraine, and the Netherlands, and has students from over 40 countries.

Since 2002, she has lived half-time in Russia where she presents her method to health professionals and to clergy regarding the treatment of trauma, abuse, deprivation, and their correlation with addictions. She was a guest professor at Moscow State University of Psychology and Education from 2004-2008; and her full Murray Method program was part of the regular curriculum at the Institute of Clinical Psychology and Psychotherapy in Moscow. She has given presentations at Moscow State University, The Russian Orthodox University and Moscow State University of Education. Murray Method International Centers are located in Moscow Russia, Poltava Ukraine, and Dushanbe Tajikistan, with certified instructors teaching this method to multitudes throughout the former USSR.

Her column, *Time to Live* was a regular feature in Russia's only English language newspaper, The Moscow Times from 2012-2014. She is the author of *Prisoner of Another War* and *The Murray Method*. She is the founder and president of Health Restoration International, Ltd. which sponsors the work in Russia; and also is the primary instructor for Murray Method, LLC which provides training for health professionals and workshops for the general public in the United States. Her two daughters and their families reside in Scottsdale, Arizona.

If you would like to work with Marilyn Murray, please contact:

Murray Method, LLC

*Professional Training Seminars,
and Workshops for the General Public*
7349 N. Via Paseo Del Sur, Suite 515-275
Scottsdale, AZ 85258
Email: **info@murraymethod.com**
English Website: **www.murraymethod.com**
Russian Website: **www.murraymethod.ru**

For more information regarding the work in the former USSR, please contact:

Health Restoration International, Ltd.

*Education and Providing Resources for
Emotional, Spiritual, Intellectual and Physical Health*
7349 N. Via Paseo Del Sur, Suite 515-275
Scottsdale, AZ 85258